THE EARLY MARTYRS

*Lives
of*

The Early Martyrs

Fr. Pedro de Ribadeneyra, SJ

Translated by
Mrs. Anne Hope
Author of *The Life of St. Philip Neri*

MEDIATRIX PRESS

MMXXIII

ISBN: 9781957066356

©Mediatrix Press, 2023, all rights reserved.

Lives of the Early Martyrs was first published by D & J Sadlier & Co., New York, 1855. The Mediatrix Press edition has been faithfully reproduced from that, and is in the public domain. Typography and editorial changes ©Mediatrix Press, 2023, all rights reserved. No part of this edition may be reproduced without the express permission of the publisher, in print or electronic format except for quotations for review in journals, blogs, or educational purposes. No part of this work may be placed on archive.org.

Cover art:
Crocifissione di San Pietro
—Michelangelo Merisi da Caravaggio
Santa Maria del Popolo, Rome

Mediatrix Press
607 E 6th Ave.
Post Falls, ID 83854
www.mediatrixpress.com

Contents

CHAPTER I
    Introduction 1

CHAPTER II
    The Persecution of the first Christians 7

CHAPTER III
    St. Mary Magdalen, St. Martha, St. Lazarus, and St. Joseph of Arimathea 14

CHAPTER IV
    St. James the Great 18

CHAPTER V
    St. James the less 23

CHAPTER VI
    St. Philip & St. Matthias 27

CHAPTER VII
    St. Peter at Rome 31

CHAPTER VIII
    St. Nazarius and St. Celsus 35

CHAPTER IX
    First General Persecution
    St. Peter and St. Paul 45

CHAPTER X
    St. Mark 55

CHAPTER XI
    St. Thomas, St. Bartholomew, St. Matthew, St. Simon, and St. Jude 63

CHAPTER XII
    The Second Persecution 72

CHAPTER XIII
    Flavia Domitilla 77

CHAPTER XIV
    St. Andrew 88

CHAPTER XV
    St. John the Evangelist 96

CHAPTER XVI
    THIRD PERSECUTION
    St. Simeon 104

CHAPTER XVII
    St. Ignatius 109

CHAPTER XVIII
    St. Clement 116

CHAPTER XIX
    Hadrian: St. Symphorosa 125

CHAPTER XX
    Marcus Aurelius: The Martyrs of Lyons and Vienne 132

CHAPTER XXI
    St. Felicitas and Her Sons 142

CHAPTER XXII
 St. Polycarp 147

CHAPTER XXIII
 FIFTH PERSECUTION
 Septimius Severus 159

CHAPTER XXIV
 St. Perpetua and St. Felicitas 168

CHAPTER XXV
 St. Cecilia 180

CHAPTER XXVI
 SIXTH AND SEVENTH PERSECUTIONS
 Maximin & Decius: St. Gregory Thaumaturgus. St. Felli. 207

CHAPTER XXVII
 St. Agatha 222

CHAPTER XXVIII
 Gallus: St. Cornelius. St. Lucius 234

CHAPTER XXIX
 EIGHTH PERSECUTION
 Valerian: Sts. Stephen, Sixtus, Lawrence, and Hippolytus 237

CHAPTER XXX
 NINTH PERSECUTION
 Diocletian: St. Sebastian. 249

CHAPTER XXXI
 St. Maurice and the Theban Legion 267

CHAPTER XXXII
 St. George 272

CHAPTER XXXIII
 St. Justus and St. Pastor 281

CHAPTER XXXIV
 St. Agnes. 286

CHAPTER XXXV
 St. Dorothea 296

CHAPTER XXXVI
 St. Boniface. 303

CHAPTER XXXVII
 Death of Galerius; Conversion of Constantine... 310

CHAPTER XXXVIII
 Maximin Daia; St. Catherine 317

CHAPTER XXXIX
 Misfortunes and Death of Maximin Daia 338

CHAPTER XL
 TENTH PERSECUTION
 Licinius: Forty Martyrs of Sebaste. 344

CHAPTER XLI
 Death of Licinius; Triumph of the Church 356

CHAPTER XLII
 Julian the Apostate 360

CHAPTER XLIII
 Julian the Apostate—Conclusion 373

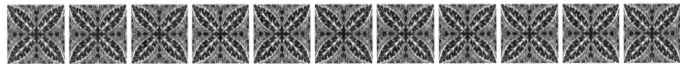

The Acts of the Martyrs in the following volume are taken from Fr. Ribadeneyra's *Flores Sanctorum*, except in the few cases in which a different authority is given in a footnote. The chronology which has been followed is that of Tillemont, not because it seemed correct in every instance, but because it was thought best to follow one uniform system.

LIVES OF THE EARLY MARTYRS

CHAPTER I

Introduction

THE interesting tale of *Fabiola* has made most readers familiar with the sufferings of the early martyrs, and desirous to know more of their history and of the victories which they achieved over the world. Every age every clime has its martyrs, for it is a distinctive mark of the Catholic Church, that the race of martyrs never dies out, and since her earliest times, a single generation has not passed without some of her children shedding their blood for the name of Jesus. Other religious bodies may have had a few individuals here and there, and at distant intervals who have died for their opinions, but it is in the Catholic Church alone, the spirit of martyrdom has ever been alive. Nor is it difficult to account for this, as the Catholic Church is the only true Church, the devil is ever ready to raise up persecutions against her; and as the Lord ever loves his spouse the Church, he bestows upon her all graces, and among them, the grace of martyrdom, with a more lavish hand than on others. The chief reason, however, is one which lies at the very root of the Christian religion; since it is connected with our Lord's motive for having redeemed the world in the way in which He was pleased to do so, instead of in some other way, which would have been equally possible and easy to Him.

When God does any great thing, He usually does it in

a different way from what men would naturally expect. Many of the pagan nations had preserved a part of the primitive tradition, which led them to expect that in the course of time God would come down upon earth to overthrow the power of the devil, but as they could not imagine that He would come except with great might and majesty, they believed that his coming would be attended with the most glorious triumphs, and that his enemies would not be able to stand for a moment before the power and the terrors of His presence. But, it was in a far different way that God was pleased to redeem men from the tyranny of Satan. He came upon earth, not as a glorious conqueror, but as a weak and helpless babe. He took for His mother, no powerful queen or noble lady, but an humble Virgin of Nazareth, espoused to a carpenter. It was by a death of shame that He chose to conquer, and His cross of agony was the trophy of His victory. He might have conquered in many other ways, which would have equally displayed His power and generosity, while they would have cost Him no suffering; but He preferred to triumph through suffering, because in this way He could best prove His surpassing love for men. Love is a priceless treasure. Even when men give us their love, we feel that they have given us their best gift. But, as for the love of God, all the joys of heaven are as nothing to it, since heaven itself would not be happiness without the love of God Who, then, can tell what a gift it was, that Jesus bestowed on men, when He suffered and died for them; for greater love than this no man hath, that a man lay down his life for his friends."

Such being the way in which our Lord Himself conquered, He appointed the same way for His Church to conquer, in order that she should be one with Him, His associate in all things, in lowliness and in suffering, as well as in glory. The men whom He chose to be the founders of His Church, were not such persons as an earthly king would choose to do a great work. For he chose, in the first place, Simon, & poor and ignorant fisherman, to whom He gave the name of Peter, which means a rock, saying to him, "Thou art Peter, and upon this rock, I will build my Church, and the gates of hell shall not prevail against it ;" and after that He chose eleven other apostles, some of them fishermen, but all of them men without any worldly power or station. He did not tempt them to follow Him by promises of earthly pleasure, or riches, or honor: but He told them, that if they would have His love, and share His glory, they must also share His sufferings. He told them that they would be hated of all men; that their fathers and brothers, and even their children, would rise against them; that they should be taken before governors and kings, and scourged, and put to death; and that they must, therefore, cast from them all love of father and mother, and wife and children, and brothers and sisters; yea, and of their own lives also, and must carry their cross, and come after Him. These were strange words wherewith to lure men to His service; but He coupled with them promises, which had a power to bind loving hearts to Him with a bond which neither earth nor hell could loose.

For He offered them the priceless treasure of His love, in return for their poor love. He opened to them the secret, unfathomable depths of His sacred Heart; and He promised them that He and the Father would love them, and would come to them, and make their abode with them, and give them an everlasting life of glory. One sees every day that when men are in pursuit of some earthly prize, they think nothing of toil and danger; and, in like manner, these sweet promises of Jesus' love, thrilled through the hearts of apostles, and saints, and martyrs, and rendering them careless of suffering, made them long for torture and death, as the richest prizes that could be offered them.

But though the heathen could never have conceived that God would have selected such a mode of triumph for Himself and for His Church, it is not hard for us to understand why He preferred it. He chose it for Himself, because He could thus best show His love for men; and He chose it for them, because it allowed them to show their love for Him. He might have subdued the unruly wills of men and asserted His just empire over their affections, in some way which they could not have resisted; but then, though He would have been honored and obeyed, He would not have been freely loved. His heart, however, yearned for man's love; and love has no value, if it be not freely given. It is a wonderful mystery that God, who possesses all things, and who is so perfectly happy that nothing can add to His happiness or take from it, should yet deign to ask man for anything, and to give him the power of refusing Him. And yet it is so; for God asks us for our hearts, and he leaves us free to give them, or to refuse them to Him, in order that if we give them, He may, so to speak, obtain from us that gift of our free love, which He has deigned to prize so highly.

We may form a true estimate of our love for a person, by what we are willing to suffer for him. We constantly see that fathers are willing to work very hard to earn food for their families; and that mothers will watch anxiously and tenderly by the bedside of their sick children; and we think it only natural that they should do so, because we know how fondly they love their families, and we all feel that we would do anything to serve those whom we love very much. In like manner, when we read how much the martyrs suffered for our Lord Jesus, and how joyfully they bore their sufferings, we feel sure that they must have loved Him very much; and what is more, when we compare all that they actually suffered for Him, with what we are willing to suffer for Him, we may be quite sure that they loved Him much, much more than we do. The martyrs were torn away from their homes and families, and shut up in prisons, and scourged, and burned, and thrown to wild beasts, and tortured and put to death in all sorts of cruel ways, and yet they thought nothing of these dreadful sufferings. Our love for God is too often cold, and weak, and wavering, while theirs was such a pure and glowing love that it consumed all other affections within their hearts; and it inflamed them with such a desire to do and suffer more for Jesus, that even in the midst of the most cruel tortures, it seemed to them as if they were suffering nothing; so that in reading about them, we almost forget what they actually endured, in our admiration of that supernatural love, which gave them such an insatiable thirst for suffering.

Nor is the spirit of martyrdom in these days, extinguished. The Annals of the Propagation of the Faith tell us, from year to year, of martyrs in the East. Only six years have passed since priests were martyred in Rome, and scarcely more than sixty, since almost all the clergy of France died for their faith. And though in England more than a century has elapsed since the blood of martyrdom has flowed on the scaffold, yet, who does not know some who have given up wealth, and station, and home, with its sweetest ties, to embrace the faith of their fathers and emulate the early martyrs and be judged worthy to join their white-robed army in heaven.

In the following pages will be given the history of the Church's first struggle with the powers of the world and of hell, entrenched, as they then were, within the stronghold of the Roman Empire. We shall see what was the character of the love which gave strength and courage to the early martyrs, and how that supernatural love enabled them to conquer and to triumph over the power of that great pagan empire. Oh, that their spirit might communicate itself to us, and that we could love with such warmth that our petty trials and sufferings would be turned into joy, and that we might thus become more generous in our offerings of love to the loving heart of Jesus.

CHAPTER II

THE PERSECUTION OF THE FIRST CHRISTIANS

WHEN our Lord ascended into heaven, He ordered His disciples to remain at Jerusalem till they should have received the Holy Ghost. They obeyed Him; and after they had waited ten days, the Holy Ghost descended on them on the Feast of Pentecost, in the form of tongues of fire, which rested on their heads. They were now consecrated to the great work to which our Lord had called them, and so they lost no time in setting about it.

That very same morning St. Peter preached to the people, who were keeping the Feast of Pentecost at Jerusalem, and made three thousand converts. A few days after, he cured a lame beggar, who used to sit at the gate of the temple, and this miracle led to the conversion of two thousand more; so that already five thousand persons had entered into the service of Jesus. The disciples were very happy to see the wonderful power of Jesus over men's hearts, for it proved to them what a great and good Lord they were serving; but still there was another very different way in which they saw that all He had said to them, and all His promises to them, were true. He had told them that they should be brought before governors for His sake; and so it came to pass. For on the same day that they had cured the lame man, the chief priests, who were frightened to think that so great a miracle should have been performed in the name of the very person whom they had crucified, put St. Peter and St. John into prison, and kept them there till the next day. Then they set them at liberty; but they ordered them not to say anything more about Jesus and threatened to punish them very severely if they did so. But the apostles answered boldly that they would go on teaching the people to believe in Jesus, because He had desired them to do so, and they must obey God rather than men. They therefore went on preaching and working a great many miracles, so that nothing but the wonders they did, and the new religion they taught, was talked about at Jerusalem. Sick persons and those possessed with devils were brought to them to be healed; and as their fame spread, the crowds who followed them became so great that the sick people could not get at them; and then their friends placed them in their beds along the streets through which St. Peter passed, and as he went along his shadow fell on them, and they were cured.

When the chief priests found that the apostles did not care for their threats, but went on preaching about Jesus, they became still more angry than before, and they seized them all, and threw them into prison. But in the middle of the night an angel came to them, and opening the doors of the prison, led them out, and told them to go and preach again in the temple. It is easy to fancy what must have been the rage of the priests the next morning when they found that the apostles had made their escape out of prison and were again teaching in the temple. They did not however, dare to show their anger openly, because they were afraid lest the people, who liked to listen to the preaching of the apostles, might make a disturbance. So, they sent for them quietly, and scourged them privately, and then dismissed them, telling them that if they dared again to mention the name of Jesus, they would treat them even worse still.

When the apostles found that they were thrown into prison and scourged for obeying Jesus, it would have been only natural for them to have thought whether, after all, they had been wise in entering His service; or, at least, they might have determined to be more prudent and more quiet for the future, and to take great care not to attract the attention of the priests. But they did not look on the matter in this way. Instead of being frightened and discouraged, they only rejoiced. Jesus had promised that they should be brought before governors and scourged, and His words had now come literally to pass. They were therefore more sure than ever that He was God the Son; their love for Him was greatly increased; and, so far from being sorry for what had happened, they only longed to suffer more for His sake, and they thought of nothing but how to spread the knowledge and love of Him through the whole world. They had already given up their homes, their families, and their worldly goods, for His sake, and all the converts they gained were obliged to make the same sacrifices. It generally happened that only one or two out of a family were converted; and then the rest were sure to treat the converts unkindly, so that they had either to leave their homes altogether, or to put up with a great deal of persecution and ill-temper from their relations. As to their worldly goods, those who had to work for their daily bread were reduced to great poverty, because no one would employ them; and even those who were rich also became poor; for they sold their estates, and gave the money to the Apostles, who made a common stock of it, and gave each of the Christians barely what was enough for his support. Though they were like sheep in the midst of wolves, yet they were very happy; for, as they had given up everything in this world, they had nothing more to lose. They hired peacefully together, having but one heart and one soul, loving Jesus, and loving each other, and caring little for the troubles that befell them. They were not frightened even at the thoughts of being put to death for their religion; because Jesus had told them that this would happen to some of them, and they knew that the more they should suffer on earth for His sake, the happier they should be in heaven.

For a short time things went on quietly, and it seemed as if the priests would take no further trouble about them. But this did not last long; for the devil could not let the apostles alone, and he soon stirred up another persecution against them. Now matters were carried further than before, and St. Stephen was stoned to death, while he prayed to God to forgive his murderers. The persecution became so hot that all the Christians, except the apostles, were obliged to leave Jerusalem. This must have been a great trial to them. It had formerly cost them a great deal to give up their homes, their families, and their worldly goods; but they had then had the consolation of gaining a great deal in exchange for all they had given up. The upper chamber, in which they used to meet for prayer and holy Communion, seemed to them the best of all homes; our dearest Lady was a mother who loved them even better than their natural mother did; the apostles were kind and affectionate fathers to them; the whole body of Christians were their brothers, and sisters, and friends; and the blessed sacraments, by which they were fed with the Body of Jesus, and washed in His precious Blood, made them much more happy than all the gold and silver in the world could have done. So long as they had these things, the loss of everything else seemed little. But they were now obliged

Persecution of the First Christians

to give up even these, and to wander alone without mother, or father, or brethren, not knowing where they would meet again, or even how they were to receive those sacraments which were their spiritual food. The heart of many a young convert must now have sunk within him and many a one whose faith and hope were weak, must have found it hard to remember that all these things were no more than what Jesus had promised them. Still, though it was a great trial, Jesus was ever with them, and He comforted them, and gave them strength to bear it all patiently.

When the priests and the rest of the Jews saw that no one followed the Apostles, they were very glad; for they believed that the new sect was quite destroyed, and that they would never again be troubled by hearing the hated name of the crucified Jesus of Nazareth.

But God is always ready to help His Church, and He never fails to turn the devices of the devil against himself. The Christians, who were scattered throughout Judea and Samaria, carried the Gospel with them, and wherever they went they made a great many converts. The number of their converts was so great that at last the priests found it necessary to send down amongst them Saul, a young man who had taken a principal part in the death of St. Stephen, and who was well known for his great hatred of the Christians, and his zeal in persecuting them. But as Saul was going to Damascus, thinking only of cruelty and bloodshed, our Lord Jesus met him. A bright light shone round him and his companions, so that they were frightened and fell on their faces; and while they lay on the ground, trembling with fear, Saul heard a voice which said to him:- "Saul, Saul, why persecutest thou Me?" Saul had never thought of persecuting anyone except the miserable followers of this new sect, and so he tremblingly asked, "Who art thou, Lord ?" And Jesus answered, "I am Jesus whom thou persecutest. It is hard for thee to kick against the goads." This loving answer so touched the heart of Saul that he was instantly converted, and offered to do whatever Jesus wished; and Jesus ordered him to go into the city, where he would be told what he was to do. He obeyed, and went to Damascus, where he remained three days blind, having lost his sight from the bright light which he had seen on his journey. At the end of that time our Lord sent Ananias, a Christian, to baptize him and to restore his sight. He was now so completely changed that he could scarcely be called the same man he had been before. His hatred for Christians was turned into the most fervent love for Jesus and for them. He gave up his high rank and good name among the Jews; he made up his mind to be despised and laughed at for his sudden conversion; he left his home, his country, and all that he loved; and he spent the rest of his life in traveling from place to place and preaching the Christian religion, which he had formerly labored so hard to destroy. In the course of his journeys, he went through many dangers and many persecutions from both the Jews and the Gentiles; he suffered hunger and thirst, cold and nakedness; he was often thrown into prison; he was frequently scourged; he was thrice shipwrecked; he was once stoned and left for dead; and yet all seemed little to him, because he always wished to do and to suffer still more and more for Jesus, who had done and suffered so much for him. At length he had the great happiness of laying down his life for Him, who had died on the cross to save him from sin and hell.

Thus we see that persecution, suffering, and death, were the lot of Christians from the very first. We learn, too, from the example of the apostles and the first

Christians, how we ought to look on any sufferings or persecutions which we also may have to bear for Jesus' sake. These early Christians, instead of being discouraged, or tempted to give up their religion, were only encouraged to hold more closely to it. For they remembered that these very trials were what Jesus had promised them; and when they saw His words come to pass they felt more certain than ever that their religion was the only true religion. Our trials are much less than theirs; but still, so long as they come on us for our love to Jesus, we may look on them as the apostles did, and then, instead of being trials, they will be turned into blessings and causes of joy.

CHAPTER III

ST. MARY MAGDALEN, ST. MARTHA, ST. LAZARUS, AND ST. JOSEPH OF ARIMATHEA

THE persecution of the Christians, after the martyrdom of St. Stephen, was a means of spreading the Gospel, not only in Judea and Samaria, and the neighboring places, but also in other distant countries.

It is mentioned in the Gospel of St. John that the priests wished to put Lazarus to death, because many people, hearing of the great miracle which our Lord had worked in raising him to life, came to Bethany to see him; and, after hearing how it had all happened, some of them became followers of Jesus. After our Lord's death Lazarus continued to draw many people into the Church, and so long as he was there, a living proof of Jesus' divine power, the priests saw that all their labor in rooting out this new sect would be lost. They also hated Lazarus' sisters, Martha and Mary, because they had such great love for Jesus ; as well as Celidonius, the man who had been blind from his birth, and had received his sight from our Lord; and also Joseph of Arimathea, who had begged His body from Pilate, and had buried it in his own sepulcher. They determined, therefore, to get rid of them all at once. So they seized them and several other Christians, one of whom was Maximianus, one of the seventy disciples, and another was Marcella, a servant of Martha's, who is said to have been the woman who cried after our Lord, "Blessed is the womb that bore Thee and the paps that gave Thee suck." But being afraid to put them publicly to death, they shut them all up on board a crazy old ship, which they allowed to drift out to sea without any sailors to steer it, making sure that they would all be lost at sea, and that no one would hear anything more about them. But He who is the Lord of the winds and the waves was with them, and bore them safely over the stormy sea, and at last carried them into the harbor of Marseilles, a city on the south coast of France, or Gaul, as it was then called. Here they landed; but a new difficulty soon met them. For the people of the country, being pagans, refused to give them food, or to let them go into their houses; so that for some time they were obliged to shelter themselves from the cold and rain under the portico of a heathen temple, trusting that God would provide for all their wants. St. Mary Magdalen stood on the steps of the temple and spoke to the people, telling them how foolish they were to worship devils and dumb idols instead of the Lord of heaven and earth. At first they would not listen to her, but after some time they began to pay attention to what she said; and when they saw the miracles which she and Martha worked, many of them were converted and baptized. From this time the Christians were better off, and they soon settled peaceably in Marseilles.

 Lazarus was made bishop of the little Church which was now founded at Marseilles, and for a short time Joseph of Arimathea and Maximianus remained with him. But all the country round them was full of people who were given up to the service of the Devil, and were living in all sorts of wickedness; and the love of Jesus would not let them rest at ease while there were souls to be won for Him. So they broke up their happy party, and St. Joseph of Arimathea, and St. Maximianus, set out to travel as missionaries through Gaul. St. Maximianus did not go very far, but settled himself down in a town in the same province, called Aix, of which he was the first bishop. St. Joseph of Arimathea, however, traveled many hundred miles, and wherever he went he made converts; and some writers have said that he even crossed into England, and was the first person who preached Christianity in that island.

The women of the party were joined by several women of the country, and gave themselves up to prayer and fasting, and works of charity. St. Mary Magdalen, however, did not remain long with the others. When Jesus had been on the earth, she had always sat at His feet, or walked close to Him, looking into His face, and listening to His words. And now she could not bring herself to live any other sort of life. So she left her sister, and went into a desert place, where she wept and did penance for her sins, just as if she had never wept for them before; and she passed all her nights and days with Jesus, speaking to Him in prayer, and looking at Him in spiritual contemplation. Thus she spent thirty years in solitude, and led a life more like that of angels than of men.

Though Martha was now very busy serving Jesus by doing good to the poor, she was not so troubled about many things as she had once been. In the midst of her works of charity, she found plenty of time for prayer; for she is said to have knelt down to pray a hundred times during the day, and as often during the night. She did not now complain that Mary left her alone to serve our Lord, for she knew that Mary was helping her as much, or even more, by her prayers, than she could have done in any other way.

The two sisters died within a week of each other. A year before St. Martha's death, God revealed to her when she should die, and immediately after she fell ill of a fever from which she never recovered. A week before her death, she heard the most beautiful music, made by the angels who were carrying her sister Mary's soul to heaven, and at the same moment St. Mary Magdalen appeared to her, and told her she was just dead. But St. Martha had even a better visitor than her sister; for a short time before she died, Jesus Himself came to visit her, and He said to her, in a loving and familiar manner, "Come, my dearest hostess, come to me; for as you received me into your house on earth, so will I now take you into mine in heaven." This joyful vision made St. Martha feel how unworthy she was to go to heaven. She insisted on being placed on the hard floor, strewed with ashes, in a spot where she could look up to the sky. While she lay in that posture, holding a cross in her hand, she desired some due to read her the account of our Lord's passion out of the Gospel of St. Luke; and just as they read the words, "Father into Thy hands I commend my spirit." she expired, and gave up her soul into the hands of her heavenly Father.

St. Mary Magdalen died on the 22nd July, and St. Martha on the 29th of the same month, on which days the Church celebrates their feasts.

CHAPTER IV

ST. JAMES THE GREAT

THE first of the apostles who had the honor of dying for Jesus was St. James, one of the sons of Zebedee. Many years before, his mother had asked our Lord to grant, that he and his brother John might sit, the one on His right hand, and the other on His left, in His kingdom. But Jesus said to her, "You know not what you ask." Then turning to James and John, He asked them, "Can you drink the chalice that I shall drink?" To which they answered boldly, "We can." Jesus then said to them, "My chalice, indeed, you shall drink; but to sit on my right or left hand, is not mine to give to you, but to them for whom it is prepared by my Father." By these words, He promised them that they should suffer for Him as He was about to suffer for them; while, at the same time, He refused to tell them what reward they should have in heaven, since God the Father would give them places according to their merits, and in any case, it would be reward enough for those who love Him, to be with Him in heaven. It was not long before His promise about suffering was fulfilled to both brothers, though St. James was the first to get his reward.

During the persecution which fell on the Christians after the death of St. Stephen, St. James left Jerusalem and preached in Samaria. He afterwards traveled through different countries, and at length arrived in Spain. He was the first to preach the Gospel in Spain, and, therefore, he has always been venerated by the Spaniards as their patron saint. While he was in Spain he is said to have had a beautiful vision. He was living in the city of Saragossa, and one night, after a long day's preaching, he went out to refresh himself by praying near the river Ebro, on which the city stands. While he was praying he saw our Blessed Lady standing before him on a jasper pillar, and all around her were multitudes of angels, shining gloriously, and singing the sweetest hymns he had ever heard. St. James wondered how our Lady could be there, because he knew that she was still alive, and was living at Jerusalem; but seeing that it was really she, he bowed down before her. Then she said to him, "Build a church in this place in my name, for I know that this part of Spain will be particularly devout to me, and from this moment I take it under my protection," and as soon as she had spoken these words, she and all the angels vanished. The apostle now perceived that it was a vision that he had seen, and that our Lady had been brought from Jerusalem by the angels for the purpose of telling him to build a church there in her honor. So he lost no time in obeying her; but he built on the very spot on which she had stood a chapel, which he called the Chapel of our Lady of the Pillar; and to the present day a chapel with this name stands on the same spot, and is held in great veneration throughout Spain.

After having spent some time in Spain, St. James returned again to Jerusalem. He preached with such fervor, and made so many converts, that the Jews were very angry with him, and plotted how to kill him. They had formerly said that our Lord worked all His miracles through the power of the Devil, and now they said the same of St. James. They, therefore, went to Hermogenes, a famous magician, who was really a servant of the Devil, and they got him to send Philetas, one of his disciples, to try what could be done against St. James by all sorts of magical incantations. But it turned out quite contrary to what they expected; for Philetas being astonished at the great works which he saw St. James do, was converted, and falling at his feet, begged pardon for his sins and was baptized. He then returned to Hermogenes, and tried to persuade him also to become a Christian. But Hermogenes flew into a great rage, and ordered the devils who helped him in his sorceries to injure St. James and Philetas. The devils would gladly have done as he bade them, but they could not; for they had no power over Christians, and instead of being able to hurt them, they were forced to obey them, and even to fly when the sign of the cross was made. For some time Hermogenes and his devils fought hard against St. James, trying in vain to work all sorts of magical incantations against him, and the less they succeeded the more angry Hermogenes became. But at last he saw plainly that the Lord Jesus, in whose name St. James worked his miracles, was much stronger than the devils who helped him. Then be became frightened to think how wicked he had been, and he resolved to have nothing more to do with sorcery and such devilish arts; and he burned all his books of magic, and after having been instructed by St. James, he was baptized.

When the Jews saw that this plot had not succeeded, they were very much disappointed. They were determined, however, that St. James should not escape, and so they laid another plot against him. They now arranged to raise a disturbance while he was preaching, and they agreed with two Roman centurions, Lysias and Theocritus, to have their soldiers ready to seize him. whenever they should give them a sign to do so. This time their wicked scheme succeeded.

St. James the Great 21

One day, while St. James was preaching and proving out of Scripture that Jesus was the Christ, some of the people seemed to be displeased with what he was saying. Then Abiathar, the high priest, thought this would be a good opportunity for seizing him, and he gave the sign which had been agreed on with Lysias and Theocritus; whereupon Josias, a scribe, rushed on St. James, and threw a cord round his neck, while, at the same moment, the soldiers seized him, and carried him off prisoner to King Herod. This Herod was not the wicked Herod who had beheaded St. John Baptist, and had insulted and mocked our Lord. He was nephew to that Herod, but he was not less wicked than his uncle had been. He saw that the Jews wished to have St. James put to death, and, therefore, without inquiring whether he was guilty of any crime or not, be ordered him to be beheaded.

St. James went joyfully to execution. He did not now think about whether he should sit on the right hand or the left of his dearest Lord, or whether he should be given a high or a low place in His kingdom. But he knew that in a few short minutes he should look again on that sweet face which he had not seen for ten long years, and he felt that it would be enough to make him happy for ever only to be with Jesus and to see Him. As he passed along the street a poor paralytic man saw him, and cried out to him to heal him, and St. James instantly did so. This miracle led to a still greater one, which was the conversion of Josias, the scribe. Josias had often heard St. James preach, and had hardened his heart against all he said; but now he was struck with the holy joy with which St. James went to die, and with the miracle worked on the paralytic man, that he was suddenly converted. He cried out that Jesus Christ was the true God, and he humbly begged St. James to forgive him all his sins, and especially what he had done against himself. St. James was so rejoiced at his conversion that he could not help crying for joy, and he answered him very kindly and affectionately, and gave him the kiss of peace, as was then the common custom among all Christians Josias was soon called to prove whether he was sincere in what he had said about believing Jesus to be God; for the Jews were so enraged at what passed between him and St. James, that they insisted that he also should be put to death. So Josias and St. James were led together to execution, and both received the glorious crown of martyrdom at the same time. Though Josias was not baptized, yet his martyrdom gave him all the blessings which he would have received in baptism, and so persons who were martyred before they had an opportunity of being baptized, were said to be baptized in their own blood. The martyrdom of St. James and Josias took place A. D. 44, about twelve years after our Lord's death.[1]

---

[1] This supposes that our Lord was crucified in the year 33. Easter, 44, would begin the twelfth year.-Tillemont, tom. i. p. 655.

CHAPTER V

ST. JAMES THE LESS

THE time was now come when the Gospel was to be preached in all parts of the world. So the apostles assembled at Jerusalem to divide the different countries between them; and then each of them set out to preach in that place which God had given him charge of. This division is said to have taken place about twelve years after our Lord's death.

But though the Jews had crucified our Lord, and had refused to believe the Gospel, which was preached to them by the apostles, our Lord did not yet quite cast them off, but still allowed one of the apostles to remain with them. This was St. James the Less, who was ordained Bishop of Jerusalem by St. Peter and the other apostles, soon after the descent of the Holy Ghost. He was the son of Cleophas, who was brother to St. Joseph, and was therefore supposed to be cousin to our Lord; and he was so like Him in face that people often came to Jerusalem to look at him, in order to see what Jesus was like. He was called the Less, to distinguish him from the other St. James, the son of Zebedee; and also *Justus*, or the Just, because he was such a very holy man.

From his birth[2] he was consecrated to God, according

---

[2] Euseb. *Hist. Eccles.* ii. 23.

to a Jewish custom, and he had therefore never drunk wine or spirits, or eaten meat, or cut his hair, or used a bath. His tongue always spoke the truth, his hands were always ready to do works of charity; and his body was always mortified with fasting. His nights and days were spent in prayer, so that both his knees and his forehead, with which he used to strike the ground when he made acts of contrition, were quite hard, like the knees of a camel. Even the Jews looked upon him as a great saint, and as he passed through the streets they used to try to touch him and to kiss his clothes.

He was Bishop of Jerusalem for nearly twenty-eight years. The holiness of his life led the Jews to listen more readily to his preaching; and he made many converts both among the common people, and among the rulers. The Scribes and Pharisees were now very much troubled to find that the Christians were increasing in number, and they feared that in a short time the whole nation would become Christian, and believe Jesus to be the Messiah. They therefore consulted with Ananus, the High Priest, a fierce and cruel man, as to what was to be done. They all agreed that it would not be safe to oppose St. James openly, because the people thought so highly of him; and they accordingly devised a plan by which they hoped either to force him to deny Christ, or to kill him without making any disturbance. They spoke fair words to him as if they had been his friends, and told him that since he was so great a servant of God, and so zealous for the honor of the Temple, in which he spent so many days and nights in prayer, he ought to do something to defend it and the Old Law. "We entreat you, therefore," said they, "to tell all the people who come up to the Passover, that they ought not to run after this crucified man, Jesus. They will be sure to listen to you, because everyone knows what a just man you are, and that you do not care for the opinion of men; and we have all the greatest confidence in you." St. James promised them that he would speak to the people about Jesus, and they were satisfied. When the appointed day arrived they took him up to the top of a very high part of the Temple, where he could be seen and heard by immense crowd of Jews and Gentiles, who were assembled below. Then the chief priests, after saying many flattering things in his praise, cried out to him, "Oh thou just man, whom we ought all to believe, since all the people are led astray after Jesus that was crucified, tell us what thou thinkest of this man, Jesus!" And St. James answered, with a loud and solemn voice, "Why do ye ask me respecting Jesus the Son of Man? He is now sitting on the right hand of God the Father, and will come again on the clouds of heaven." Many of those in the crowd who were inclined to be Christians, were very glad to hear these words, and they cried out, "Hosanna to the Son of David." But the Pharisees and priests said: "We have done foolishly in letting this man bear witness to Jesus. But let us now go and throw him down, so that the people may be afraid to believe him." So they rushed up to St. James, and making a great noise, they cried out, "Ah! Justus himself is deceived;" and laying hold on him, they flung him down headlong from the height on which he stood. Though the fall hurt and bruised him very much, yet it did not kill him; whereupon his enemies began to stone him. But he, remembering how Jesus had prayed for those who were crucifying him, had no sooner reached the ground than he placed himself on his knees, and lifting his hands and heart to God, he prayed, "I entreat Thee, my Lord God and my Father, forgive them, for they know not what they do." The Jews, however, did not listen to his words, but went on stoning and beating him, till at last one of the priests, who was a

Rechabite, cried out to them, "Stop! what are you doing? Justus is praying for you." But just at that moment a fuller fell upon him, and beat out his brains with the club he used to beat out clothes. Thus did this holy apostle die, and win his crown of martyrdom, on Easter-day, A.D. 62.

By this murder the Jews filled up the measure of their wickedness in persecuting the Church. A few years after, the Romans sent an army to besiege Jerusalem, and after putting to death more than a million of Jews, they destroyed the city and left not one single stone of the Temple standing upon another. Many of the Jews believed that these misfortunes happened to them because they had murdered James the Just; but we know that they had all been foretold by our Lord, and were the just vengeance of God on them, for having rejected and put to death One who is infinitely higher and holier than St. James, even our Lord Jesus, God the Son Himself.

CHAPTER VI

ST. PHILIP & ST. MATTHIAS

THE Church celebrates the feast of St. Philip on the same day as that of St. James the Less, though St. Philip's martyrdom took place ten years before that of St. James.[3] Very little is known of St. Philip either before or after our Lord's death. It is mentioned in the Bible, that it was he who brought Nathaniel to our Lord, and that he also showed our Lord to the Gentiles, who wished to see Him after they had heard of Lazarus being raised from the dead. Thus from the first he acted like a true apostle in bringing souls to Jesus. When the apostles divided the world between them, Upper Asia fell to him. Here, then, he preached for several years, and by his holy life, his heavenly doctrine, and the miracles he worked, he converted a great many people. He also went into Scythia, a part of which is now called Russia, and which was then inhabited by ignorant, uncivilized nations, who lived in huts, or tents, or covered wagons. Here, too, his preaching brought forth great and wonderful fruit; and many of these wild people, who knew nothing else, knew all that was worth knowing, when they learned from this apostle how to love Jesus, and to save their own

---

[3] That is, supposing that he was martyred in the twelfth year of Claudius, as Baronius supposes. Tillemont gives no date, but inclines to a much later one.

souls.

At length St. Philip came to the city of Hierapolis in Phrygia, where he preached as he had done in all the other places. In this city there was a temple, and in it a strange and horrible serpent, which the people worshiped as a god, and to which they were in the habit of offering sacrifices of human beings. It was a sad sight to see so many people devoured by this serpent, and it was still more sad to see such a multitude worshiping the Devil in the form of this serpent, and offering to him the adoration which belongs to God alone. St. Philip was filled with pity for these poor deluded creatures, and prostrating himself before Almighty God, he prayed to Him with many sighs and tears, to open their eyes, and to deliver them from the tyranny of Satan. Our Lord heard his prayers, and caused the serpent to fall down dead. At first the people. were in great consternation at having lost their god; but when St. Philip spoke to them, and showed them how foolish they were to call such a poor beast as that a god, instead of worshiping the only true God who had made heaven and earth, they began to see their folly, and listened eagerly to all he had to tell them about this true God and Lord, Jesus Christ. But when the idolatrous priests saw that all the people were running after this new teacher, they became frightened lest their own credit with them, and their profits from the false religion, should be diminished. So they went to the magistrates, and persuaded them to seize St. Philip and throw him into prison. This, however, was not enough to satisfy them; for even in the prison St. Philip would go on preaching, and so long as he lived he would continue to fight against their master, the Devil, and to persuade people not to worship him. They, therefore, Scourged him very cruelly and crucified him, and as he hung upon the cross, they threw stones at him, and laughed at him, and reviled him. But even now they were not satisfied, for St. Philip did not seem to care for all they did to him. Instead of being conquered by them, it actually seemed as if he had the best of it; for as he hung on the cross he spoke joyfully and triumphantly, giving thanks to Jesus for having granted him the great honor of imitating Him by dying upon a cross. And while he was thus praising God, the earth began to quake and tremble, and the houses swayed backwards and forwards like ships in a storm at sea, and many of the finest buildings in the city were laid in ruins, and the ground opened, and swallowed up alive all the wicked men who had fastened him to the cross. The people of Hierapolis were dreadfully terrified, for all that St. Philip had told them about the great day of judgment rushed into their minds, and they thought that God was coming to judge them for their sins. Then they smote their breasts, and cried to God to have mercy on them; and some of them ran to the cross, and begged St. Philip to pray for them, while they made all the haste they could to take him down. St. Philip, however, was very sorry to be kept any longer alive; and while they were taking him down, he prayed to Jesus, begging Him not to disappoint him of the pleasure of dying on the cross, and not to keep him waiting longer for the bright martyr's crown which seemed to be almost within his grasp. His prayer was granted, for before the people could loose him, our Lord set him free in a better way; for He allowed his body to die, and took his blessed soul to Himself in heaven. The converts he had made carried away his body and buried it reverently, and many years after it was removed to Rome, where it lies in the church of the Twelve Apostles, together with that of St. James the Less

St. Matthias, the apostle, suffered martyrdom a few years after St. Philip. Still less is known about him than about St. Philip.

He was not one of the twelve apostles whom our Lord first chose; but after our Lord's ascension he was chosen in the place of Judas by St. Peter and the other apostles. to whom our Lord had given authority to appoint their successors. For some time, he preached in the neighborhood of Jerusalem, and afterwards he went into the most distant parts of Ethiopia. This country, which was to the south of Egypt, was then little known; but many Jews had gone there at different times; and we read in the Scriptures that one of these, a servant to Candace, the Queen of Ethiopia. was converted and baptized by St. Philip, the deacon. It may have been this man who persuaded St. Matthias to go to Ethiopia, though we do not know that it was. We know, however, for certain, that the Church founded there by St. Matthias and others of the apostles continues to exist even to the present day, while all the nations round it are either heathens or Muslims. St. Matthias made many long and fatiguing journeys in Ethiopia, and he underwent a great deal of persecution both from the Jews and the Gentiles. At last, he was stoned and beheaded, suffering martyrdom joyfully, on account of the great love he bore to his dear Lord Jesus. After many centuries, his body was brought to Rome. His death is said by some to have taken place about A.D. 60.

CHAPTER VII

ST. PETER AT ROME

WHEN the apostles assembled at Jerusalem, to divide between them the different countries in which they were to preach the Gospel, Rome, which was then the capital city of the world, naturally fell to St. Peter, the chief of the apostles. For seven years before this time he had been living at Antioch, the principal city of the East; but now he removed his bishopric to Rome. He entered that splendid city as a poor man, and its proud nobles did not notice him as they passed him in the streets. But our Lord had appointed him to reign in Rome for many centuries, and so it came to pass, that though he was such a poor and humble man, he, in the course of time, took away their city from those proud nobles, without their knowing how, so that instead of being, as before, the queen of the heathen world, and the capital of Satan's kingdom, Rome became the mother and mistress of all the Catholic Churches, and the head of the kingdom of Christ on earth.

But though the Roman nobles did not notice St. Peter, as he entered their city, the Devil had his eye on him; and knowing that he was going to do a great work for Jesus, he lost no time in guarding against the danger which threatened his own kingdom.

It is mentioned in the Acts of the Apostles that there was a great magician called Simon Magus, who bewitched the people by his sorceries, and made them believe that he himself was the great power of God, or, in other words, the Messias, whose coming was generally expected in the East. Simon having heard St. Philip preach, believed and was baptized. But he did not give his whole heart to Christ, for he wished still to keep up his credit with the people as a magician, and he therefore offered money to St. Peter and St. John, if they would sell him the power of giving the Holy Ghost to whomsoever he laid hands on. St. Peter reproved him very sharply for this sacrilegious thought, and told him to do penance for his wickedness, lest the curse of God should fall on him. But though Simon Magus was very much frightened, and begged Peter to pray God not to punish him, yet he did not repent. He had been accustomed to be thought a great man, and he could not bear to be nobody; so he soon returned to all his old wicked ways, practicing magic and working miracles by the help of the Devil; till at last, going on from bad to worse, he founded a sect of heretics, from which all other sects of heretics have sprung, and thus he became the head end leader of all the heretics that have since been in the world.

This Simon Magus, the head of all heretics, was the person whom the Devil sent to Rome to oppose St. Peter, the head of the Catholic Church. While St. Peter was busy preaching in every part of the city, Simon also was as busy preaching; but while St. Peter told the people that he himself was only a poor fisherman, and that Jesus was the God whom they were to worship, Simon told them what was to his own honor alone; for he said that he himself was the great God, and that a wicked woman, called Helen, whom he took about with him, was the Spirit of God. While St. Peter worked miracles to show the power of the true God, Simon worked all sorts of magical wonders to show his own power, and to make the people admire him and follow him. So St. Peter had enough to do in undoing all the mischief that Simon was doing. But though the Devil gave Simon a great deal of power, our Lord Jesus gave St. Peter still more; and thus it came to pass that at last St. Peter completely conquered Simon. This is said to have happened in the following way:

After they had been several years in Rome, St. Peter challenged Simon to try which of them could bring a dead man to life. Simon agreed, and the body of the dead man was brought into the room where they were. Simon made the first trial; but, though he was able by his sorceries to make the corpse move its head, yet still it remained as dead as before. St. Peter then prayed to our Lord for some time, and, after having done so, he ordered the dead man to rise; and instantly he got up perfectly alive and well. Then the people cried out that Simon was nothing more than a juggler, but that St. Peter was a great man, and that all he had told them about Jesus was true. Simon was in a great rage at having been conquered, and, fearing that he had quite lost his credit with the people, he determined to make a bold attempt to recover it. He pretended not to care about what they thought of him, and he spoke in a very scornful and majestic tone to them, telling them that since they were so foolish as to reject him and follow Peter, he would command his angels, even in their presence and before their very eyes, to carry him up in the air; and that he would go up into heaven, and would send down on them all sorts of misfortune as a punishment for their ingratitude. He even fixed a certain day, one Sunday, when he would take his flight up to heaven. On hearing of this impious boast, St. Peter gave himself to prayer and fasting, and all the Christians did the same, beseeching our Lord in some way or other to confound the diabolical arts of their great enemy.

On the appointed day Simon Magus went up to a very high place, and immense crowds assembled to see what he was going to do. The Devil was very anxious that Simon should recover his power with the people and lead them away from Jesus; so he sent his wicked angels to help him, and they lifted him up from the ground, so that he seemed to be flying up to heaven, as he had said he would do. When the people saw this wonderful sight they were very much astonished, and they cried out, "Simon is the only true God." But St. Peter was filled with grief, and, raising his eyes to heaven, he prayed very humbly and fervently; and then, speaking in a loud voice so that everyone could hear him, he ordered the devils to leave Simon, and to let him fall. The evil spirits were forced to obey St. Peter, and the moment they quitted Simon he fell down to the ground and broke both his thighs. Though he was so much hurt by the fall that he could not recover, yet it pleased our Lord not to let him die without giving him time for repentance. He was carried to Ariza, a village a short distance from Rome, and here he lingered on in great pain till the next day; but the unhappy man had so long been thinking only of his own glory, that he had made self his God, and he was now too hardened to humble himself even before the God of heaven and earth. So he died miserably without having repented of his horrible wickedness. His dreadful end was, however, the means of saving many other souls; for a great many of those who saw his fall were converted by it and became Christians. Among them were two of his disciples, Marcellus and Apuleius, who were baptized by St. Peter, and never left him till his death. They lived nearly thirty years after their conversion, and, at last, had the honor and happiness of dying for Jesus. They were martyred A.D. 90, on the 7th October, on which day the Church keeps their feast.

CHAPTER VIII

ST. NAZARIUS AND ST. CELSUS

ONE of the converts which St. Peter made at Rome was St. Nazarius. He was a Roman noble, and his father and mother were very rich. At that time the whole civilized world had been conquered by the Romans, and the Roman nobles were a very proud set of people. They had thousands of slaves who had nothing to do but to wait on them; and if any of these slaves disobeyed them, they punished them very cruelly, and sometimes even killed them. Besides this, numbers of persons who were not so well born as themselves, used to enter their service and call themselves their clients; and these clients made it their business to please them, in hopes of gaining their favor, and getting in return whatever they wanted for themselves. And so a Roman noble was always surrounded by flatterers, who praised whatever he did, and helped him to do whatever he liked, however wicked it might be.

This was the way in which Nazarius was brought up and so, before he became a Christian, it was scarcely possible for him to be otherwise than proud and selfish, and no doubt he lived a very wicked life, as the rest of the heathens did, thinking only of eating and drinking and all sorts of sinful pleasures. But at last he happened to hear St. Peter preach, and, moved by the grace of God, he was filled with sorrow for the sins of his past life, and longed to become a Christian. So he went to St. Peter and asked to be baptized; and when he had been baptized, he gave up all that he had, and took up his cross and followed Jesus.

Nazarius had more to give up than most people, and so it must have cost him more to leave it all for Jesus' sake. He was very rich and clever, and as he was not obliged to work for his livelihood, he was accustomed to think that his time was his own, to do as he liked every hour and all day long. But now that he had given up all that he had—his time, his talents, and his wealth, to Jesus—he spent the whole day in praying, or visiting the sick, or preaching to the heathen; and he gave all his money to be shared with the poor Christians, so that he had no longer anything which he could call his own. He had formerly been too proud to associate with anyone who was below him in rank; but now he spent his life with poor and common people, such as the Christians mostly were, loving them as his brothers, because they loved Jesus. It also cost him a great deal to leave his parents and his joyful and noble friends. The Romans had mixed up the worship of their false gods with every action of their daily life, so that Nazarius could not live with his parents as he had formerly done. He could not eat at their table, because all the meat had been offered to idols; he could not go with them to any party of pleasure, because there were sacrifices to the false gods; nor could he walk with them in shady groves, or sit beside the fountains in their gardens, because these, too, were dedicated to their gods. It almost broke their hearts to hear that their son had become a Christian, and was about to leave them; and they besought him with tears and caresses not to disgrace them, and bring their gray hairs with sorrow to the grave. It was a dreadful trial to Nazarius to make them so unhappy, and to appear so ungrateful to them for all their love and the care they had taken of him from his birth. When he saw his parents' grief, his heart would sometimes almost fail him, but he would strengthen himself by thinking that he saw Jesus bleeding on the cross for his sins, and he would remember our Lord's words: "He that loveth father or mother more than Me is not worthy of Me." And then he would make up his mind that it was better to grieve his parents than to grieve Jesus, who had loved him and done so much more for him than even his parents had.

After this great trial was over, it seemed a little one to separate from his friends; but often little trials are harder to bear than great ones. For some time the young Roman nobles wondered why Nazarius dressed so shabbily, and lived so meanly, and spent all his time in out-of-the-way parts of the town, where only poor people lived; but at last they came to know that he was a Christian, and then they were very angry with him for taking up such strange notions about a Jew who had been crucified, instead of worshiping the gods as all respectable people did. So, when they met him in the street, they would pass him as a low fellow who was a disgrace to his rank, or they would speak to him in a contemptuous, sneering way, which was even more trying to a proud young nobleman.

But Nazarius bore all these trials nobly, and he gave up generously all he had to Jesus, and Jesus repaid him with His grace a hundred-fold even in this life. He now increased in virtue from year to year, and his fame spread all over Italy, so that Christians from distant places used to come to ask his advice and received instructions from him. He was so holy that he was said to shine among the Christians at Rome like a star in the sky.

After Nazarius had been several years a Christian, our Lord told him to leave Rome and go to preach the Gospel in other places. He obeyed, and set off to travel through various parts of Italy, teaching the people and making converts wherever he went. When he left Rome he took with him a large sum of money; but he soon gave it all away to the poor in the places through which he passed, while he allowed himself only the coarsest food and most ragged clothing, and depended even for these on the alms that he picked up from day to day.

At last be arrived at Milan, which was then the second town in Italy. Here his preaching made such a stir that he was seized and taken before Anolinus, the governor of the city. Anolinus asked him his name and station. "I am a Roman noble," answered Nazarius, "my name is Nazarius, and the name of my family is known to all who have been in Rome." "A Roman noble, indeed," cried Anolinus, with a laugh, "A pretty fellow you are to be a Roman noble! Do Roman nobles wear such ragged old clothes as those?" And then Anolinus and his officers began to make sport of him as a fool and a madman. When they were tired of their joke, Anolinus asked him how he dared to make such a disturbance in the town, and to say such wicked things against the gods. "Because," answered Nazarius boldly, "Jesus, the only true God, has ordered me to come here, and to tell you that the gods you worship are not gods, but devils." Anolinus asked who Jesus was, for he had never heard of a god by that name. But when he learned that Jesus was a Jew, and had been crucified by Pontius Pilate, he was more convinced than ever that Nazarius was a madman and an impostor. He ordered him, therefore, to be cruelly beaten in the face, till the blood flowed down in streams, and he was driven out of the town amid the shouts and jeers of a mob, who thought it fine sport to mock and pelt him. It was contrary to the laws to strike a Roman noble, and once upon a time Nazarius could not have submitted for an instant to such an insult. But now he thought it a great honor to be insulted and buffeted as Jesus had been, and he therefore only prayed to God to forgive his persecutors, and shaking the dust off his feet, he set off to preach in some other place.

God now sent him into France. He traveled through different parts of that country, and wherever he went great numbers of people were converted. At one time, when he was in a town in France, a lady of high rank, whose name was Marianilla, came to see him. She brought with her a beautiful child, who was her son, and she said that she was come to give him to Nazarius. What made her do so, we do not know. It may have been that her husband was a pagan, and she knew he would not let her bring up her son as a Christian. Or it may have been that she was afraid that when the boy came to be a man, he would be proud of his high rank and his riches, and would not have the courage to give them up and follow Jesus. Or it may have been the pure and simple love of Jesus which moved her to do it. But at all events, we know one thing very certainly, which is, that this dear boy was the most precious thing she had in the world, and she wished to give him to Jesus. So she took him up to Nazarius, and putting his little hand within that of the Saint, she said :-"My father, I give you this child in charge for Jesus. He shall always go with you wherever you go, until you come to present him to the Divine Majesty." Then she said a short prayer, asking Mary to be his mother, and bidding all the saints and angels take care of him, and she kissed him and went away alone. And Nazarius took the dear little child, and baptized him by the name of Celsus.

From this time little Celsus never left Nazarius, but always traveled about with him, and shared all his dangers and hardships. Before this, Celsus had always lived in warm rooms; he had slept in a soft bed; he had eaten nothing but the best food; and he had been taken care of and petted by a kind nurse and a fond mother. But now he led a very different life. Sometimes he lodged in the house of some kind Christian, but more frequently he was with pagans, and then he was ordered off to the barn or stable, as being the place most fit for poor ragged people like himself and Nazarius. There were times when he would have been most thankful even for a stable to sleep in, for occasionally they would be turned out of doors, and would have to sleep under a hedge, or at the foot of a clump of trees. He very seldom got a comfortable meal, for he and Nazarius depended entirely on the alms they picked up, and they lived chiefly on the cold scraps from the tables of the rich, and too often they had scarcely enough even of these to satisfy their hunger. The warm clothes he had on when his mother gave him to Nazarius soon wore out, and no one gave him new ones. His shoes became full of holes, and at last dropped off his feet, and then he had to walk barefoot over stones, and through thorns and brambles, which cut and tore his feet and made them bleed in winter, he was drenched with rain and frozen with cold, and in summer he was scorched by the burning rays of the sun. This was a sad life for a delicate creature like Celsus to lead, and it would have been no wonder if he had sometimes longed to be back in his father's comfortable house, with his dear mother to take care of him. But the little saint never for one moment thought of such a thing. When his mother gave him to Nazarius, he had offered himself up to Jesus; and though he was so very young, he had determined to take up his cross and follow Him. He did not seem to feel cold or hunger, nakedness or fatigue; he did not care for the winter's cold, or the summer's heat; he did not notice that his food was bad; that his lodging in a stable was cold and dirty; that his clothes were tattered;

Sts. Nazarius and Celsus 41

or that his poor little feet were cut and bleeding. A bright smile was always on his face, and as he walked along by the side of Nazarius, or ran joyfully before him, he was always singing hymns of love and praise. But though he was so happy and cheerful, he did not care for playing like other children. He appeared to be always talking with God, and the holy angels and saints; and the greatest treat he could have was to collect round him little pagan children of his own age, and to tell them about the Heavenly Babe who was born at Bethlehem, and wh had no other home than a stable, and no better bed than a manger. Then it seemed as if he could never stop talking, and he would go on to tell them how this sweet Babe loved little children, and all about His mother Mary's happiness in nursing Him, and St. Joseph's care of Him, and about the glorious choice of angels who sang the hymns of triumph at His birth, and about the shepherds and the kings of the East, who came to worship Him in His lowly shed. As he spoke about other things, those who were listening would become so interested that they could not go away without hearing more about this Jesus; and so it came to pass, that many a soul was converted and saved, by the preaching of this holy little child.

But besides the hardships of his everyday life, Celsus went through many other trials with Nazarius. Sometimes he was roughly handled by mobs, who attacked them and pelted them with stones and dirt. At others he was thrown with him into cold and damp prisons; and on one occasion, he was taken before one of the Roman governors of France, who ordered him to be whipped till he would offer sacrifice to the heathen gods. When the governor gave this cruel order, he thought that a few sharp strokes would bring the boy to his senses, and make him give up all the nonsense that the old man had taught him. But he soon discovered his mistake. Little Celsus did not cry, or wince, as the rods fell on him, but he kept his eyes fixed on heaven, as if he saw beyond the blue sky sights which those around him could not see; and the only words he said, were, "Thou wicked man! the God whom I serve will judge thee." The savage governor was very much enraged at the boy's obstinacy, as he called it, and he would not let the executioners stop whipping him, till they were quite tired, and the blood was streaming from his wounds.

It was not long after this, that the first great persecution of the Christians, of which more will be said in the next chapter, broke out. The Emperor Nero, having heard that Nazarius was a Christian, ordered him to be brought, prisoner to Rome; and as Celsus could not be persuaded to leave him, he, too, was brought with him. The emperor knew Nazarius' rank, and was acquainted with many persons of his family, and he, therefore, determined to speak to him himself, thinking that he should easily persuade him to give up his folly. But Nazarius did not care for all the gold and silver, and all the honors with which the emperor tried to tempt him, because nothing less than the bright crown of martyrdom, and the high honor of serving the King of kings, could satisfy him. The only answer he gave to all the emperor's offers was, "What doth it profit a man if he gain the whole world, and suffer the loss of his own soul?" Nero was a cruel tyrant, and very few people dared to contradict him, so he was the more angry with Nazarius; and finding that his words had no effect on him, he flew into a great rage, and ordered him and Celsus to be thrown into the sea.

There is something very dreadful in being drowned, in being plunged into the deep sea, and in fighting and struggling hopelessly for breath; but Nazarius and Celsus did not think about the cold dark waves, or the deadly struggle of suffocation, but only about the bright heaven to which they would go. The emperor's officers took them out to sea in a boat, and when they were at some distance from the land, they threw them overboard. There was a great splash, and Nazarius and Celsus disappeared for a minute; then they rose, straining for breath, but no one tried to help them, and they quickly sank again. In another minute they rose a second time, and their breathing was hard, and there was a gurgling noise as if the water was choking them; but the cruel boatmen only laughed at their death struggle, and they sank a third time to rise no more. Then the men rowed towards the shore, and kept up their spirits by joking, or counting how much money they would get for their bloody day's work.

In this thoughtless mood they went along, and had almost reached the land, when suddenly looking up, they saw Nazarius and Celsus, the very persons whom they had just drowned, walking on the sea, and coming towards them. They thought they must be evil spirits, come to punish them for their sins; and so, throwing down their oars, and falling on their knees, they called on the gods to have mercy on them, and begged those who were risen from the dead to forgive them what they had done against them. Nazarius ordered them not to make such impious prayers to devils, for that it was the Lord Jesus who had saved him and Celsus from drowning, and that He would forgive them all their sins, if they would repent and be baptized. It was some time before they could listen to Nazarius, or be comforted by what he was saying; but at last they became more calm, and rowed to shore. And when they were landed, they threw themselves at Nazarius' feet, and begged him to tell them who was this mighty Jesus, whose name they had never heard before. Then Nazarius instructed them in the Christian faith, and, by the grace of God, they were converted and baptized.

Nazarius and Celsus, being now at liberty, set off again to travel through Italy, preaching the Gospel wherever they went. They came at last to Milan, where they were seized by Anolinus, the same governor who had formerly treated Nazarius so roughly. As Anolinus now knew that Nazarius had spoken the truth in calling himself a Roman noble, he did not dare on his own authority to punish him; be therefore threw him and Celsus into prison, and wrote to inform the emperor of what he had done, and to ask what more he was to do to them. Nero was very much enraged to hear that the persons whom he believed to have been drowned were alive, and he desired that they should be beheaded. His order was immediately obeyed, and St. Nazarius and St. Celsus were beheaded together, on the 28th of July, A.D. 68, on which day their feast is kept by the Church. More than three hundred years after their death, their bodies were found at Milan by St. Ambrose.

CHAPTER IX

First General Persecution

ST. PETER AND ST. PAUL

IT has been said that St. Nazarius and St. Celsus were martyred at a time when there was a general persecution of the Christians. There were several of these general persecutions, and this one, which was the first, took place in the reign of the Emperor Nero, A.D. 64. Before this time there had been no edict against the Christian religion; and though the Christians had often been persecuted, yet it had always been done in an irregular way; for they had never had a fair trial according to the laws, but had been ill-treated either by wicked governors or by mobs of people, who believed all sorts of false charges against them. Besides, these chance persecutions took place only in single cities and at particular times, so that if a Christian was in danger in one city he might escape to another, and very often he might return home after a short time, when people's minds had got quieter. But now the case was very different. For an edict was issued against the Christians; and though no law can make it just to put innocent persons to death, yet people often fancy that when the law is against a man he must be in the wrong; and many quiet folks, who had never before troubled their heads about the Christians, now began to think that they must be very wicked, and must be doing a great deal of harm, since the emperor had actually been obliged to issue an edict against them. Every one, therefore, set about persecuting them, giving information against them, and helping to have them put to death.

This persecution began in the following way. A dreadful fire, such as had never before been known at Rome, suddenly broke out and burnt down the greater part of the city. The public distress was very great; for thousands of persons had lost everything they had in the world, and were turned out to live for weeks in the fields, without a roof to cover them or any clothes to keep them warm. There were, of course, many inquiries into the way in which the fire had begun, and people wondered that nothing had been done to stop it. And then it began to be whispered about that the emperor himself had had the city set on fire, and had forbidden his officers to do anything to put out the fire; and that while the place was all in a blaze, he had looked down on it from a high tower, and had enjoyed extremely the grand spectacle which the flames presented. Nero had actually killed his own mother, and his wife, and many of the Roman citizens, so there was nothing too bad for him to do. The people, therefore, believed that he was the cause of all their misery, and they began to hate him very bitterly.

Nero was frightened when he found that all the Roman citizens hated him, for he was afraid they might rebel against him, and kill him, as they had done to several other emperors; and he was therefore at some pains to make them think better of him. He opened his own gardens to receive the people whose houses had been burnt down; he gave them houses to live in till their own should be rebuilt; and he distributed corn among them. But all in vain; for nothing would persuade them but that he had set the city on fire. He then determined to shift the blame from himself to some innocent persons, and as the Christians were very generally disliked, he accused them of having done it, and he ordered them to be very severely punished for having done such a wicked thing.

Numbers of persons were now seized and put to the torture, to make them confess that they were Christians; and as they did not wish to deny their religion, but were only too happy to suffer for it, the prisons were soon full of them. Every kind of torture was invented to increase their sufferings. Some were scourged, others were nailed to crosses, others had to fight in the amphitheater with wild beasts, while others again were sewed up in skins and thrown to dogs to be torn to death. But this cruel monster invented even a more horrible kind of death for them. He gave a grand entertainment to the people of Rome; he threw open his gardens, where there were chariot and horse races, and all sorts of amusements; and when night came on there were splendid illuminations, and then, shocking to relate! the Christians, smeared over with pitch and other combustibles, were put in various parts of the gardens and were set on fire, to burn as torches to give light in the darkness to the people who were walking about and amusing themselves.[4] The very pagans turned in horror from the sight, and began to pity the poor Christians whom they had hitherto hated.

It was now nearly twenty-five years since St. Peter had first come to Rome. He had not, however, remained there all this time. Some say that he went into Spain and Britain, but this is not at all certain. There is, however, no doubt that he went into the East to visit the churches in Asia, and that he held the first council of the Church which met at

---

[4] Tacitus, *Annal*, i. 15.

Jerusalem A.D. 51, for the purpose of deciding some disputes that had arisen between the converts from Judaism, and those from paganism.

After he had spent some years in the East he returned again to Rome, A.D. 58; so that he was there when the persecution broke out.

Another apostle was also in Rome at this time, namely St. Paul. He had been brought a prisoner to Rome several years before, and had been confined for two years in a house under the charge of a soldier. During that time he had frequent disputes with the Jews who came to see him; he was examined by the Senate, and from one of his Epistles it appears that he was taken before the Emperor Nero. At the end of the two years he was set at liberty, and joined St. Peter in preaching at Rome. He did not, however, stay there long, but traveled into Italy, France, Spain, and some say even into Britain, spreading the Gospel to the furthest parts of the West. After spending eight years in this way he returned to Rome a short time before the persecution began.

It was a great comfort to the poor Christians to have these two great apostles with them at this dreadful time. Both St. Peter and St. Paul were remarkable for their great love of souls. St. Paul remembered that he had once persecuted the Christians, and so, though he was so great an apostle, he called himself the chief of sinners, and thought he never could do enough to make reparation for his sins. St. Peter, too, could not forget that he had formerly denied Jesus; and though he knew that his dear Lord had forgiven him, he could never forgive himself. There never passed a day in which he did not weep for having grieved so kind and good a Master, till at last his eyes became quite red from constant crying, and looked as if they had been dyed in blood. So both these apostles, out

Sts. Peter and Paul 49

of gratitude for Jesus' great love in forgiving them, labored hard to convert sinners, and to bring them to love Him as they themselves did. They now went about from house to house, and prison to prison, encouraging those who were frightened on account of the persecution, and comforting those who were being tortured, or who were in grief because their relations had been killed or imprisoned.

Happily St. Peter and St. Paul were left at liberty till towards the very end of the persecution. They were at last seized and thrown into the Mamertine prison, where they were kept shut up for nine months. During this time they were not idle, for they took every opportunity of preaching the Gospel to their guards and the other prisoners, and several persons were converted by their words, and by the miracles they worked. Among these were Processus and Martinianus, two soldiers who guarded them, and who, being converted, threw themselves at their feet and begged to be baptized. The apostles were very willing to baptize them, but it did not seem possible, because there was no water in the prison. But St. Peter made the sign of the cross on the rock on which the prison stood, and immediately there sprang out of it a fountain of clear water, which may be seen there to the present day. Forty-seven other persons were converted and baptized at the same time.

The Christians could not make up their minds to lose both their great apostles at the same time; and so they did everything they could to persuade St. Peter to make his escape from prison, which he could easily do now that his guards, Processus and Martinianus, were Christians. For a long time St. Peter would not hear of such a thing, because he longed to die for Jesus, and was very glad to think that he would soon have that pleasure; but at last the tears and entreaties of the Christians got the better of him, and he consented, like a good shepherd, to save his life for the sake of his flock. So Martinianus and Processus let him secretly out of the prison, and he passed through the gate of the city without being observed by any one.[5] But as he was going along, walking away from Rome, and had arrived at a place called Sancta Maria ad Passus, where a small chapel now stands, he met our Lord walking towards Rome, as if He were going into the city. As soon as St. Peter saw Jesus he knew Him, and said to Him, "Lord, whither dost Thou go?" And Jesus answered, "I go to Rome to be crucified again." This seemed a strange answer, for Jesus was now ascended into His glory, and could not be crucified again in Rome. What, then, could He mean by saying that He was going to be crucified again? But St. Peter understood what he meant, and he knew that as Jesus could not be crucified again in His own person, He wished to be crucified in that of His servant Peter. So he immediately turned to go back to Rome, and returned to the prison, determined to wait there to be martyred according to his Master's will.

At length the day fixed for the execution of the apostles arrived. The sentence against them was, that Peter, being a Jew, should be fastened to a cross; and that Paul, because he was a Roman citizen, should be beheaded. They were taken to the spot where the church of Santa Maria Transpontina now stands, and there they were cruelly scourged. They were then led forth to execution. On reaching the gate Trigemina or Ostiensis, which leads to Ostia, they had to separate, because they were to be executed at different places. So they embraced each other, and gave each other the kiss of peace, and parted joyfully

---

[5] Rohrbacher, *Hist. Eg. Cath.* xxv.; Origen. *In Joan*, c. 21; Ambr. *Serm.* 68.

knowing most certainly that in a few minutes they would meet again in the presence of Him, whom they both loved so dearly.

St. Peter was led to a high place, near the Vatican, where they stripped him of his clothes and nailed him to a cross. Though he was very happy to die in the same manner as his Master had done, yet he thought himself so unworthy of such a great honor, that he wished some little difference to be made between them; and so he begged the executioners to place his cross in such a way, that he should hang with his head downwards and his feet up in the air. In this position he would suffer much more pain; but he did not care for that, so long as he could have an opportunity of being humble, and of placing himself in a worse posture than his Lord and Master had been in. In this manner died St. Peter, the Prince of the Apostles, watering and sanctifying with his blood the city which was destined to govern the Church in his name, and over which he has ever since watched from his place in heaven. His body was taken away by a priest called Marcellus, who embalmed it, and buried it on a part of the Vatican at some distance from the spot where he was crucified.

Meanwhile St. Paul was led to the place appointed for his execution. When he came to the gate of the city he met a Christian lady, called Plautilla, who was crying very bitterly because he was going to be put to death. He asked her to lend him a handkerchief to blind his eyes, as was the custom with those who were beheaded, and he promised that it should be returned to her. She was very glad to do the least thing for him, and so she immediately gave him her handkerchief. As he went along he converted three soldiers, Longinus, Acestus, and Megistus, who were martyred a few days after. When he arrived at the place of execution, he prayed to God with great joy and fervor, and then bowing his neck to the executioner's sword, his head was severed from his body. St. Chrysostom mentions that when his head was cut off not a single drop of blood, but fountains of milk flowed from it; and as during his life he had had but one thought, which was Jesus, so now in death the same one thought followed him. For tradition says that when the head was severed from the body, it gave one leap, and then a second, and then a third, and at each leap the loved name of Jesus burst from the quivering lips, while on each spot on which the head rested a fountain of water sprang up, which three fountains are to be seen to the present day. His body was taken away by a devout lady called Lucina, who buried it with great reverence in her own garden. After his death St. Paul appeared to Plautilla, and gave her back the handkerchief which she had lent him.

There is an old fable about a monster called Hydra, which had a great many heads, and which never could be killed, because, as soon as one of its heads was cut off, two new ones sprang up in its room. The Church was like this fabulous monster, for as fast as one Christian was put to death, others sprang up in his place. The martyrdom of one Christian was so often the cause of a great many conversions, that it passed into a proverb that "the blood of the martyrs was the seed of the Church." Thus the martyrdom of St. Peter and St. Paul led to the conversion of above forty persons.

A few days after they had been put to death, Processus and Martinianus, the soldiers whom St. Peter had baptized in prison, were brought before Paulinus, one of the judges. Longinus, Acestus, and Megistus, who had been converted by St. Paul, as he went to martyrdom, were seized at the same time.

Paulinus at first tried to persuade Processus and

Sts. Peter and Paul

Martinianus to deny their religion. "Give up this folly," said he, "and return to the worship of the immortal gods who guard the Roman Empire, and to the religion in which you were born and bred; for be assured that if you do not, you will lose your rank and even your lives, whereas if you do as I bid you, the emperor will show you his favor, and bestow great riches and honors on you." The Christian soldiers, however, answered him, that they thought the faith and love of Christ worth much more than all the riches and honors the world contained; and as for death, it was long since they had learned not to be afraid of it. The Roman soldiers were trained in very strict discipline, and these bold words sounded strangely in the ears of a Roman judge like Paulinus; so he did not waste any more time in arguing with such men, but ordered their mouths to be struck, and all their teeth to be knocked out with large stones. Though such heavy blows on so tender a part as their jaws, gave them excruciating pain, yet they did not care in the least for all that they suffered, but only said, "Glory to God in the highest." Paulinus then ordered an image of the heathen god Jupiter to be brought, and commanded them to adore it; but instead of obeying him, they spat in its face. Here upon Paulinus flew into a great rage, and had them stripped naked and stretched upon the rack, so that their bones were all pulled out of joint; their sides were also burnt with plates of red hot iron, and their bodies were torn with a kind of whips called scorpions, and many other cruel tortures were inflicted on them. But they endured them all with great patience, singing songs of joy and triumph, and saying, "Thy name, O Lord! be forever blest. Let all Thy angels praise Thee, and let all Thy creatures bless and glorify Thee for ever and ever."

While these things were passing, the wicked Judge, Paulinus, was suddenly struck blind, and at the same time he was seized with such dreadful pains all over his body, that it seemed as if he was beginning, even in this world, to suffer the torments that were awaiting him in hell. He lived three days in this horrible state, and then he died most miserably. Pomponius, his son, instead of being frightened by the judgment that had fallen on his father, thought only of revenging his death. He, therefore, went to the emperor, and told him that Processus and Martinianus were magicians, and had killed his father by their enchantments. So Nero ordered Cesarius, the governor of the city, to put them to death immediately; and Cesarius had them beheaded in the Via Aureliana, outside of the city. Their bodies were left to be devoured by dogs, but Lucina, the same devout lady who had buried St. Paul, took them up and buried them in her garden. They were afterwards laid in a church dedicated to their honor, and at last they were removed to the great church of St. Peter's at Rome.

St. Peter and St. Paul were martyred on the 29th June, A.D. 66, and St. Processus and St. Martinianus three days later, on the 2nd of July, on which days the Church keeps their respective feasts.

CHAPTER X

ST. MARK

AMONG those who suffered martyrdom about this time was St. Mark the Evangelist. Though he was not one of the twelve apostles, yet he is a very remarkable person on three different accounts. First, he was the companion and interpreter of St. Peter, who loved him so much as to call him his son; secondly, he wrote one of the four Gospels; and thirdly, he was the person sent by St. Peter to found the patriarchal see of Alexandria.

It has always been the custom of the Catholic Church to appoint certain bishops to be archbishops, and to have authority over all the other bishops; and these archbishops, again, are under the jurisdiction of patriarchs, who, in their turn, are subject to the Pope; and so the whole church comes to be governed by St. Peter, and his successors, the Popes. The consequence of this is, that no Catholic priest or bishop can teach any doctrine he chooses, but only what has been taught by the whole Church, in all places and at all times; and so it comes to pass that there are no divisions in the Catholic Church. This is one great thing which distinguishes the Catholic Church from all heretical bodies; for heretics are always changing their doctrines, forming new sects, running after new teachers, and trying to reform their religion; and thus, in fact, they are always making a new religion for themselves.

At first there were only three patriarchates in the Catholic Church, viz.-those of Rome, Alexandria, and Antioch, all of which were founded by St. Peter.

The patriarchates of Rome and Antioch were founded by him in person; for, during seven years he fixed his bishopric, or his chair as it is called, at Antioch, and he afterwards removed it to Rome, where it has remained ever since. But he could not go himself to Alexandria, and so he sent St. Mark to found the patriarchate there in his name; and he gave it the second rank among the patriarchates, oven above that of Antioch, which he had founded himself.

St. Mark the Evangelist was one of our Lord's seventy disciples, and he afterwards became a follower of St. Peter, to whom he was very useful as an interpreter. For while St. Peter would be preaching in the language of the town in which he was, and which was understood by most of the people, there were often present strangers who did not understand what he was saying, and yet who, having seen his miracles, longed to know something about this wonderful new religion; and then St. Mark would be at hand to tell them in their own language all that St. Peter was saying. Sometimes, too, it happened that persons were inclined to become Christians, but could not quite make up their minds to be baptized; and then St. Mark was ready to listen privately to all they had to say, and to explain things more clearly to them. It was in the following way that he was led to write his Gospel. After great numbers had been converted at Rome by the preaching of St. Peter, they wished to have in writing what they had heard him say about our Lord Jesus, and they begged St. Mark to write it down for them. He did as they wished, and wrote in his Gospel what he had heard St. Peter preach; and, when St. Peter came to know what St. Mark had done, he highly

St. Mark 57

approved of it, and confirmed the truth of all that this Gospel contained.

After St. Mark had lived for some years at Rome, St. Peter sent him to Egypt to preach the Gospel among the Egyptians, who, more than any other nation, were given up to the most absurd and wicked superstitions. He went first to Cyrene and Pentapolis, and afterwards to Alexandria, the capital city of Egypt. He converted great numbers by his teaching and holy life, and by the miracles he worked; and because he was so good in the midst of such wicked people he was said to shine gloriously like the sun, which always looks brightest when it is surrounded by dark clouds.

St. Mark did a great work in Egypt; for he not only converted great multitudes from heathenism, but he led many of his converts to practice the evangelical counsels of perfection in a way which was not done at that time in other places. Everyone who became a Christian in those days had to make such heavy sacrifices of all sorts, that people did not generally think of leaving their Christian friends, and going to live alone in order to lead more perfect lives.[6] But many of the Christians of Egypt wished to give themselves up more entirely to God; and so they left their families, and gave all their property to the Church, and went away to live in solitary places, taking with them nothing for their bodies, but only the Scriptures and spiritual books which would feed their souls. Here their food was dry bread, and sometimes a few herbs; their drink was water; their clothing was barely enough to cover them; they kept up a continual fast, never eating till after sunset, and often passing three, and sometimes even six

---

[6] Marin.— "Vies des Peres des Deserts," Tom. i., liv. i., c. i

days without food. They observed the strictest silence; they spent their whole time in prayer, and were so absorbed in spiritual meditations, that their life was more like that of the angels and saints in heaven than that of men upon earth. In course of time there were so many of these hermits and monks, that the desert was peopled with saints, and the sound of prayers and hymns of praise was to be heard like beautiful heavenly music in every part of this wild and barren district. In one city called Oxyrynchus[7] there was actually no one except monks and nuns; and at Easter, when the monks and hermits assembled, 50,000 persons used to receive holy communion together.

The devil could not bear to see all that St. Mark was doing to save souls, and he would not let him go on long without trying to hinder his work. So he set his servants to persecute him; and several wicked men joined together to kill him. St. Mark was warned by God of the plot against his life, and he therefore prepared himself for death, and made arrangements that in case he was killed, his flock might not be left without a pastor. He ordained Anianus bishop, and appointed him to be his successor; and he ordained several priests and deacons, and other ministers of the Church; and when he had thus put all things in order in Alexandria, he set off to do the same at Pentapolis, which was at some distance. He had formerly preached at Pentapolis, and now all the Christians of the town were rejoiced to see him again. He remained with them two years, and during this time he confirmed the faith of the old converts, and added many new ones to their number. Here also he ordained a bishop, and priests, and deacons,

---

[7] Rohrbacher, *Hist. Eg. Cath.* xxxvli.

to instruct the people and govern the Church when he should be taken away from them.

At the end of two years, when all appeared to be quiet, and the pagans seemed to have forgotten all about St. Mark, he returned to Alexandria. He found that during his absence the Church had been very prosperous, and that the number of Christians was very much increased. This was a cause of great joy and thankfulness to him, and it made him doubly happy to be with his children again; and the Christians of Alexandria were not less happy to have their dear father and bishop once more among them. But their happiness did not last very long; for his old enemies no sooner heard of his return than they laid a new plot to kill him.

The day which they fixed on for the execution of their wicked plot was Sunday, the 24th of April. It happened to be a great festival in honor of the pagan god, Serapis, and crowds of people were assembled in the temple of Serapis, amusing themselves, and committing many horrible sins under the name of religion. It was always easy to raise a tumult in Alexandria, because the citizens were a very restless set of people; and they were so devoted to their god, Serapis, that it needed very little to stir them up against anyone who did not reverence him as they did. St. Mark's enemies told them that he was a great enemy to Serapis, and in a few minutes the whole town was in an uproar. Nothing but threats and curses on the Christians were to be heard, while the furious crowd rushed with shouts and yells to the Church. Here they found St. Mark saying Mass. They seized him roughly; they tied a halter round his neck; and, throwing him down, began to drag him about the streets. All day long the saint was in their hands, buffeted, pelted, pulled over the rough stones, half smothered in mud and filth; bruised and cut from head to foot, till his flesh was so torn that it hung, as it were, in rags about him, while the blood streamed from every part of his body. At length night came on, and the mad crowd, wearied out with their wicked sport, threw their helpless victim into a dungeon.

They went to spend the night in feasting and drunkenness, rejoicing at the thought of the plight in which they had left the hated Christian. But though there was not one sound part in his flesh, or a single bone which was not broken or bruised, or a single sinew which was not strained and aching, yet it was his body only which these servants of the Devil could hurt. His soul was free, and far above their reach; and as he lay in the damp and filthy dungeon, an almost shapeless mass of bleeding flesh, his spirit rose joyfully to Jesus, and he gave Him hearty thanks that He had allowed him to suffer for His sake. His little flock were weeping at home, or praying in the Church for their beloved bishop, while he lay alone on the damp floor, with no kind friend to bind up his bleeding wounds, to bathe his aching limbs, or to give him one drop of water to quench his burning thirst. But the saints of God can never be alone. At midnight when the prison gates were locked, and the guard was set, and the jailer felt certain that no one could enter, the earth began to quake, and a bright and beautiful angel stood by St. Mark, and gently touching him, said to him, "Mark, servant of God, your name is written in the book of life. You shall have your share and rank among the apostles, and your memory shall live forever. The angels will receive your soul and carry it into heaven, and the relics of your body shall be honored on earth." Oh! how calm and sweet did that holy voice sound after the angry and wicked shouts, which St. Mark had been hearing all day long. It filled his heart with such joy, that he forgot all his pains and aches, and lifting his hands to heaven, he thanked our Lord for having granted him so great a favor, and he besought Him to receive his soul. Then Jesus appeared to him, looking kind and loving, just as he was accustomed to do when St. Mark used to be with Him on earth, and He spoke to him in the same sweet and gentle voice which he knew so well, saying, "Mark, my evangelist, peace be unto thee;" and Mark answered, "Peace be with Thee, my good Lord Jesus Christ."

As soon as the morning dawned, the wicked crowd assembled to continue their cruel sport of the day before St. Mark heard them coming, when they were still a great way off, and their shouting was like the roar of a stormy sea. But it sounded to St. Mark even sweeter than the angel's voice; for it told him that he was going to suffer more for the love of Jesus, and that he should soon be with Jesus. In a few minutes the furious mob rushed into the prison, and they seized the old man, and tying the halter round him, they began once more to drag him about as they had done the day before. He was already so bruised, and cut, and exhausted, that he could not endure much more of this rough treatment; and in a short time his happy soul took its flight to heaven, and he was far beyond the reach of his cruel enemies. Even when they saw that he was dead, their rage was not satisfied, and they determined to burn the mangled body which was still in their power. But just as they were about to execute their wicked purpose, there arose a whirlwind, with a storm of thunder and lightning, and a shower of great stones which threw down several houses and quickly dispersed the crowd, wounding some, and killing others. In the confusion the Christians got possession of the body of their martyred bishop, and gave it honorable burial. After many centuries, when Egypt fell into the hands of the Muslims, the body of St. Mark was taken to Italy, where it was buried in the town of Venice. A beautiful church was built over it, and the republic of Venice placed itself under the special patronage of St. Mark, taking for its motto, the words of our Lord, "Pax tibi, Marce, evangelista meus." "Mark, my evangelist, peace be unto thee." Thus was fulfilled the promise of the angel, that St. Mark's relics should be honored upon earth. St. Mark is supposed to have been martyred in A.D. 68.

CHAPTER XI

ST. THOMAS, ST. BARTHOLOMEW, ST. MATTHEW, ST. SIMON, AND ST. JUDE.

VERY soon after the martyrdom of St. Peter and St. Paul, the Romans rebelled and murdered the Emperor Nero. After his death there were great troubles in the empire; for as soon as one emperor was chosen, another was set up against him. Three emperors, Galba, Otho, and Vitellius, thus came to be made emperors, and to be killed after each had reigned only a short time. They were succeeded by Vespasian, who found everything in great confusion, and had enough to do to put it all in order. He had, also, on his hands a great war with the Jews, which ended in the destruction of their city and temple. During all this time the Christians were left pretty much to themselves, for people were too busy with other things to trouble themselves much about them. It must not, however, be supposed that they were quite happy and free from every kind of trial. They had still to bear all sorts of little persecutions, such as their relations being unkind to them, and being refused employment on account of their religion, and not being able to get justice from the pagan magistrates, and many other things, like what Catholics in a Protestant country are now obliged hear patiently. But besides all this, they were sometimes cruelly punished and put to death by unjust governors, so that no great length of time passed without some of them being martyred.

It was during this time of comparative peace that the apostle, St. Thomas, suffered martyrdom in a distant country, far beyond the limits of the Roman Empire. St. Thomas' love for our Lord was of a very generous and impetuous kind. When Jesus was going to Bethany to raise Lazarus from the dead, the other apostles reminded Him how dangerous it was for Him to go there, because the people of Judea had lately tried to stone Him; but St. Thomas cried out courageously, "Let us go and die with Him." And when Jesus told the apostles, at the last supper, that He was going away from them, but that He would prepare a place for them, and that they knew the way to come to Him, St. Thomas was so eager to follow Him, that he cried out, half impatiently, "Lord, we know not whither Thou goest, and how can we know the way?" And after our Lord's resurrection, even though at first he would not believe what the other apostles told Him, yet when he did actually see Him alive, he was so overcome with joy that he could not contain himself, and he was the first to make that glorious confession, "My Lord, and my God." "He saw one thing," says St. Augustine, "and believed another: he saw a man, and believed that he was God."

St. Thomas had formerly cried out, "Let us go and die with Him;" and after Jesus' death, the same generous thought remained in his mind. He did not stop to think whether the countries he was going to were well known, or whether the people who lived in them were wild or civilized, or whether it would be dangerous to go among them; the only thing he thought of, or wished for, was to live and die for Jesus. And so he set off for countries which were scarcely at all known, and preached among nations who were very uncivilized. None of the other apostles traveled so far as he did. He is said to have preached to the Ethiopians, the Abyssinians, and Parthians, the Medes, the Persians, and the Hircanians; and one of the Jesuit fathers declares, that when he was in Brazil he saw with his own eyes, and heard from the natives, things which convinced him that St. Thomas had been there. But India is the country where he made the most converts.

There is a very pretty legend showing how he came first to go to India, and what happened to him on his arrival there. It is said, that when St. Thomas was at Caesarea, a town in Syria, our Lord appeared to him and said to him, Thomas, the King of India Gondofurus, has sent for the best workmen that can be found, to build him a more beautiful palace than that in which the Emperor of Rome lives. Behold, now, I send thee to him." St. Thomas did not ask how he, who was neither a mason nor a carpenter, could build such a palace as the king wanted; but he set out at once, in obedience to our Lord's command. After he had traveled several months, and journeyed over many hundred miles, he arrived at the part of India which belonged to Gondofurus. He went to the king, and told him why he had come so far, and the king was very much pleased to hear what he said, for though he was a heathen, he felt certain that a man who was sent to him from such a distance by God, would be sure to build him a much finer palace than anyone else could. It happened that Gondofurus was just then going into another part of his dominions, where he expected to remain two years; but before he went, he gave a great deal of gold and silver to St. Thomas, desiring him to hire workmen, and to buy whatever he required for the work. St. Thomas took the gold and silver, and promised the king that on his return he should find that be had built him a much more magnificent palace than even that of the

Emperor of Rome.

But as soon as the king was gone St. Thomas seemed to have forgotten all the promises he had made; for he hired no workmen, and bought no building materials, but gave. away to the poor and the sick all the treasures which the king had entrusted to him. The people of the place did not know what to make of him, for he was so kind and charitable that they thought he must be a good man; and yet, it seemed to them that he was cheating the king by spending all his money, and not building the palace as he had promised to do.

At the end of two years Gondofurus returned, longing to see the magnificent palace which St. Thomas had promised to have ready for him. He found, however, that instead of the palace being finished, the foundations had not been dug, nor had a single stone been laid, and that St. Thomas had spent all the money he had charge of. So he was very angry, and ordered St. Thomas to be thrown into prison, and to be put to a very cruel death. Just at this time the king's brother happened to die; and as the king was very fond of him, be took no more thought about punishing St. Thomas, but gave himself up to grief for the loss of his dear brother. And it came to pass after four days, that as the king and the courtiers were standing round the coffin and crying, the dead man opened his eyes and sat upright, and turning to the king, said to him, "The man whom you are going to torture and kill is a servant of God; for I have been in Paradise, where the angels showed me a wonderfully beautiful palace, built of gold, and silver, and precious stones, and they said to me, "This is the palace that Thomas has built for your brother, King Gondofurus." When the king heard these words he was very sorry that he had been so angry with St. Thomas, and he ran immediately to the prison and set him at liberty, begging his pardon, and asking him to pray to God to forgive him for all that he had done against him. Then St. Thomas said to him, "Dost thou not know, that those who would have heavenly things, must care very little for earthly things? There are in heaven a great many rich palaces prepared from the beginning of the world for those who will buy them through faith and charity. If, then, O king thou wishest for one of these palaces, thou must send thy riches before thee in thy lifetime to buy it, for after thy death they cannot follow thee, and will not profit thee in Paradise."

It is on account of this legend that St. Thomas is chosen to be the patron saint of masons and builders, and that he is often drawn in pictures with a builder's rule in his hand.

St. Thomas traveled to the farthest parts of India, and after preaching in the Malabar coast, he crossed over to the Coromandel coast, and at last settled himself at Meliapore, where he built a church. He underwent so many hardships during his long journey, that he made a very miserable appearance when he reached the peninsula of India. His hair was long and rough, his face was pale and thin, his body was more like that of a skeleton than a living man; he was covered with a patched and ragged garment, while his manner was humble and lowly, like that of the very poorest of the people. Wherever he went he worked miracles, and preached to the natives that the gods they adored were false gods, and that there was but one living and true God, the Creator of heaven and earth, and one Savior of mankind, Jesus Christ. He made a great many converts, and when the Portuguese arrived in this country more than one thousand years afterwards, they found there several Christians who were descended from these converts.

St. Thomas at last came by his death in the following

way. Sagamus, the king of that part of the country, and a great many persons of rank having been converted, the idolatrous priests and the Brahmins, who were the persons of highest rank in the kingdom, became very angry, because they found that they and their gods were not thought so much of as they had formerly been. They, therefore, hated St. Thomas, and determined to get rid of him somehow or other. They first tried to destroy his character, by telling all sorts of wicked lies about him, but no one would believe them, for everyone knew what a holy man St. Thomas was. They, therefore, determined to kill him. Accordingly, one day when he was in a cave about a mile and a half from the city, and was praying, as was his custom, before a cross, they fell on him with stones and cudgels, and wounded and bruised him, and at last one of them having run a long lance into him, he fell down dead. His disciples took up his body, and buried it in the church which he had built, and they buried with it a piece of the lance with which he had been killed, and his walking staff, and a vessel in which they put some of the earth which had been watered with his blood.

Hundreds and hundreds of years passed away, and no one knew where the body of this great apostle lay. But that was of no consequence, for wherever it lay, whether to the north, south, east, or west, the sound of the great trumpet on the judgment day would be sure to reach it, and it would arise and take its seat on one of the thrones beside Jesus. Time rolled on, and century after century passed away, till at last, about fourteen hundred years after St. Thomas's death, the Portuguese made their way to India, and settled themselves in this very city of Meliapore. And it came to pass, that one day as some workmen were clearing away some rubbish, they met with an old wall, and in digging through it, they found two large stones, and one of them was sprinkled with blood, and on it was carved a cross, the ends of which were ornamented with fleurs-de-lis, and in the middle of it was a dove, and over it an arch, on which was some writing in a character which no one could understand. They removed the stone with great care, and under it they discovered a dead body, together with a walking-staff and a piece of a lance. They lost no time in giving notice to the viceroy who governed the country for the King of Portugal, and crowds of people flocked to see the body and the two stones. The pagans looked at them with curiosity, thinking, perhaps, that the body was that of some ancient king or warrior. But the Christians knew very well, by the cross and the dove, and the drops of blood, that it must be one of that noble army of martyrs, who stand before the throne of God, clad in white robes, with palms in their hands. Then all eyes were turned to the writing, but none could read it. So there was search made for someone who could make it out; and all the most learned men in the country were sent for to see whether they could tell what it meant. At last two Brahmins, who did not know each other, were brought separately to look at it, and both said that the unknown writing was as follows:-"Thomas, a divine man, sent by the Son of God, and His disciple, went to King Sagamus, to give the knowledge of the true God to his people, where he wrought great wonders; and at last, as he was kneeling upon this stone, and making his prayers to God, he was thrust through with a lance by a Brahmin and killed." The joy of the Christians on discovering the body of the apostle was very great. They buried it on the spot where it had been found, and the viceroy had a church built over it; and many of the Portuguese, from devotion to the saint, came to live near the place where he was buried, and they almost gave up calling the town Meliapore, and loved to call it the city of St. Thomas.

Many people have often wished to know more about the minute details of the apostles' lives. But for some good purpose, God has not thought proper to gratify this wish; and the fact is, that we know less about their sayings and doings than about those of many others of the saints. Of several of them we know nothing, except that they left all to follow Jesus, and after founding Churches in distant lands, laid down their lives for Him; but where they preached, or where or how they attained to martyrdom, is so uncertain, that it is not possible to give any credit to the accounts which have reached us. Of this number were St. Bartholomew, St. Matthew, St. Simon, and St. Jude.

Of St. Bartholomew nothing is known for certain, except that, when the apostles divided the world between them, Lycaonia, a part of Asia Minor, was the country which fell to his share; and that he afterwards went into India and Armenia, in which last place he was martyred, as is generally supposed, by being flayed alive.

St. Matthew traveled into Ethiopia, the king and queen of which were converted in consequence of his raising their son from the dead. Their daughter, Iphigenia took a vow of virginity, and consecrated herself to the service of God. But after the death of the king her father, Hirtacus, her uncle, came to the throne, and as she was very beautiful, he wished to marry her; and he desired St. Matthew to go to her, and persuade her to marry him. But St. Matthew told him that it would be very wicked of him to marry Iphigenia, who had made herself the spouse of Jesus Christ, by taking the vow of virginity, and equally wicked of her to break her vow. On hearing this, Hirtacus flew into a great rage, and soon after sent one of his officers to kill St. Matthew. The apostle was pierced with a lance as he was standing at the altar, so that the altar

Sts Thomas, Bartholomew, Matthew, Simon and Jude

itself was sprinkled with his blood. His martyrdom took place on the 21st September.

We know very little for certain about St. Simon and St. Jude, except that St. Simon preached in Egypt, and St. Jude in Mesopotamia; and that afterwards they are supposed to have gone together into Persia, where they made a great many converts, and were at last crowned with martyrdom. The Church keeps their feast on the 28th October.

CHAPTER XII

𝕿𝖍𝖊 𝕾𝖊𝖈𝖔𝖓𝖉 𝕻𝖊𝖗𝖘𝖊𝖈𝖚𝖙𝖎𝖔𝖓

ON the death of the Emperor Vespasian, his eldest son, Titus, succeeded him. He was a very wise and good prince, but he reigned only two years. He was succeeded by his brother Domitian, under whom the second great persecution of the Christians took place. Domitian was naturally of a cruel and suspicious temper. He always wished to be the first in every way, and he was jealous of any one who was superior to himself. If a general was very brave and was gaining a great many victories, he was called away from the army, and was kept idle at home. If a senator was known to be very clever or very good, some frivolous accusation was found against him, and he was banished or put to death. So that, in fact, the greatest crime in the eyes of Domitian was to be good, or clever, or brave, or great in any way whatsoever.

At the beginning of his reign he tried to make himself beloved by his people, and for two years he governed very well. But every now and then his jealous temper would get the better of him, and make him do some cruel thing, so that it was impossible for people to love him. He was not really good and kind, but was only pretending from selfish motives to be so; and this made him so uncertain in his moods, that people never knew what sort of temper they might find him in, and thus they came to fear him and to tremble in his presence, almost without knowing why. Domitian quickly perceived this, and it only made him

The Second Persecution

more jealous and suspicious than ever: his dark moods came more frequently on him; and at last he gave up trying to make himself loved, and became one of the greatest tyrants that ever lived. But, while he made other people unhappy, he himself was the most unhappy man in the empire. He worked himself up into such a state of suspicion that he could not trust his servants or his most intimate friends; and at last he had a room built, lined with marble, which was so highly polished that it reflected objects like a looking-glass, so that no one could come near him without his perceiving them, and there he sat, constantly watching those who were waiting on him, and literally trembling at every shadow.

It was his suspicious temper, and not any thought about religion, that led him to persecute the Christians. He had two cousins, Flavius Sabinus and Flavius Clemens, who were both very good young men. The elder, Flavius Sabinus, was consul with Domitian the first year of his reign but the herald who was proclaiming their names made an unlucky mistake, and said, Flavius Sabinus, emperor, instead of Flavius Sabinus, consul; and this trifle being enough to alarm Domitian, some excuse was soon found for putting the unfortunate young man to death. Flavius Clemens was of a very different character from his brother. He did not care for worldly honors or riches, and it was impossible to make him angry like other young men; so people thought him stupid and idle, and even cowardly and without proper spirit, as they said; and though they could find no positive fault in him, yet they secretly despised him. Domitian was very glad of this; and, as he saw that he had nothing to fear from him, he took him into his favor made him consul, and gave him his niece, Domitilla, for a wife, and adopted their children to be his heirs.

But though Domitian was right in thinking that he had nothing to fear from Flavius Clemens, he was quite wrong in thinking that it was because he was stupid and cowardly. The fact was, Flavia Clemens was a Christian, and his heart and his treasure were in heaven, so that it would have seemed to him a very small thing to be emperor of the whole Roman world. For some time his religion was very good for him in a worldly point of view, for it was the means of saving his life. But Christ has called all His disciples to take up their cross and follow Him, and sooner or later He will send each of them a cross, and give them the opportunity of suffering for Him.

So it was with Flavius Clemens. In proportion as Domitian became more and more suspicious, he began to look more and more closely into the conduct and character of Flavius Clemens; and then he noticed many strange things in him which he had formerly thought nothing of. Flavius did not mix with the other courtiers; he had strange friends who came constantly to his house, who were very fond of him, and with whom he used to spend many hours shut up alone. Domitian did not know how much all the Christians loved each other, and that they spent a great deal of time in prayer; so he thought Flavius and his friends could not be doing anything else than plotting to kill him, and make Flavius emperor. It was impossible to make out that Flavius had done anything against the laws, so it was necessary to invent a new crime to accuse him of. As the Christians did not believe in the heathen gods, they were said to be atheists and because our Lord and His first disciples were born in Judea, they were often called Jews. So Flavius Clemens was accused of atheism and Jewish manners, and was put to death. His wife, Flavia Domitilla, was banished to the island of Pandataria, and his niece, whose name also was Flavia

Domitilla, was banished to the island of Pontia. Of this second Flavia Domitilla, more will be said in another chapter. Several other persons of high rank were either banished or put to death; and among the martyrs were St. Cletus, the second Bishop of Rome after St. Peter, and the apostle St. John.

As Domitian now inquired more closely into the religion of the Christians, he discovered several things which frightened him terribly; for he found out that they obeyed a king called Jesus Christ, who was descended from David, one of their ancient kings; and that they expected this Jesus to set up a kingdom which would conquer all the other kingdoms of the world. He was very much troubled to hear this, and was very anxious to find out who this Jesus could be; and he therefore ordered that all the persons who belonged to the family of David should be seized and brought before him, so that he might question them, and see if there was any chance of their trying to dethrone him and kill him.

Among those who were brought before him, were two grandsons of the apostle, St. Jude, and who were, therefore, cousins to our Lord. The emperor asked them whether they were of the race of David; and they answered, that they were. He then asked them what property they had, and how they supported themselves. They told him that they had nothing except a piece of land, of the value of about £280, which they cultivated, and from which they got enough to pay their taxes and support themselves. Then, in order to prove that they spoke the truth, they showed him their hands, which were hard and rough like those of laboring men. The emperor almost smiled at his own fears, for such poor fellows as these did not seem likely to be very dangerous to him. Still, however, he could not quite get out of his head all that he had heard about the kingdom which one of their family was to set up; and he began to ask them what sort of kingdom that of Christ would be, and when and where it would be set up. They had now no difficulty in setting him at rest; for they assured him that the kingdom they looked for was not an earthly kingdom, but a heavenly one; and that it would appear at the end of the world, when Christ would come in His glory, and would judge the living and the dead, and reward every one according to his works. Domitian was not afraid of such a king as this, for so long as he was left in quiet possession of his empire in this world, he cared little for what would happen in another world, since he did not believe in the resurrection from the dead, or in life everlasting. So he dismissed the grandsons of St. Jude with contempt, looking upon them as simpletons, who were so foolish, that they were not worth punishing.

CHAPTER XIII

FLAVIA DOMITILLA

THE name of Flavia Domitilla, the younger, has already been mentioned, as having been one of those who were banished by Domitian. The story of her life is very interesting. She was a person of high rank, being cousin to the Emperors Titus and Domitian, and what was much better, many of her relations were saints and martyrs; for she was daughter to St. Plautilla, and niece to Flavius Clemens, who also was a martyr. She had two servants, Nereus and Achilleus, who were brothers, and had been converted by the preaching of St. Peter. They were so much more faithful and well-conducted than any of her other servants, that she could not help noticing them; and when she came to speak to them, she was even more pleased with them. They said that they were Christians; and when she asked them what it was to be a Christian, they told her all about a future state, and the great day of judgment, and Jesus Christ's having become man, and having died on a cross to save sinners. She liked very much to hear them speak about these things, and she used very often to escape from her happy companions, and go to talk quietly with them, till at last she was converted, and was baptized.

As Flavia Domitilla was of the Emperor's family, and was besides very rich, many young noblemen wished to marry her; and after some time, her friends engaged her to

Aurelian, a handsome and agreeable young man of high birth. Domitilla was very much pleased with the idea of this marriage, and being a joyful young girl, she thought only of dressing herself and making herself look as beautiful as she could, in order that Aurelian might be the more in love with her. One day when she was busy choosing the most elegant dress she could think of, and arranging all her jewels, so as to be most becoming to her, her two faithful servants, Nereus and Achilleus, said to her, "Ah! dear Madam, if you would but take the same care to adorn your soul with virtues, as you do to deck out your body, you would not fail to win the love of Jesus Christ, the King of heaven; and He would take you to be His spouse, and then this beauty of yours, which will now so quickly fade, would last forever, and you would become even much more beautiful than you are now, and would shine gloriously in the Court of Heaven." Domitilla did not much fancy this sort of advice, and she answered: "All that is very true; but still there is no sin in marrying; and if I am to marry, I may just as well take pains to set myself off properly, and to win the love of my husband, so that I may be happy in my marriage." Then Nereus, replied: "You look only on the pleasures of this life, which so quickly pass away, and do not think about the everlasting happiness of Heaven; you look on the advantages of marriage, and not on the trouble and misery which it may bring on you." And then he and Achilleus went on to show her how, when she became a wife, she gave herself up to a man of whom she could know but little till she went to live with him, and who would perhaps treat her very unkindly. For if he took a fancy, he might shut her up and not let her see her father and mother or any of her old friends; or if he were jealous, he might be angry with her for every word she spoke, and everything she did innocently; or if he were ill tempered, he might beat her, and use rough and harsh language to her. And then, if she should have children, they would be a continual cause of anxiety and trouble to her, from the very time of their birth, for they would be ill, or they would be hurting themselves, or they would be disobedient and unruly, or they would not be so clever or so handsome as she wished them to be; and then there would be the care of nursing them, and teaching them, and putting them forward in the world; and perhaps, after all, they would die young, or what is worse, they might live to be a disgrace to their family, and a curse both to themselves and to their parents. They said all this, and much more, which might well make a young girl think twice before she married.

After they had gone through all the troubles and anxieties of marriage, Nereus began to speak of the blessed state of virginity. "A virgin," said he, "lives on earth the life which the angels live in heaven, and she will have in heaven a bright crown which is given to no one but virgins. She has God for her husband, and she knows that He can never treat her unkindly; whatever she tries to do for love of Him, He will be pleased with; He will never neglect her or forsake her, but he will always be with her, speaking sweetly to her, and putting happy and holy thoughts into her heart; and she will be free from all the cares of this world, and will not be afraid of sickness or of any misfortunes that may happen to her, for His arms will always be round her, His beautiful countenance will always be smiling on her, and the thought of His love will be a paradise of unspeakable happiness to her. Think then, my dear young mistress, which husband is the best, and choose him whom you think you can love most-either a mortal man, who, be he ever so good, will one day die and leave you, or Jesus Christ, who will never die, but who will rejoice and bless you with His company for ever and ever."

Domitilla was very much struck with what Nereus and Achilleus said. Her conscience told her that they were right, and a voice within her seemed to call her to be the spouse of Jesus. But how could she give up all the things of which she was so fond- her beautiful dresses, her costly jewels, the happy company she was in the habit of keeping, and, above all, the love of Aurelian? It was a hard struggle between the love of God and the love of the world; and for a short time it seemed as if the world must conquer. For the Devil whispered to her that, after all, there was no need to give up all these things, for why could not she marry Aurelian, and yet love Jesus, as many married women did. But then there flashed across her mind the words of the apostle St. Paul, "The virgin thinketh on the things of the Lord, that she may be holy both in body and in spirit. But she that is married thinketh on the things of the world, how she may please her husband." And she felt and knew that it was her whole self that our Lord was asking of her, and that He would not be satisfied if she gave Him only half her heart. So she tried to look at the matter simply and earnestly, and she prayed to God to guide her, and to give her strength to do His will, whatever it might be. At last, the grace of God triumphed, and she exclaimed, "Would to God I had heard all this before I was engaged to be married. But even now it may not be too late, and God may yet open to me some means by which I may get free from Aurelian." On hearing these words, Nereus and Achilleus gave fervent thanks to God, who, by His grace, had brought their dear mistress into such a good disposition of mind; and they earnestly exhorted her to make an offering of herself to God, and to trust confidently and lovingly in Him. The next question was how she was to break off her marriage. This was a subject which required some consideration, for it was not to be supposed that Aurelian would submit quietly to lose his rich and beautiful young wife; and if he made any disturbance about it, her change of religion would come to the ears of the emperor, who was beginning just then to persecute the Christians. And now the Devil set before her the trials that she was going to draw on herself the dark dungeon, the scourging, the rack, the wild beasts, the fire, and all the horrible torments that were inflicted on Christians; and he asked her how a thoughtless young girl like herself, who had spent her life in dressing and amusing herself, could bear such things as these. All that he put into her head seemed very sensible, and when she thought about the tortures she could not help shuddering, and she felt that if she thought much about these things she should not have the courage to keep to her resolution. So she determined to put away all these thoughts with which the Devil was tempting her, and not to trouble herself about consequences; and she committed herself gently to the care of her dearest spouse, Jesus, trusting entirely to His love, and beseeching Him to take care of her and to give her strength to do His will and to bear whatever trials He might send her.

Nereus and Achilleus, meanwhile, had gone to the Pope, St. Clement, and had told him that she wished to consecrate her virginity to Jesus, and to become His spouse instead of marrying Aurelian. The Church of Rome was now in great trouble on account of the persecution, and the Holy Father was in constant anxiety for those of his flock who were being persecuted, lest they should not bear their trials with fortitude. It was, therefore, a great joy and encouragement to him that a young girl like Flavia Domitilla, should wish, in a time like this, to consecrate herself to God's service, for he knew that nothing but the grace of God could lead her to make such a holy resolution.

He was filled with joy and courage, and he exclaimed: "It seems to me, that the time is not far off, when our Lord will be pleased to crown you, and me, and Domitilla with martyrdom; and since He commands us not to fear those who kill the body, but cannot hurt the soul, let us not care for the displeasure of the emperor, but let us boldly obey God, who is the Sovereign Lord of heaven and earth." He then went with Nereus and Achilleus to the house of Flavia Domitilla, and after talking to her, and finding that she had a true vocation, and was ready to suffer everything for the love of Jesus, he consecrated her to be His spouse, and to spend her life in loving and serving Him.

It was not long before the troubles which Domitilla expected came upon her. At first, Aurelian would not believe that she really meant to break off the marriage; he thought it was a whimsical fancy, and he did not doubt but that he should soon bring her round by flattering words and beautiful presents. But when he found that she would not listen to his words, and that she refused his presents, he began to look more seriously on the matter, and complained to the emperor. Domitian was very angry when he learned that she was a Christian, and he ordered her to be brought before his tribunal. Then this gentle and timid girl, who had never before appeared in public, and had always been treated with the greatest respect and kindness, was roughly seized and brought a prisoner into a public court of justice. Domitian spoke to her in coarse, insulting language; he encouraged the people who were present to laugh at her and revile her, and he tried to frighten her by threatening to inflict the most horrible torments on her. But she remained quite unmoved; till at last Domitian, finding he could do nothing with her, gave her her choice either to sacrifice immediately to the gods, or to be banished to the island of Pontia. The choice was made without a moment's hesitation, and Flavia Domitilla was sent off to Pontia.

In these days, when people have broken the laws, they are sometimes banished; and though it is a great punishment to them to be taken away from their homes and their families, and to be obliged to work very hard, yet they have the comfort of knowing that they will at all events meet with just and fair treatment. But it was quite different with those who were banished by the Roman emperors. They were put in charge of some wicked man who thought only how he could make them most wretched; and he would often torture them or kill them secretly if he knew that the emperor wished to get rid of them. This was the sort of way in which Flavia Domitilla was now treated. She was not allowed to see any of her friends; she was lodged in close, unhealthy rooms; she was fed with coarse, unwholesome food; she could not walk in the garden or move a step without being watched; she was treated rudely by the servants and soldiers who waited on her and guarded her and if it was noticed that she took pleasure in one thing more than another, she was immediately deprived of it. Most people would have been very much fretted by this sort of petty persecution, carried on every day and all day long. But Domitilla did not seem to notice or to feel the things that were done to vex and annoy her. She gave herself entirely into the hands of her dearest Spouse, Jesus Christ, and she knew that whatever happened to her, was ordered by Him. When we love a person very much we like to do what he wishes; and so Domitilla was very happy to live in closed rooms, and to eat coarse food, and to be watched by the soldiers, and treated rudely by the servants, because she loved Jesus, and knew that it was His will that these things should happen to her. She had still one great consolation, which was the company of Nereus and Achilleus who had followed her to Pontia. They waited on her most affectionately; they did all they could to make her more comfortable; and above all, they talked to her about Jesus, who was so dear to them all.

After some time Aurelian came to see her, hoping to find that she was tired out with all that she had suffered in her banishment, and was ready to marry him. He was very much surprised to see how calm and joyful she looked, and to hear her talk of the great happiness she was enjoying. He looked round at the wretched room in which she was confined, and he was puzzled to think what could make her so happy where other people would have been very miserable. He saw, however, that she had still one consolation, which was the company of Nereus and Achilleus, and he was so selfish and cruel as to take them away from her.

As Nereus and Achilleus were only slaves, he might do whatever he liked to them. So he had them cruelly scourged, and then sent them to Terracina, to a friend of his called Memmius Rufus, who was governor of the place, and he told him to punish them as severely as he could, because they were very obstinate Christians. Memmius Rufus at first tried to persuade them to sacrifice to the gods; but they declared that nothing in the whole world would ever induce them to give up what the Apostle St. Peter had taught them. He, therefore, determined to see what would come of these brave words when they were put to the torture, and he ordered them to be placed on a horrible wooden machine called the horse, which was used for torturing slaves. Here their limbs were drawn out of joint, and their sinews were strained to their farthest stretch, and at the same time plates of red hot iron were applied to their sides and other parts of their naked bodies,

Flavia Domitilla

so as to burn them dreadfully. But in the midst of their agony they remained unmoved, and broke out into songs of triumphant joy as each fresh torture was inflicted on them. Memmius Rufus, at last, saw that it was hopeless to conquer their constancy, and he had them beheaded.

Aurelian hoped that now that Nereus and Achilleus were gone, Domitilla would soon make up her mind to marry him, and to return to the happy life she used formerly to live at Rome. But he was again mistaken. Though Nereus and Achilleus had been a great comfort to Domitilla, yet it was in Jesus that her real strength and comfort lay; and now that He had been pleased to let her friends be taken from her, she looked only the more simply to Him for support and consolation. And so it came to pass that when Aurelian again visited her, expecting to find her dull and out of spirits, she was even more firm in her faith and more happy than she had been when he was there before.

Aurelian was now convinced that there was no hope of conquering Domitilla's obstinacy by keeping her in the island of Pontia, and so he determined to take her away and marry her by force. He therefore carried her with him to Terracina and invited a large party to be present at his wedding. Aurelian and his friends began to feast and make merry, while poor Domitilla was shut up in a room, alone, sad and trembling, waiting till Aurelian should come to her and force her to marry him. It seemed now that all hope was lost, and that she must at last be obliged to marry him. But still Domitilla's heart did not sink, and she continued to hope and trust in Jesus. She had vowed herself to Him, and she was sure that He would defend her, because she was His own spouse. She knelt and prayed in her solitary chamber, while the jovial party in the banqueting room drank and feasted. At last they began to dance, and

Aurelian was the merriest of them all, dancing and laughing with all his might, and rejoicing to think that he had at last conquered this proud Christian girl. But in a moment the merry scene was changed. God struck Aurelian, and he fell down dead. Then there was a sudden cry of alarm, followed by a loud weeping and wailing, which ran through the house, and told Domitilla that our Lord had heard her prayer, and had delivered her from the great danger which had threatened her.

This was not, however, the end of all that Domitilla had to suffer for Jesus' sake. Luxorius, Aurelian's brother, was very angry with her, because he said that she had been the cause of his brother's death, and he accused her to Trajan, who at this time was emperor, and he got leave to question her, and put her to death if she would not sacrifice to the heathen gods. He came to Terracina, where she was living with two other young women, Theodora and Euphrosina, whom she had persuaded to be Christians and to vow themselves to a life of chastity. They were all three brought before Luxorius, who told them that the emperor ordered them to sacrifice to the gods, and he advised them to obey at once, for if they did not, he would put them to a cruel death. They refused to do so, and answered boldly and firmly to all he asked them about their religion. He knew there was little chance of making Domitilla change her mind, and besides, he was not sorry to punish her for the death of his brother. So he ordered them all three to be shut up in a room, which was then set on fire, and thus they were burnt to death. The next morning Cesarius, a deacon, came to the place, and upon going to the room in which they had been shut up, he found them dead, lying on the floor on their faces, just as they had prostrated themselves in prayer, but without a hair of their head being singed or any part of their body being burned. The fire had released their souls from this mortal life, but it had been miraculously prevented from burning their bodies. Cesarius took up their bodies, and buried them with great honor. The Church keeps the feast of St. Flavia Domitilla, together with that of SS. Nereus and Achilleus, on the 12th May.

CHAPTER XIV

ST. ANDREW

ST. ANDREW is supposed to have been martyred about this time. He was a very great apostle, because, though he was not the first who was chosen to be an apostle, yet he was the first who knew our Lord and talked to Him, and he it was who brought St. Peter to Jesus. The way in which this came to pass shows what a simple, straightforward person St. Andrew was. He was a disciple of St. John Baptist, and he was living a strict life and looking out for the great Messias, about whom St. John Baptist had told his disciples. One day, as our Lord was passing, St. John Baptist pointed to Him, and said: "Behold the Lamb of God. Behold Him who taketh away the sin of the world." Andrew heard these words: he did not wait to ask how a poor carpenter of Nazareth could be the great Messias; but he immediately believed what St. John said, and he set off with another disciple to follow Jesus. When Jesus saw them following He turned round and spoke to them, and took them home to spend the day with Him. This was St. Andrew's first act of faith, and he lost no time in following it up by a work of charity; for the very next day he went to St. Peter, and told him that he had found the Messias, and took him to Jesus.

Scythia, the country of the Tartars, was the country where St. Andrew chiefly preached. The Scythians were rude, ignorant savages, who knew nothing except about hunting, and fishing, and fighting, and if anyone had set about arguing and talking learnedly to them they could not have understood him, and would not have listened to him. But St. Andrew was the man to suit them, for he spoke so plainly and simply that they easily understood him; and when they saw how much he was in earnest, and that he himself always did the things he told them to do, they thought he was a very good man, and many of them were converted by his holy example and by the miracles he did. Besides this, St. Andrew preached also to the Sogdians on the confines of India, and also to the Galatians, the Epirots, and the Thracians, who were more or less uncivilized people, and he made many converts among them too. At length he left these wild countries and came to Greece, the inhabitants of which were the best educated and most refined people in the Roman Empire. St. Paul had told these same Greeks that he did not come to preach to them with learned and wise words, but to tell them about the cross of Christ, which appeared foolishness to those who would not believe; and he warned them that God had not chosen many wise men, but had chosen the foolish things of the world to confound the wise. So St. Andrew now found it; for these Greeks were so proud of their learning that they thought themselves a great deal too wise to listen to the plain, simple things that St. Andrew told them; and it seemed to them very foolish to believe that God the Son had been crucified, or that men would rise from the dead. So St. Andrew did not make so many converts among them as he had done among the Scythians; and, though they pretended to be very civilized people, yet they treated him much more roughly than the barbarous Scythians had done.

After traveling through various places, St. Andrew

arrived at Patras, in Achaia. The Roman governor in this town was Egeas, the proconsul of Achaia, who was a great enemy to the Christians, and was in the habit of torturing them and putting them to death. St. Andrew was very much grieved to hear how he was persecuting the Church, and looking on the matter in his own simple, loving way, he was filled with pity for the soul of Egeas; and without thinking of the danger he would himself be running, he determined to make an attempt to convert him. He therefore went to him, and spoke thus: "It is only reasonable, O Egeas! that you who are a judge of men, should know your own Judge who is in heaven, and that you should honor Him as the only true God, and cease to honor those that are not gods." Egeas was very much pleased to see this man, of whose miracles he had often heard, and he said to him: "Are you Andrew, the man who destroys the temples of the gods, and persuades men to receive that superstitious sect, which the Roman princes command to be banished out of their empire?" The apostle said that he was Andrew; and then he went on to speak to Egeas about the great judgment day, and about the wonderful love of Jesus Christ in becoming man, and dying on the cross to save sinners from going to hell. The Greeks were fond of listening to all sorts of opinions, provided only they were new, and for some time Egeas was greatly interested in what St. Andrew was telling him, looking upon it only as a new system of philosophy. But when St. Andrew spoke of our Lord's Crucifixion, and His glorious Resurrection, the Greek began to smile, for he was much too wise in his own conceit to believe such things; and at last, losing all patience, he burst out into a contemptuous laugh, and said: "Tell these things to those who will believe them; but do you believe me, if you will not sacrifice to the gods, I will command you to be placed on this same cross

St. Andrew

which you are praising so much." St. Andrew replied, "I sacrifice every day to the only Almighty and true God, not the smoke of incense, nor the flesh of bulls, nor the blood of goats, but the Immaculate Lamb, Jesus Christ and I will not sacrifice to your false gods, which are not gods, but devils." When Egeas heard him speak against the gods, he became very angry, and ordered him to be put into prison. As soon as the news of St. Andrew's imprisonment was spread through the city, the people, who had been very much interested in his preaching, began to make a tumult and they ran to attack the prison, in order to take him out by force. But St. Andrew begged of them not to be so wicked as to rebel against the magistrate whom God had set over them, but rather to imitate the meekness and patience of Jesus, who bore all the wrongs that were done Him without saying a single word; and as for himself, he entreated them not to deprive him of the crown of martyrdom which he hoped to win very soon. His words calmed the populace, and they dispersed without committing any violence.

After St. Andrew had been some time in prison Egeas ordered him to be brought before him; and he said to him: "You have now had some time to consider this matter, and I dare say you have thought better of it, and are ready to give up your folly, in order to escape the cruel death which I will inflict on you, if you still persist in saying that Christ is God." But the apostle answered boldly; "He who does not believe in Christ can never have either happiness or life, as I have always preached in this province." "It is for this very reason," said Egeas, "that I will force you to sacrifice to the gods, so that all the people who have been deceived by you may give up your false doctrines, and return to the worship of the ancient gods. For there is not a temple in Ashaia which is not deserted through your false preaching; and seeing you have deceived the people, it is only right that you should undeceive them. So now make up your mind at once, either to sacrifice to the gods, or to suffer the most cruel torments, and to die at last on a cross." St. Andrew fixed his eyes on Egeas, and for a few moments he did not say a single word. Then with a stern look and a solemn voice he answered thus: "Wicked and miserable man, listen to me. Hitherto I have spoken gently to you, thinking that as a man of reason you would profit by my words, and leave the adoration of your false gods. But since you are so hardened and obstinate, I tell you plainly you must not think to move me with your threats and terrors. Here I am, do what you will with me; the greater the torments are which you will inflict on me, the greater will be the reward which Jesus will give me for having suffered them for His love, and the hotter will be the place in hell which will be prepared for you."

On hearing these bold words, Egeas flew into a great rage, and commanded St. Andrew to be scourged by seven men, and as soon as they were tired seven others were to take their place. The executioners were thus changed three times, and the blows they gave the Apostle were so many, that his bones were laid bare, and the blood flowed in streams from all parts of his body. Notwithstanding the severity of this torture St. Andrew was unmoved, for he was so occupied in prayer that he did not seem to feel the blows that fell on his flesh, and tore it up in the most horrible way. Egeas was more and more provoked at the sight of his constancy; so he commanded him to be crucified, and in order to make his death more lingering, he desired that he should not be nailed to the cross, but only tied on it with cords.

As he was being taken to martyrdom, the people flocked round him, crying out, "What has this just man,

St. Andrew

this friend of God done, that they should crucify him?" But St. Andrew entreated them not to rob him of the glory of martyrdom that was awaiting him. When he came in sight of the cross on which he was to suffer such a horrible death he was not the least frightened, as he might well have been, and as many a brave man has been at the thought of being crucified. His blood did not run cold, nor did he turn pale, nor did his voice tremble; but he was so transported with joy that he could scarcely contain himself. His heart seemed to be on fire with the love of Jesus, and the longing desire he had to imitate Him in His death, made him cry out even when he was at some distance from the cross: "I adore thee, precious cross! that wast consecrated with the body of my Lord, and adorned with His limbs, as with precious jewels. Before Jesus was put on thee, men were afraid of thee; but now they love thee, and thou makest them happy. I rejoice to come to thee, O good cross! whom Christ's body has made so beautiful. I have long wished for thee, I have long sought diligently for thee; and now that I have found thee, receive me into thine arms, take me from among men and present me to my Master, so that He may receive me by thee, who by thee redeemed me.

When St. Andrew arrived at the place of execution, he pulled off his clothes and gave them to the executioners. He was then lifted up, and tied to the cross. There stood round about nearly twenty thousand people, who wept and mourned over the grievous sight; while he, who was the great sufferer, seemed to suffer nothing. Here he hung for two long days and nights, scorched with the sun by day and chilled with the cold of the November nights; the sharp wind blowing on his raw and smarting wounds, without any food to stay his hunger, or a drop of water to quench his thirst. Still, however, death seemed to be far off.

In the midst of his agony he never ceased to comfort the weeping multitude, and to encouraged them to be ready to suffer torments for Christ's sake. At last, in spite of all his efforts to keep them quiet, they began to cry out again, "Why is this man, who is so holy, and who taught such good doctrine, put to death?" Egeas, hearing that the crowd were beginning to lose all patience, was frightened, and thought he had better set St. Andrew at liberty, and so he went to the place of execution, and ordered the executioners to take him down. They set about obeying him, but could not do as he told them; for whenever they came near St. Andrew, and stretched out their arms to untie him, a strange sensation came over them, their strength left them, and they fainted. Meanwhile the saint, raising his voice, cried out, "My Lord Jesus Christ, I beseech Thee do not let me be taken down from this cross, to which I have been fastened for love of Thee; and since Thou hast shown me Thy power by this cross, do not let me be buried by a wicked man like Egeas. But, my Lord and Master, whom I love, and in whom I am all that I am, do Thou receive my soul; for it is time that I should go to Thee, since I have so long desired to see Thee," When he had finished these words, a glorious cloud, brighter than lightning, was seen to come down from heaven, and it covered his body, so that no one could even look at it. There it remained for half an hour, at the end of which time it disappeared; and, as it was vanishing, St. Andrew's soul mounted up to heaven, and was received into glory.

A rich and holy woman, called Maximilla, took his body and gave it honorable burial. Egeas heard what she had done; and, though he did not dare to punish her at once, because she was a person of rank, he determined to accuse her to the emperor. But while he was preparing to do so, he was taken suddenly ill, and died a miserable death.

The martyrdom of St. Andrew took place on the 30th November, A.D. 95, in the beginning of Domitian's persecution.[8]

---

[8] Tillemont places it much earlier, in A.D. 66 or 70, tom. i. 624. Gallandius places it in the last year of Vespasian.

CHAPTER XV

ST. JOHN THE EVANGELIST

ST. JOHN the Evangelist was one of the martyrs in the reign of Domitian. Our Lord had promised him and his brother St. James that they should both drink of His chalice and be baptized with His baptism; but the promise was very differently fulfilled to each of them. St. James was martyred a few years after, being the first of the apostles to receive his heavenly reward; while St. John lived to a very great age, long after all the other apostles, and at last died a natural death. Still he is always looked on as a martyr, both because of our Lord's promise, and because he actually suffered what would have killed him, if it had not pleased our Lord to save his life by a miracle.

Every Catholic knows that St. John was the disciple whom Jesus loved in a peculiar way; that he leaned on Jesus' breast at the Last Supper; that as Jesus was hanging on the cross He gave our dear Lady into his charge; and that during the fifteen years that she lived after our Lord, St. John waited on her, and took care of her, like a most dutiful and affectionate son. When we think of all these things we cannot wonder that St. John should have been the apostle of love. One of the fathers of the Church says, that even the Cherubim and Seraphim learned many things from St. John, and listened to him with great attention.

St. John preached the Gospel in Phrygia and Parthia

and some say that he traveled as far as India. But his chief charge was Asia Minor, where he founded the seven Churches of Ephesus, Smyrna, Pergamus, Thyatira, Pala Delphia, Sardis, and Laodicea. He spent most of his time in Ephesus, where there was a famous temple dedicated to the goddess Diana. This temple drew a great many people of all classes to Ephesus; so that the city was both a very rich and very wicked place; for the worship of the pagan gods was so very impure, that wherever it flourished the most horrible sins were practiced under the name of religion. It was, therefore, no easy task to preach the Gospel at Ephesus. But St. John did not despair that the grace of God could convert even such hard hearts as those of the Ephesians; and so he went on month after month, and year after year, preaching to them, setting them a very holy example, and winning them by the sweetness and gentleness of his conversation, till at last in this place, which had been filled with evil spirits and devoted to the service of the devils, a flourishing Church was established, and prayers and hymns rose night and day in honor of the one True God.

St. John had a great many enemies among the wicked men who worshiped the goddess Diana, and when the Emperor Domitian began to persecute the Christians, they accused him of being a very dangerous sort of person who had great influence with the people. Domitian, therefore, ordered him to be sent to Rome, in order that he himself might question him. St. John was now about ninety years old, and though his mind was as strong as ever, his body was feeble and bowed down with age. But the Roman soldiers who had charge of him were a hard-hearted set; they took no notice of his holy and venerable countenance, or of his great age, but they loaded him with heavy chains, which bent him double, and made his whole body ache.

When St. John arrived at Rome, he was taken before the emperor, who asked him several questions, to all of which he gave bold and straightforward answers. Domitian, however, was not satisfied. He was of such a suspicious temper that the more simple were St. John's answers, the more certain he felt that there must be something very deep hid under them. St. John also worked several miracles before him, casting out devils, healing the sick, and even raising the dead to life. But this only made his case the worse; for Domitian now hated him because he was so superior to himself; and he, therefore, condemned him to be put to a very cruel death.

It was the Roman custom to scourge all persons who were condemned to die; and, accordingly, St. John was stripped, and, in spite of his age and weakness, was scourged till his bones were bare and the blood poured from him. He was then taken to a place in the city, near one of the gates, which is still called the Latin gate. The fame of his preaching and his miracles was widely spread abroad, and the whole Senate and an immense crowd of people were assembled to look at him, and to witness the horrible punishment which was going to be inflicted on him. It was indeed a horrible death; for the Devil had put it into Domitian's head to invent a new kind of torture for the apostle, whom he hated more than any of the others only because Jesus loved him most. A great cauldron of oil was prepared, and a large fire was placed under it; and when the oil was boiling St. John was roughly stripped and thrown in. His wounds from the scourging were raw and bleeding, and it makes one shudder to think how they would naturally have smarted when the boiling oil touched them, and how great would have been the pain of the burns all over his body, for nothing penetrates and burns more than boiling oil. But as soon as the saint touched the

St. John the Evangelist

oil the fire seemed to lose its force, and the oil appeared to be changed into a gentle dew from heaven, so that it felt soft and soothing to his wounds, and instead of being a torment it was only a refreshment to him. When the executioners saw this strange sight they thought that perhaps they had not made the fire hot enough, so they went to stir it up and add fresh fuel to it. But God was resolved to show that St. John was preserved by a miracle, and not through any fault in the fire. So He caused the fire to blaze up so fiercely that it caught some of those who were stirring it up and burned them to death; while at the same time St. John remained unhurt. At last finding there was no use in keeping him any longer in the cauldron, they took him out, shining like an angel, and stronger and more vigorous than when he went in.

The emperor was in a furious rage at what had happened; and as the miracle made a great noise in Rome, and set every one talking about this wonderful saint and his new religion, he became more suspicious and afraid of him than ever. But what could he do against such a man? It was plain that there was no use in trying to kill him. Still he must be got out of the way somehow or other; and so he was banished to Patmos, a small island near Crete, where he was set to work in the mines. This banishment was not much of a punishment for St. John; for he knew that wherever he went our Lord went with him; and it was while he was at Patmos that he was favored with the wonderful visions which are described in the Apocalypse. Here, too, St. John could find work to do for Jesus, and while he was working in the mines he found opportunities of preaching the Gospel to the poor and ignorant miners, many of whom were converted and baptized.

After St. John had spent some time in the island of Patmos, Domitian was murdered by his own servants, and the new Emperor Nerva allowed all those who had been banished by him to return home. The people of Patmos were very sorry to part with their dear apostle, but he could not remain longer with them, because he had a great deal to do in looking after the Churches which he had founded in different places. So he returned to Ephesus, and spent the few remaining years of his life in going from time to time to visit the neighboring Churches for the purpose of seeing that sound doctrine continued to be taught by the priests, and of warning the people not to be led away by heretical teachers, who, even so early as St. John's time, began to deceive foolish people, and to persuade them to wander away from the true fold of Christ, which is the Catholic Church.

The following story shows what love St. John had for souls, and what care he took of those who were under his charge. It happened once that when he was paying one of his usual visits to a city in Asia, he saw a youth of a very pleasing countenance. He spoke to him, and found that he had good abilities, and that if he were well educated he might turn out to be a very good minister of the Gospel. Accordingly, when St. John was about to leave the city he gave this youth in charge to the bishop, and said to him; "Take charge of him, and train him carefully; for I commend him to you with all earnestness in the presence of the Church and of Christ." The bishop promised to do what St. John bade him, and taking the youth home to his own house, he began to teach him how to live a Christian life. At first he looked after him very carefully, and the youth seemed to be going on very well; but after some time the bishop began to look after him less strictly, and to let him have more and more liberty, and the consequence was that he fell into bad company, and was led away to all the feasts, and merry-makings of the pagans. The bishop now tried to check him, but it was too late. The youth was headstrong, and like a restive horse which has got the bit between his teeth, nothing would restrain him and prevent his taking his own way. He went on from one thing to another, and from venial sins to mortal sins, till at last he became the captain of a band of robbers who infested the neighborhood, plundering and murdering everyone who fell into their hands.

Time passed on, and, at length, St. John came again to the city. After having finished all his other business, he turned to the bishop, and said to him: "Come, return me my deposit, which I and Christ committed to thee in the presence of the Church over which thou dost preside." The bishop was puzzled and distressed when he heard St. John's words, for he thought that St. John was asking about some money which he had given him to take care of, and as he could not remember that he had received any money, it was impossible for him to give an account of it. But at last he understood that St. John was asking him for an account, not of money, but of the soul of the young man who had been committed to him; and as soon as he found this out, he began to cry and groan, and he said, "Alas alas! he is dead, he is dead." "Dead!" cried St. John, "how, and by what death did he die?" "He is dead to God," replied the bishop, "He has turned out a very wicked man, and he has at last become a robber: so that, instead of serving in the church, he now wanders about the neighboring mountains at the head of a band of robbers." On hearing this grievous news the apostle tore his clothes for grief; and, making great lamentations, he exclaimed: "To a fine keeper, indeed, did I commit the soul of my brother! But get a horse ready immediately and hire a trusty guide to show me the way to the mountain."

The horse and guide were instantly got ready, and St

John rode away quickly from the church to the mountain where the robbers lived. When he reached their out-guard, the robbers came up to him to make him prisoner; but, instead of trying to run away from them, he only cried out, "For this very purpose am I come; take me to your captain." The robbers led him to their captain, who stood armed in the middle of the company, ready to receive the prisoner. But the moment the young robber cast his eyes on the apostle, he remembered him; and, being very much ashamed of himself, he fled from him. St. John, however, forgetting his old age, ran after him with all his might, crying out, "Why dost thou fly, my son, from me, thy father, thy aged, defenseless father? Have compassion on me, my son; fear not, there is still hope for thee; I will intercede with Christ for thee. I am ready to die cheerfully for thee, as our Lord Jesus Christ died for me, and to give my soul for thine. Stop! stop! for believe me, Christ hath sent me." The hard heart of this prodigal son was touched with these loving words. He stopped, stood like a culprit with downcast looks-hid his right hand with which he had shed so much blood—and, trembling all over, threw himself at the feet of the apostle, and prayed for mercy. St. John raised him up, and embracing him, kissed the hand which he was hiding for shame, and assured him that Jesus would pardon all his sins. He then desired him to fast and pray constantly for several days, while he himself did the same; and he never left him till he was perfectly contrite and was restored to the Church.

Some writers say that St. John lived to be a hundred years old, and others that he was only ninety-three when he died. His precise age is of little consequence. We know that he lived to be so old and infirm that he was unable to walk, and yet his love of souls was still so great, that he could not bring himself to give up the charge of the churches. He was so filled with love to his neighbor, that no other word or precept seemed ever to pass his lips. When he used to be carried into the church, and was so weak that he could hardly speak, he constantly repeated to the people who gathered round him for instruction, "Little children, love one another." His disciples, tired with always hearing the same words, asked him why he never said anything else to them; and he answered, "Because it is the precept of our Lord, and, if it be fulfilled, it alone is sufficient."

Some people fancy that it is very charitable to be as good friends with heretics as with good Christians; but St. John did not think so. Though he was so filled with the love of Jesus, and with love for the souls of heretics, that he would have done anything to turn them away from their sins, yet he could not bear to be in their company, except for the purpose of converting them. It happened that one day he went to the public bath at Ephesus; but, on entering it, he found that a great heretic, called Cerinthus, was there. As soon as he saw him he instantly turned round, and went out in great haste, saying to those who were with him, "Let us flee, lest the bath should fall while Cerinthus, an enemy of the truth, is in it."

St. John had to wait a long time to receive the reward which Jesus had promised him so long before; but at last the happy hour arrived. A short time before he died, God revealed to him that he was going to take him to Himself so he called together his disciples, and gave them his last instructions and his blessing, and, after taking leave of them, he expired peacefully, on the 27th of December, A.D. 100.

CHAPTER XVI

Third Persecution

ST. SIMEON

AFTER the death of the Emperor Domitian the Senate repealed all his wicked laws, and so the general persecution of the Christians came to an end. Still, however, they were so much hated by the pagans, that they continued to be persecuted in places where there were so many of them as to attract the attention of their enemies; and in less than ten years another great persecution broke out.

The Emperor Trajan was now on the throne. Though he was a pagan, yet he was such a kind prince, and was so much beloved, that for many hundred years after his death it was the custom of the Romans to wish, that each new emperor might be "happier than Augustus and better than Trajan." But though he was so humane in other respects, yet he was an enemy to the Christians, and strange to say, he thought it his duty to persecute them. He had a friend called Pliny, whom he appointed governor of Bithynia and Pontus. When Pliny arrived in the countries he was to govern, he found himself rather at a loss to know how to treat the Christians who were brought before his tribunal, and he wrote to the emperor to ask what he was to do with them. His letter and Trajan's answers are very interesting, because they show what good and clever pagans thought about the Christians. Pliny did not at once believe everything that people said against them, but he took a great deal of trouble to find out the real truth about them. He did not trust to common reports, but he made inquiry of persons who had formerly been Christians, but had become apostates, and he also put to the torture two female slaves who then filled the office of deaconesses in the Church, in hopes that they would be forced by the pain to tell him all they knew. He wrote to Trajan that he could discover no crime against the Christians; and that all that he had learned about them was, that they were in the habit of assembling one day in the week before daybreak, to pray and sing hymns in honor of one Christ whom they adored as God; that they bound themselves by an oath not to commit any crime, neither to steal, nor to murder, nor to cheat, nor to break their promise; that they afterwards assembled to eat a simple and innocent meal; and that in all things they acted according to the laws.

Pliny was a just and humane man, and it seemed to him, on the one hand, very hard to punish such persons as these. But on the other hand, everyone seemed to think that they were dangerous people, and other governors were in the habit of putting them to death; and besides, their religion had spread so widely, that in many places the temples of the heathen gods were quite deserted, and it seemed as if the pagan religion would soon be forgotten. So he wrote to Trajan to inquire what he was to do, whether he was to punish them or not; and if he was to punish them, whether any difference was to he made between young children and grown persons; whether those who gave up their religion and offered sacrifice to the gods were to be pardoned; and whether they were to be punished simply for being Christians, or only if they were found guilty of some other crime. Now it seems to us there was only one answer to be given to this letter, which was, that persons who committed no crime against the laws ought not to be punished. But Trajan judged otherwise. He ordered that no search was to be made for Christians; but that whenever they happened to be brought before the tribunals, they were to be punished, simply for being Christians, without being found guilty of any other crime; but that those who gave up their religion were to be pardoned.

Trajan did not decide in this way because he was an irreligious man, or because he was bigoted to one form of religion above all others, but because he thought it his duty as a good governor to put down the Christians. As the Roman Empire was made up of a great many countries which the Romans had conquered, and each country had its own religion, so it came to pass that there were a great many different religions in the Roman Empire. Every person was allowed to worship what god he liked, and to follow what religion he liked best; but no one thought of saying that his own god or his own religion was the only true one, because the Roman laws said that all the religions were equally true, and all gods equally to be worshiped, provided they were licensed by the State. The Christians, however, knew there can be only one true religion, and all other religions which are different from it must be false and so they always said that the Christian religion was the only true one, and that those of the pagans were false. The pagans would not have cared if the Christians had simply believed Jesus to be God, but they were very angry when they were told that He was the only true God, and that all their own gods and all their own religions were false; and so the followers of all the different pagan religions, who agreed in nothing else, agreed in at least one thing, which was, to hate and persecute the Christians; just as now-a-days Protestants of all sects agree in hating Catholics, for saying that the Catholic Church is the only Church, and that there is no salvation out of it. Trajan felt like the other pagans, and as he did not choose that any one should blame all the different religions which the State sanctioned, he gave orders to punish the Christians, even when they had done nothing else against the laws.

Several very good bishops suffered at this time. One of them was St. Simeon, the brother of St. James the Less, who had been appointed Bishop of Jerusalem after the death of St. James, and had governed that Church ever since. He was one hundred and twenty years of age when he was taken before Atticus, the Proconsul, and was accused of being a Christian and of belonging to the family of David, from which the great Messiah was to be born. Atticus talked a long time to the old man, trying to persuade him to give up his religion, and to save his life by obeying the emperor and sacrificing to the gods. But St. Simeon had known and loved Jesus too long to think of such a thing. As he belonged to the family of St. Joseph, he must have known our Lord from the time of His birth, even during those thirty years which He had spent at Nazareth, when so few other people knew Him. He had loved Him, and had followed Him on earth for a long life of above one hundred years, and he would not deny Him now, when he was so old that he must soon be called to see Him in heaven. Instead of caring for what Atticus said to him, he thought only of the honor and happiness of suffering for Jesus, and of the glorious martyr's crown which he should gain. So he refused to sacrifice to the gods, and begged Atticus to lose no time in putting him to death. He was then scourged, and put on the rack, and tortured in several other ways, while, at the same time, the executioners took great care not to kill him, wishing him to live the longer, in order that they might torture him the more. Day after day he was brought out to be scourged, and racked, and tortured; and day after day, just when he seemed to be on the point of dying and escaping out of their hands, the tortures were stopped, and he was sent back into prison to recover his strength a little, and be able to stand another day's torturing. He bore it all with such extraordinary patience, that even the hardhearted Atticus wondered how such a feeble old man could stand out against such sharp and lingering torments. At last Atticus was wearied out with what he called the obstinacy of the old man, and he ordered him to be crucified. The sentence was executed on the 18th February, A.D, 117, on which day the Church keeps the feast of St. Simeon.

CHAPTER XVII

ST. IGNATIUS

ANOTHER celebrated Saint, who suffered in the reign of Trajan, was St. Ignatius, Bishop of Antioch. Some persons have said that he was the child whom our Lord took in His arms and blessed, saying to His disciples, "Unless you be converted and become as little children, you shall not enter into the kingdom of heaven." He was very intimate with some of the apostles, and, more especially, with St. John, whose disciple he was. He was afterwards made Bishop of Antioch, being the second bishop of that city after St. Peter. He was remarkable for the perfect way in which he performed the duty of a good pastor. He comforted the afflicted, visited the sick, instructed the ignorant, and led quite a heavenly life. On account of his great love for our Lord, he was called Theophorus and Christophorus, which words mean one who carries God, or carries Christ within him. He once had a very beautiful vision. He saw a multitude of angels singing hymns in praise of the Blessed Trinity, and he noticed that one-half of them sang one verse and the other half the next verse; and so he taught the Christians in his Church at Antioch to sing the psalms in the same way, and, ever since then, this has been the custom in the Catholic Church.

It happened that the Emperor Trajan came to Antioch at this time. He was a great soldier, and after having gained a number of victories over a barbarous people, called Dacians, who were at the north of the empire, he was now passing through Antioch on his way to conquer the Parthians, another barbarous nation who lived to the east of it. He was now in the very height of his pride and power, and it was not to be supposed that he would allow anyone to disobey him. He was, therefore, very angry when he was told that, in spite of all the orders he had given against the Christian religion, St. Ignatius would persist in calling himself a Christian, and in teaching that Jesus Christ was the only true God. He therefore ordered him to be brought before him, and having heard a great deal about him he said to him:— "Are you Ignatius, who call yourself Theophorus, and are the leader of those who speak against the emperors, and will not acknowledge the gods whom we worship?" Ignatius answered, "I am Ignatius, and I am Theophorus, because I bear on my heart Jesus Christ, who is my God." What," replied Trajan, "and do not you think that we also have within us the immortal gods, who help us in all that we do?" "Oh! my Lord, do not say so," cried St. Ignatius, "do not call those dumb idols gods. There is only one true God, who is the Creator of heaven and earth, the sea, and all things that we see, and His only Son Jesus Christ, who made Himself man for love of us. If you did but know Him, your empire would be safe from all dangers; for He would take care of you, and would give you great victories over all your enemies." "Enough of such silly talk," said the emperor impatiently; "I will hear no more of this folly; but if you wish to do what will be most pleasing to me, and most for your own advantage, you will come and offer sacrifice to the immortal gods; and if you will do so you shall always be my friend, and I will make you great Jupiter's priest, and will give you the title of the father of the Senate." St. Ignatius answered, "I know very well that we ought to be thankful to great princes when they offer us their favor; but if what they offer us would hurt our souls, it would be very wrong of us to accept it. Now what you offer me is just such a thing. I am a priest of Jesus Christ, and I can be priest to no other god. I daily offer sacrifice to Him, and I wish to sacrifice myself to Him, by dying for Him as he died for me." Much more passed between Trajan and St. Ignatius. They were both great soldiers, the one a great conqueror of earthly kingdoms, and the other Christ's soldier, fighting bravely for His heavenly kingdom. Trajan was very ambitious, and did everything he could to gain the earthly glory which Satan offered him; while St. Ignatius thought all the best things on earth poor and worthless, in comparison with the glory of heaven. Neither would give up to the other, and at last Trajan, finding that he could not make St. Ignatius change his opinions, ordered him to be taken to Rome, and thrown to lions in the Amphitheater.

When the Christians of Antioch heard that their dear bishop was to be put to death, they were filled with sorrow. Antioch was a very wicked place, and they were surrounded with all sorts of temptations, and they were afraid that they should never be able to struggle and fight against them, without the help of their good bishop who had taken care of them for forty years. But while they were all crying and mourning, St. Ignatius was very joyful, and he tried to comfort them by telling them to put all their trust in their Divine Shepherd, Jesus Christ, who would never leave them, and would take much better care of them than he had ever done.

After he had given them his blessing, and had taken leave of them, he put on, with his own hands, the irons with which he was to be loaded, and cheerfully followed the soldiers who were to take him to Rome. These soldiers were so cruel that they did everything they could to make his imprisonment more severe, and his journey more fatiguing; so that he wrote to his friends that during the whole journey, whether by land or by sea, he seemed to be fighting by day and by night, being tied in the midst of ten soldiers, who were like ten leopards. The Christians gave presents to the soldiers in hopes of making them treat the saint kindly; but all in vain, for the more they got, the more cruel they were to him. On his way to Rome, St. Ignatius passed through many countries, and wherever he arrived all the Christians came out to meet him; and churches which were at a distance sent their bishops and some of their clergy to visit him, for all looked upon him as their spiritual father and master. They listened eagerly to every word he said; they threw themselves at his feet; they kissed his hands, his clothes, and the chains that bound him; they begged his blessing, and they looked reverently on him, as on one who was so wonderfully filled with the love of Jesus, that he seemed to be a living image of Him. At Smyrna St. Polycarp, the bishop, came out to see him. St. Ignatius and St. Polycarp had known each other when they were both disciples of St. John, and they had been friends ever since. It was a great joy and comfort to them to meet, and to talk to each other about the love of Jesus, in a way in which only such great saints can feel and talk.

St. Polycarp could not help crying; but he did not cry, like the other Christians, because St. Ignatius was going to leave them. He longed so much to die for Jesus that it made him sad to think that St. Ignatius had got the start of him, and would soon be martyred, and would see Jesus, while he himself would be left behind for perhaps a great many years, shut out from the sight of Jesus' loving face, and from the sound of His sweet voice. These saints longed for torments as other men do for riches and pleasures, and therefore the sight of St. Ignatius, on his way to martyrdom, filled St. Polycarp with a holy envy of him; and he said, "Would to God that I too were found worthy to suffer for this cause." But St. Ignatius comforted him, saying, "Doubt not, my dear brother, but your time will come at last; but for the present the Church has need of you."

St. Ignatius longed for martyrdom even more than other great saints and martyrs have done. He seemed actually to tremble lest some accident should happen to rob him of the martyr's crown. He was afraid lest the Christians of Rome, some of whom were noblemen and friends of the emperor, might ask to have his life spared; or lest the wild beasts might lose their fierceness and refuse to tear him to pieces, as had actually happened more than once, when they had been brought into the Amphitheater to devour other Christians. So he entreated his friends to pray to God that the wild beasts might tear him to pieces, just as they would do any pagan; and he wrote to the Christians of Rome begging them not to prevent his being put to death, since it was much harder for him to live without Christ than to die the worst kind of death, and telling them that if they let him suffer for Jesus, he would take it as a sign that they loved him, and if they did not let him do so, he would take it as a sign that they hated him. He also said to them in the same letter, "The only thing I wish for is that the wild beasts were very hungry, and that I were in the midst of them; for everything else in the world seems to me less than dust, because I long so to embrace Jesus Christ, my Savior. As for fire, wild beasts, breaking of my bones, quartering of my limbs, tearing of my body, and all the other torments the Devil can invent, let them all come upon me, only let me enjoy my Jesus. For it is far better to die for Jesus than to be king of the whole world."

At last St. Ignatius arrived at Rome, and the soldiers who had brought him from Antioch gave him up to the governor of the city. St. Ignatius had traveled as fast as he could, and had always begged the guards to hurry on to Rome, because he was afraid that the games might be over before his arrival; and in that case, he would have had to wait for many weeks, or even months, before he should have an opportunity of being martyred. But he was thankful to find that he was still in time, and would not have more than a few days to wait. During this time he underwent many cruel and horrible torments. His whole body was cut and bruised by being beaten with whips, to which pieces of lead were tied; his flesh was torn with iron hooks and rubbed with flints and sharp stones; and in order to add to the pain of his wounds they were washed with salt and water. He was also kept for three days without food, or a drop of water to quench the feverish thirst which was caused by his wounds. But he did not care for all this suffering, because he was so happy to think that, before many days were over, he should die for Jesus. While they were torturing him, the holy Name of Jesus was always on his lips, and being asked why he constantly repeated it, he said, "Because it is engraved on my heart, and I cannot forget it." Some of those who heard him say this, had the curiosity after his death to examine his heart; and it is said that they actually found the name of Jesus engraved on it.

At last the joyful morning of his martyrdom arrived, and he was led into the Amphitheater where the games of wild beasts took place. The whole city was astir, and crowds were assembled to witness the spectacle. The saint entered the arena with a firm and bold step, and a calm and cheerful countenance. He looked round on the multitude who were thirsting for his blood, and fixing his eyes on them he said, "Think not, O Romans that I am condemned to the wild beasts for any crime unworthy of a Christian, but only because I desire to join and unite myself to God, after whom I thirst insatiably." While he was speaking he heard the roar of lions who were about to be let loose on him, and he cried out with great fervor, "I am God's corn, and the teeth of these wild beasts must grind me, in order that I may become pure and white bread fit for Christ's table." He had scarcely uttered these words when the lions seized him, and tore, and devoured his flesh, but without breaking his bones. He was martyred on the 20th December, A.D., 107, and the Church keeps his feast on the 1st February.

CHAPTER XVIII

ST. CLEMENT

ANOTHER great bishop who suffered martyrdom during this persecution was the Pope St. Clement. He is said to have been of high family, and also to have been very rich and learned. But he loved Jesus so much that everything else seemed to him of no more value than so much dust. So he gave up his high station, and divided his riches among the poor; and putting aside all his learned books he spent his whole time in preaching the Gospel. Even on earth he got his reward for St. Paul said that his name was written in the book of life, and so he had the happiness of hoping securely that he would be granted the grace of final perseverance. He was first a disciple of St. Paul, and afterwards of St. Peter, who appointed him to be his successor as Bishop of Rome. But St. Clement was so humble that he thought himself unworthy to succeed so great an apostle; and, therefore, after St. Peter's death he gave up his place first to St. Linus, and afterwards to St. Cletus. Both of these Popes were martyred, and when St. Clement saw how much danger there was in being Bishop of Rome, he was not so unwilling to fill that high office, and he consented to become Pope.

It was of great consequence in such troubled times as these, that the Pope should be a very holy and prudent man, such as everyone would look up to. St. Clement was

St. Clement

just such a person. He was very bold, and was not the least afraid of persecution; but at the same time he was a great lover of peace. In these times of persecution people were apt to get excited and agitated, some thinking only of how to keep themselves out of trouble, and others running themselves uselessly into it, by talking in a foolish, boasting way; but St. Clement was always calm and quiet, and kept the whole Church steady, by teaching courage to the timid, and humility to the proud and presumptuous.

St. Clement preached the Gospel with such fervor that numbers of the pagans were converted. Among the converts was Theodora, a lady of high rank. Her husband, Sisinnius, was very angry when he was told that his wife was a Christian, and at first he would not believe it; so, in order to make quite sure of it, he determined to go to the house where the Christians were in the habit of meeting, and to see with his own eyes whether his wife really was there; but ad scarcely entered the room when God struck him stone-blind. He was dreadfully frightened for his conscience told him that this sudden blindness was a judgment from God. He, therefore, fell on his knees before St. Clement, and begged him to pray for him; and St. Clement did so, and God was pleased to hear his prayer, and to restore Sisinnius' sight. At the same time the grace of God touched his heart, and he was converted and baptized. Many others were converted by his example, and by the sight of the miracle which the prayers of St. Clement had worked.

For many years St. Clement went on preaching and making a great many converts, without being hindered by the pagan magistrates. But, at last, several heathen priests and other wicked people joined together to get rid of him, and they accused him before Mamertinus, the prefect of Rome, of being an enemy of the gods. Mamertinus was a very prudent man, and he did not at all like to meddle with St. Clement; for though, on the one hand, the emperor had ordered the Christians to be punished, and he might be very angry if St. Clement was not punished; yet, on the other hand, things were not done fairly at Rome, and great favor was constantly shown to people of rank, and, therefore, Mamertinus was afraid that he himself might get into a scrape, if he dared to punish a person like St. Clement, without the emperor's express order. He was also puzzled to know what to think of him, for the whole city was divided about him one party accused him of being a very wicked, irreligious person, while the other party praised him as being a very holy man, who was very kind to the poor, and cured sick persons, and did nothing but good. Thus, Mamertinus found himself in the same difficulty as Pliny had been in, and, therefore, he also wrote to Trajan to know what he was to do. Trajan answered that was to call on Clement to sacrifice to the gods, and if he would not do so, he was to be banished to the Chersonesus, a wild, out of the way place, at the farthest extremity of the Black Sea, now called the Crimea.

Mamertinus had always behaved very kindly to St. Clement on account of his noble birth; and in the course of his conversation with him he had become very fond of him. He now did all in his power to induce him to worship the gods of Rome; but St. Clement, instead of consenting to do so, answered him by entreating him to become a Christian. Mamertinus and St. Clement argued together for a long time, each trying to persuade the other to change his religion, but neither could succeed; and at last Mamertinus was obliged to obey the emperor, and to pass sentence on St. Clement. He could not, however, do so, without shedding tears; and he said to him: "The God whom thou worshippest will favor thee in this affliction which thou sufferest for Him." At the same time he did everything he could to make St. Clement suffer as little as possible; and he ordered that the ship which took him to the Chersonesus should be fitted out with all those things which would make him more comfortable in that wild country.

There were loud lamentations among the Christians of Rome when they saw the Holy Father step on board the ship which was to carry him away from them; and they sorrowfully and anxiously watched its white sails as they gradually went further and further, and became smaller and smaller, till at length they looked like a little speck on the horizon, and then vanished in the distance. It was indeed a dreadful trial to the Church to be deprived of its head, and more especially in this way. For if St. Clement had been put to death they might have chosen another Pope; but so long as he lived they could not do so; and therefore they could only pray to God to take care of His Church while the Pope was in exile, and to give him patience to bear this greatest of all misfortunes that could have befallen them.

But God looks on things very differently from what men do. Men think that it is a great thing for the Church to have holy men in large cities preaching and doing a great work for God in the sight of the whole world-and so it is. But God cares quite as much for the souls of poor people who are not known in the world, and whose conversion seems to do little good to the Church, as He does for those of great and noble people, whose conversion makes a great stir. St. Clement had been doing a great deal among the rich and noble citizens of Rome, but there were some souls in the wilds of Chersonesus for whom Jesus had shed His precious blood, and whom He loved very dearly; and so He allowed St. Clement to be carried away from Rome and taken to the Chersonesus, that he might look after and feed these poor sheep in the wilderness, who had no one else to look after them or feed them.

In that dreary country there happened to be two thousand Christians who had been banished there on account of their religion, and were kept hard at work in the stone quarries. Some of these Christians were of noble birth, and had formerly lived in ease and luxury, while others had been slaves, accustomed to poverty and labor. But now they were all equal, all alike poor and friendless; all alike condemned to wear away their lives in hopeless, daily toil. What made their life of labor the harder was, that there was no priest among them, and so they could not receive the Sacraments, which would have strengthened them, and enabled them to bear their trials with patience. It is impossible, then, to say how overjoyed they were when St. Clement arrived among them; for our Lord had now sent them not only a priest who would give them the Sacraments, but a bishop, and that Bishop no less a person than the Holy Father himself, the successor of St. Peter, and Christ's vicar upon earth.

St. Clement's arrival changed the tone of their whole lives; for now every morning, before going to work, they were strengthened by receiving the Body of their dear Lord; and every evening, when they were weary with the day's toil, they were refreshed by meeting together to pray and sing hymns. Then, too, it was a great encouragement to see this holy man working patiently and humbly among them; and if any of them were sometimes tempted to complain, they were cheered by looking at his calm, joyful face, or by listening to the sweet words of comfort which he spoke to those around him.

But it was not in spiritual matters only that St. Clement assisted these poor, unhappy people. The nearest spring was six miles off, and after a tiring day's work it was very hard to have to go so far to fetch water; and also very often during the day the Christians were hot and thirsty, but had nothing with which to quench their thirst, and this made their work appear the harder. When St. Clement heard the state of the case, he assembled the Christians, and desired them all to pray to God to show them where they were to find water. While they were praying, St. Clement raised his eyes, and he saw a beautiful Lamb standing on a point of the rock, with one of his feet raised up as if it were pointing to a certain spot. No one saw the Lamb except St. Clement; but he knew that it was a vision, and that this Lamb was no other than the Lord Jesus, who was pointing with His foot to the place where they would find water. So he told the Christians to dig on the spot to which the Lamb had pointed. They immediately began to dig, one here and another there, but no water came; for as they had not themselves seen the Lamb, they could not hit on the exact place which St. Clement meant; till at length St. Clement took a mattock, and he struck the very spot to which the beautiful Lamb had pointed, and immediately there sprang up a fountain of clear, fresh water, which swelled gradually till it grew into a river, which was more than enough to supply all their wants.

The fame of this miracle spread over the country, and crowds came to inquire into it, and to see this new and wonderful fountain. St. Clement preached the Gospel to all who came, and thousands were converted, so that in one year no less than seventy-five new churches were founded in this country, which had so lately been a spiritual desert. In course of time, the news of these conversions reached the emperor, and he was very much enraged to find that there was no keeping St. Clement quiet, for he was no sooner sent away from Rome, because he had been working so hard for his new religion, than he must needs go and spread it among these poor, ignorant barbarians. Trajan did not really care about these barbarians, and it mattered little to him what was their religion, or whether they had any religion at all. But he hated this new sect of Christians, and he would not allow this Bishop of Rome to disobey his orders. So he sent to the Chersonesus a new governor, whose name was Aufidian, and he ordered him to put down the Christian religion, by killing all who would not give it up.

Aufidian obeyed these cruel orders very faithfully, for he made a great slaughter of the Christians, putting them to the most dreadful tortures, and inventing new and horrible punishments to inflict on them. But his cruelty was all in vain. For the Christians stood firm to their religion, and they suffered the tortures so bravely, and died so joyfully, that their blood was like the seed of the Church, and brought about the conversion of a great number of pagans, so that the more Christians Aufidian killed, the more Christians there were left behind. Aufidian soon saw that he was not getting on with his task of getting rid of the Christians, and so he thought the best plan would strike at the root of the matter, by killing St. Clement, who was the leader and master of all the others. He, therefore, ordered him to be brought before him, and gave him the usual choice of sacrificing to the immortal gods, or being put to death. St. Clement had made his choice many years before when he became the soldier of Christ; and so he instantly answered, that he was quite ready to die, but that he would never sacrifice to what were devils, and not God. He was accordingly sentenced to be thrown into the sea, with a heavy anchor tied round his neck, in order that is body might sink to the bottom, and not fall into the hands of the Christians, lest, as Aufidian said, they should worship him as a god. The Christians were in despair when they heard that St. Clement was condemned to death, for he had been not only a father to them, but a brother and a friend, and the greatest comfort of their lives. The Holy Father was very much grieved to see their grief; he wept with them, and did his best to comfort them. But they would not be comforted, and just as he was on the point of being thrown into the sea, the multitude who had followed him to the shore raised a loud cry, saying, "Lord Jesus, save him." At the same moment St. Clement said, "Eternal Father, receive my soul," and our Lord heard the prayer of His faithful servant, and received his blessed soul into glory, while, at the same moment, his body sank to the bottom of the sea. The Christians, who had hoped that he would have been saved at the last moment by a miracle, were in the greatest despair, and for some time nothing but cries, and groans, and loud wailings were to be heard. But after a time they became more calm, and then they began to mourn that the precious body of the martyr should be buried in the depths of the sea, and that they could not have the pleasure of possessing his relics. At last Cornelius and Phebus, two of St. Clement's disciples, said to them, "Brethren, let us to pray to God that He would be pleased to give us the relics of this holy martyr." The people entered heart and soul into this proposal, and the voice of the whole multitude rose in one united and fervent prayer to Heaven; and immediately, the sea retired three miles from the shore, so that the Christians could walk into it as upon dry land.

They went boldly forward over the place which had just before been covered with waves, and when they came to the spot where St. Clement had been drowned, they saw a wonderful sight, which showed them how God loves and honors His saints. They found a little chapel of pure, white stone, built by no other than angels' hands, and within it was a chest of stone, in which lay the body of the Holy Father and beside it, the anchor which had been tied round his neck. They took up the body with great joy, and buried it as honorably as they could; and many years after it was taken to Rome, and was placed with great solemnity in a church, which was called by the name of this blessed martyr. St. Clement was martyred on the 23rd November, on which day the Church keeps his feast. The year of his martyrdom is not quite certain, but it is supposed to have been A.D. 100.

CHAPTER XIX

HADRIAN: ST. SYMPHOROSA

AFTER the death of the Emperor Trajan there came better times for the Church, and for above forty years Christians were free from any general persecution. The emperors and magistrates in those days were very much puzzled to think how they were to get rid of this new religion; and it is no wonder that they were puzzled, because, though they did not know it, they had set themselves to fight against God, and to pull down what He was building up. Trajan had tried to root out the Christians by putting to death all who would not give up their religion; but this was soon found to be of no use, because, as has been before said, the Christians were like the fabulous monster Hydra, and as soon as one head was cut off, several others sprang up in its stead. So the next two emperors, Hadrian and Antoninus Pius, tried another plan, and determined to see what could be done by treating the Christians fairly and justly.

Several philosophers and learned men had now become Christians, and they wrote books in defense of their religion, showing how unjustly they were treated. These books were called Apologies, and the most celebrated of them were written by Quadratus, Bishop of Athens, and by Aristides and Justin, both of whom were philosophers. The Emperor Hadrian also called himself a philosopher; so he ho read these apologies with attention, and he thought there was some truth in what the Christian writers said. It happened that at this time Serenius Granianus, the proconsul of Asia, wrote to him, as Pliny had written to Trajan, to inquire what he was to do with the Christians, because it seemed to him very unjust to put them to death when they had done nothing wrong, merely to please the people who raised an outcry against them. Hadrian agreed with Serenius Granianus, so he wrote back to Minucius Fundanus, who meanwhile had succeeded Granianus, desiring him not to let the Christians be harassed by malicious people. He ordered that if any regular accusation was brought against them, they should have a fair trial; and if it were clearly proved that they did anything contrary to the laws, they were to be punished; but if it were found that there was no ground for the accusation except the malice of the person who made it, the accuser was to be punished in the stead of the Christian whom he had accused.

This edict of the Emperor Hadrian was a great blessing to the Christians, for it gave them at least a chance of just treatment. Still they did not always get the protection to which the laws entitled them. It was as easy in those days to get up a cry of, "The Christians to the lions," as it is now to get up a cry of, "No Popery." Because the Christians said that their own religion was the only true one, and they chiefly lived alone, and never went with the rest of the people to the temples or the public games, they were said to be very uncharitable, and to hate their neighbors. If any public misfortune happened, the blame was laid on them. If there was an earthquake, or a famine, or a plague, it was said to be a punishment from the gods for the impiety of the Christians. If the barbarians who lived on the borders of the empire made an irruption into it, people said it was because so many persons had become Christians and thought only about saying long prayers, instead of doing their duty and fighting for the emperor. Besides this, they were accused of many shocking crimes, such as eating human flesh, and killing little children to offer them up as sacrifices to their God, and other things too horrible to be mentioned. The pagans generally believed these things without inquiring into them; it was enough for them that everybody said so, and what everybody said, they thought must be true. So it often came to pass that at the public. games, or on other occasions where great crowds were assembled, people would talk against the Christians, till, at last, a great outcry would suddenly be made, and then numbers of them would be seized and hurried before the judges, who would condemn them, and let them be executed without a fair trial.

Though the Emperor Hadrian wished in a general way that the Christians should have justice, yet sometimes his passions got the better of him, and then he himself behaved to them in the same cruel and unjust way as other people did. It was thus that St. Symphorosa and her seven sons came to be put to death by him. Their history is as follows.

Hadrian built at Tivoli a magnificent villa, the ruins of which are still to be seen; and when it was finished, he dedicated it to his false gods. He was very superstitions, and was in the habit of consulting the devils, whom he worshiped as gods, and who used in those days to speak to their worshiper by means of oracles and imposters of various kinds. Now it came to pass on this occasion, that the devils told Hadrian that a certain lady, called Symphorosa, never ceased to torment them by worshiping her God. Symphorosa was a Christian, widow of St Getulius Zoticus, and sister to Amantius, both of whom had been martyred some time before, and she had seven sons of whom she might well be proud. This answer of the devils, however, settled her fate and that of her sons. She was brought into the presence of the emperor, who being unwilling to proceed to extremities, with her, tried by gentle words to persuade her to sacrifice to his idols. But she answered firmly, "My husband, Getulius, and my brother, Amantius, endured many tortures rather than sacrifice to your idols, and by their deaths they triumphed over your demons, choosing to be beheaded rather than to commit sin. Though they were disgraced before men, yet they were clothed by the angels with immortal glory, and they now enjoy an endless life in the presence of the King of Heaven." Hadrian replied, "Either sacrifice to the immortal gods or I shall offer you in sacrifice to them." But Symphorosa exclaimed, "What! am I and my sons to have the honor of being offered up us a sacrifice to God?" "I shall not sacrifice you to your gods but to mine," replied the emperor. "Your gods," rejoined Symphorosa, "cannot receive me in sacrifice; for if you burn me for the sake of Christ, my God, the fire which consumes me will torment your devils much more than it will me." Hadrian began to lose all patience when he found that whatever he said to frighten St. Symphorosa was turned against himself, so he cried out very angrily, "Come, come, I will have no more of this foolish trifling. Choose at once which you prefer, either to sacrifice to my gods or to die a cruel death." Symphorosa answered joyfully, "My most ardent desire is to die for the name of Jesus, my Lord and my God."

Hadrian, finding that his threats had no effect on Symphorosa, determined to put her to death, as a sacrifice by which he hoped to please the devils, whom he worshiped as gods, She was accordingly led to the temple of Hercules, where she was first cruelly beaten about the mouth and face, and then hung up by the hair of the head.

Her seven sons were forced to stand by, and look on at her sufferings, because Hadrian wished them to see what would happen to themselves, if they imitated her example and stood firm to their religion.

During the many years that Symphorosa had been a widow, these seven sons had been her greatest joy and comfort. When they were little babies she had nursed them in her arms, and had fondly watched over them in their cradles, and when they had grown older, she had given herself up to educating them, and had taken the greatest pains to teach them to love and serve Jesus. She was so anxious to keep them pure from sin that she had scarcely ever let them out of her sight, but had made herself their companion, joining them in all their merry plays, or drying up their childish tears with her kisses; and now in this last trying hour her love for them did not fail, and she still thought more about them than about herself. Though she loved their bodies dearly, yet she loved their souls much more; and she would rather have seen them torn to pieces, than have heard them deny the name of Jesus. She was afraid that, as they were still very young, the sight of her sufferings might frighten them, and tempt them to give up their religion; and so, though she was in the greatest agony, while the whole weight of her body was hanging from her hair, yet she did not mind the pain she was suffering, but thought only of how she should encourage them to bear every torment for Jesus' sake. She exhorted them to imitate their father's example and hers; she said it would be a shame to them if she, who was only a weak woman, should have more courage than they; and she assured them that the tortures she was suffering were not near so bad as they appeared to be. The executioners ordered her to hold her tongue, and they struck her on the face, and they scourged her most cruelly while she was hanging by her hair. But all in vain, for the love of her children would not let her be silent. She still went on saying all she could to encourage them; till at last the executioners saw that there was no use in torturing her any longer, because her example, instead of frightening her sons, would only make them more brave; and so they took her down, and tying a great stone round her neck, they threw her into the river, where she was drowned. Her body was afterwards taken up and buried by her brother Eugenius.

The morning after her death her seven sons were brought into the presence of the emperor, who offered them the usual choice of sacrificing to the gods, or being put to death. Their mother's example had not been lost on them, and though they were so young, they all firmly refused to sacrifice to the gods.

Hadrian accordingly ordered them to be carried off to the temple of Hercules and put to death. Seven stakes were placed round the temple, and to each of the stakes one of the seven brothers was fastened. They were then killed one after another in sight of each other, but in different ways. Crescentius, the eldest, had a lance thrust through his throat; Julian was run through his chest; Nemesis was pierced through his heart; and Primitivus through his stomach; Justin was cut to pieces; Eustatius was wounded all over his body and then quartered; while last of all, Eugenius' chest was opened and his body was divided into two parts. Thus did these seven youths win their crowns of martyrdom.

Hadrian died very soon after he had put St. Symphorosa and her sons to death. He was succeeded by Antoninus Pius who was one of the best of the Roman emperors and behaved very kindly to the Christians. He wrote to the governors of Asia, bidding them not to persecute the Christians, but to leave it to the gods to punish those who would not worship them; and he said that when earthquakes or other public misfortunes befell the empire it would be well if the pagans, instead of throwing all the blame on the Christians, would look to themselves, and see how they neglected their own religious duties, while the Christians became on these occasions only more cheerful and resigned to God's will. Under such an emperor the Church prospered, and went on quietly and steadily increasing, and drawing many souls into the service of Jesus Christ.

CHAPTER XX

MARCUS AURELIUS: THE MARTYRS OF LYONS AND VIENNE

THIS season of peace to the Church ended with the death of Antoninus Pius. He was succeeded by Marcus Aurelius, who was a Stoic philosopher, and prided himself on being too wise to have much feeling, or to be glad and sorry like other people. He has been considered a pattern of pagan virtue, and in some respects he was better than the people around him. But when he is compared with Christians, he appears to be very proud and selfish. The Christians left their homes and gave up all they loved best, in order to preach the Gospel to strangers, and to save them from going to hell; but Marcus Aurelius allowed his own wife, his son, and many others of his family and friends to lead most horribly wicked lives, because he would not take the trouble of checking them, and would not disturb the peace of his own mind by caring about their wickedness.

Marcus Aurelius was very proud of his own learning and wisdom, and so the Christian religion was too humble and simple a religion to suit him. He hated the Christians, and they were cruelly persecuted during the whole of his reign. No new law was passed against them; but as soon as it was known that the emperor hated them, and would not be displeased at any injustice that was done to them, the edicts. of Hadrian and Antoninus Pius were disregarded, and the Church was given up to the fury of savage mobs, and bigoted magistrates. Several Popes, one after the other, suffered in this reign, and Christians were martyred in all the provinces from one end of the empire to the other.

There has come down to us a letter which was written at this time, and which gives a most interesting account of what befell some of the Christians in Gaul, by which name France was then called. It is from the Churches of Lyons and Vienne to their brethren in Asia and Phrygia.[9]

The writers begin by saying, that it is impossible fully to describe the greatness of their own sufferings, and the madness of the heathen against the Christians; because their great adversary, the Devil, had attacked them with his whole strength. He began by gradually exciting his servants against the Christians, so that they were shut out from the houses of pagans, and from the public baths and markets, and everything belonging to them was prohibited from being seen in any public place. But the grace of God was with the Christians, and these trials only served to prepare them for the greater ones which were at hand. Before very long the populace proceeded to violence against them; their houses were plundered, their goods were carried off, they were hunted down with furious cries, and were beaten and stoned, and given up defenseless to bear all that a savage mob could inflict on them. Several of them were seized, and after being examined by one of the inferior magistrates, they were thrown into prison till the return of the governor, who happened just then to be absent.

On the governor's return they were taken before him, and were treated by him in the same cruel way as they had

---

[9] Euseb. 1. v. c. 5.

been by the mob. The unjust treatment they met with was so evident, that Vettius Epagathus, a young man of high rank, who was secretly a Christian, filled with indignation.

And forgetting the danger to which he was exposing himself, demanded to be heard in their defense, boldly declaring that they had done nothing against religion and the laws. A loud cry from the mob rose in answer to his words; but the governor quickly cut the matter short, by asking him whether he also was a Christian. Epagathus confessed in a clear voice that he was, and instantly he was placed among the martyrs, while the populace hooted him; calling him contemptuously the advocate of the Christians. He and his companions were then led to torture. Most of them bore the tortures with great constancy; but ten of them, whose faith was weak, could not stand out against the intensity of their sufferings, and to the great grief of their brethren, they were tempted in an evil moment, to offer sacrifice to the gods. The others, including Epagathus, died amid the tortures, confessing Christ and rejoicing at dying for Him.

The persecution did not end with the execution of these first martyrs. Some heathen slaves, who lived in Christian families, were seized and brought before the governor; and, on being questioned, they accused the Christians of eating human flesh, of sacrificing little children, and of committing other crimes too horrible to mention. Up to this time several of the more respectable pagans had not joined in the persecution, because some of the Christians were their relations or friends; but after these fresh accusations became generally known, all ties of blood and friendship were forgotten, and the whole population seemed only to be vying with each other who could be most cruel to the Christians. Then was fulfilled our Lord's prophecy, "The hour cometh, that whosoever killeth you, will think that he doth a service to God."

Every day more and more persons were seized and thrown into prison, till at length all the principal members of the Churches of Lyons and Vienne were collected there. The bishop, Pothinus, was more than ninety years of age, and he was so infirm that he could scarcely breathe. But he longed so for martyrdom, that he roused his little remaining strength, and had himself dragged before the judge. Though his body was nearly worn out, partly by age, and partly by disease, yet he still retained enough of life in him to suffer for Christ. When he was carried before the tribunal he did not shrink from the blows and clamor to which he was exposed; and on being asked by the governor, who was the God of the Christians? he answered, "If thou art worthy thou shalt know." After this he was dragged away and mercilessly scourged, while those of the mob who stood near him kicked him and struck him with their hands and feet, and those at a distance pelted him with stones and filth, till at last he was thrown almost dead into prison, where he expired at the end of two days.

It would be endless to narrate all that the martyrs suffered. They were thrown into the darkest and most dismal dungeons; they were stretched in the stocks till their limbs were out of joint; some of them were so tortured that they were kept alive only by the supernatural strength of body and mind, which God gave them; and numbers of them who had been rich, and had not been accustomed to hardships, died in prison from suffocation and want of the commonest necessaries of life.

Four of the martyrs were more particularly distinguished by their constancy and their sufferings. These were Sanctus, the deacon of Vienne; Maturus, a recent convert; Attalus, of Pergamus, a Roman citizen of high rank; and Blandina, a slave. Maturus and Attalus suffered the usual tortures, which they bore with great firmness. As Sanctus was a deacon, the pagans were very anxious to conquer him, or at least to make him say something he ought not to say; so, while he was being tortured, they kept on asking him all sorts of questions. But he saw what they wanted, and was determined to disappoint them; and so he would not tell them what was his name, or his nation, or the city whence he came, or whether he was a slave or a freeman, but answered them only with the words, "I am a Christian." This confession was to him instead of name, and city, and race, and every other thing; and no other word was heard to pass his lips. Then there arose a diabolical contest between the governor and the tormentors, to see who could invent the most horrible tortures for him, till at last, when all their ingenuity was exhausted, and they did not know what else to do, they fastened red-hot plates of brass to the most tender parts of his body. But through it all he continued unmoved, firm in his first confession, "I am a Christian," and constantly refreshed and strengthened by the fountain of living water which flows from the Heart of Jesus. By this time his whole body from head to foot was one great wound, and it was so mangled and shriveled that it had no longer the form of a man. It needed but a little more to set him free; but his cruel tormentors denied him this little; for just as he seemed to be on the point of expiring, they stopped the tortures, and sent him back again to prison. After a few hours, when they supposed he had recovered a little strength, they brought him out again, and prepared to put him once more to the torture. His wounds were now so swollen and inflamed, that the tenderest touch of the softest hand gave him excruciating pain; and they thought that if they were to repeat the former tortures while he was in this state, he must either give way under them or die, and his death would at least strike terror into others. But the supernatural power of Christ, who dwelt and suffered in him, now appeared in such a wonderful way, that the devices of the devil were defeated, and his fellow sufferers saw plainly that there is nothing terrific where the love of God dwells, and nothing painful where the glory of Christ reigns. For, when the tortures were applied a second time, his body, which just before had been a shapeless mass, suddenly resumed its accustomed form, his limbs recovered their natural strength, he stood erect, and was able to endure all that was inflicted on him; so that, through the grace of Christ, these second tortures, instead of being a torment, became the means of curing him.

As for the slave Blandina, she had always been a gentle and unpretending person, and she had never said much about her love for Jesus, or about her readiness to suffer martyrdom. When she was seized, the rest of the Christians, and especially her mistress, who was herself among the martyrs, were afraid that she would not have courage or strength to stand firm. But she cherished in her heart a deep though secret love to Jesus, and He, in return for this love, filled her with such supernatural power, as made it evident that He prizes most the things which appear mean and contemptible to men. Her tormentors inflicted on her all the usual tortures; they racked their brains to discover new and unheard-of modes of suffering; they took her in hand by turns, relieving and succeeding each other from morning till night. But all in vain. This blessed saint seemed to gain fresh strength and courage by constantly repeating, "I am a Christian, no wickedness is carried on among us," these words appeared to refresh her and to ease her pain. At last her tormentors confessed that they were fairly beaten, for they knew of nothing more which they could do to her. It was only a wonder, they said, that she continued to breathe, after her whole body was thus pierced and torn asunder, since one single torture such as they had inflicted on her was enough to have killed her.

The public games were now about to be exhibited, and, on the day appointed for the fight with wild beasts, Maturus, Sanctus, Attalus, and Blandina were led into the Amphitheater to be torn to pieces by them. Maturus and Sanctus now underwent a second time a repetition of all the same tortures as on the former occasion, just as if they had suffered nothing before; and whatever torments the mob called for, were inflicted on them. At last, when they had been scourged and torn by wild boasts, and tortured in every conceivable way, they were placed upon an iron chair, which was made red-hot, so that they were literally roasted alive, while the fumes of their own scorching flesh almost suffocated them. In this position they expired; and thus, after having fought and conquered nobly, they won the glorious crown of immortality.

Blandina, meanwhile, being bound and hung upon a stake, was exposed as food to the wild beasts. While she was thus hanging as it were on her cross, she prayed so earnestly that she inspired her fellow-sufferers with fresh courage and love; for, as they looked at her, they seemed to be contemplating Him who was crucified for them, and her holy joy served to remind them that those who suffer for Christ will forever enjoy communion with Him. But the beasts were less savage than the men who goaded them on; for they refused to touch her, so that after she had hung for some time she had to be taken down and sent back to prison, to be reserved for another trial.

Attalus, too, was sent back to prison, after he had been led round the Amphitheater amid the shouts and hootings

Marcus Aurelius: Martyrs of Lyons and Vienne   139

of the brutal mob; for, as he was a Roman citizen, the governor would not venture to throw him to the wild beasts without express orders from the emperor.

Attalus and Blandina were very sorry to be thus kept waiting, and not at once to have the happiness of dying for Jesus; but our Lord ordered it so from love to those unhappy persons who had forsaken their religion at the beginning of the persecution. These wretched apostates had gained nothing even in this world by their sin; for, though they had been let off at first, yet they had afterwards been seized on various pretenses, and had been thrown a second time into prison. They were downcast and hopeless, for they were not supported as the martyrs were, since they knew that their present sufferings were only the beginning of much greater ones, which were awaiting them in hell. Attalus and Blandina had been very much grieved at the fall of these apostates; but now, instead of despising them, and refusing to have anything to do with them, because they were so wicked, they felt very sorry for them, and spoke kindly and gently to them. By these means these poor sinners were brought back to repentance, so that the love of Jesus revived in their hearts, and they were enabled at their next trial to make a good confession, and to recover the glorious crown which they had formerly lost.

In course of time the emperor's answer arrived, and then all the prisoners were led out to be questioned by the governor. A few, but only a very few, denied their faith, and they were at once dismissed. As for the others, those who were Roman citizens were ordered to be beheaded, while the rest were sentenced to be thrown to the wild beasts. When it came to the turn of those who had formerly apostatized, the governor was about to dismiss them after very slight questioning; but they cried out boldly that they were Christians, and would not give up their religion, so that they were led away to death with the other martyrs. There happened to be among the crowd a physician called Alexander, a Phrygian, who had been for several years in Gaul, and was well known to the Christians for his love of God and his boldness in speaking the truth. He was not, however, at once recognized by the mob, and thus he was able to stand near the tribunal, and to encourage by signs those who were led up to be questioned. But he was at last noticed; and, when the former apostates made a good confession, the mob cried out that it was Alexander who had made them speak in this way. Then the governor asked him who he was, and he answered that he was a Christian ; whereupon he also was condemned to be thrown to the wild beasts.

The following day he and Attalus were led into the Amphitheater; for although Attalus was a Roman citizen, and ought to have been beheaded, the governor gave him to the wild beasts in order to please the people, who were very much exasperated against him. Alexander and Attalus now endured all the tortures that the savage cruelty of the mob demanded, and at last their torn and bleeding bodies were placed on the red-hot iron chair. Not a word, or a groan, or any other sound, was heard from Alexander, who, during all his torments, held silent and sweet communion with God. As for Attalus, when he was placed upon the chair, and the suffocating fumes rose round him, he said to the surrounding multitude, "Lo, this is to devour men, and you are doing it; but as to us, we neither devour men nor commit any other evil." When he was asked what was the name of God, he answered, "God has no name like a man." They were at last put to death with the sword.

On the last day of the games, after all the other martyrs had been dispatched, Blandina, and a boy of fifteen, called

Ponticus, were brought into the Amphitheater. They had been brought in each preceding day to witness the torments of the rest, and the pagans had tried to force them to swear by the idols. They were now put to the whole round of tortures; but all was in vain. Blandina openly encouraged Ponticus by her words and example, so that he bore the whole bravely, till at length he expired. And then Blandina, who had been like a mother animating her children, and had now seen them all conquer and go to Jesus, hastened herself last of all to His sweet presence. After having been scourged, torn by the beasts, and roasted on the iron chair, she was put into a net and thrown to a wild bull; and, finally, after she had been repeatedly tossed by this animal, she, too, was dispatched by the sword. Even the heathens confessed that no woman had ever endured so many and such great sufferings as she had done.

The savage fury of the mob did not cease with the death of their victims. They watched the bodies of the martyrs day and night, lest they should be taken away and buried by their friends; they gnashed their teeth at them; they mocked at them, saying, "Where is now their God?" and "What good has their religion done them?" They allowed the dogs to gnaw them; and at last, after having abused and insulted them during six days, they burned them and threw their ashes into the River Rhone, in order, as they said, to prevent their resurrection, exclaiming, with fearful impiety, "Now we shall see whether they will rise again, and whether their God is able to help them and to rescue them out of our hands."

CHAPTER XXI

ST. FELICITAS AND HER SONS

THERE lived at Rome, in the reign of Marcus Aurelius, a noble lady called Felicitas. She was a widow and had seven sons. On her husband's death she took a vow of chastity, and gave herself up to a life of prayer, fasting, and good works. One of her principal occupations was the education of her seven sons, whom she loved very dearly. Felicitas' love for her sons was not merely such as all women feel for their children. She remembered that they were not her children only, but that they were the children of God, who had lent them to her, and would one day ask her an account of them. She did not wish to see them rich and great in this world, but she wished to lay up in store for them the inestimable riches of eternal glory in the next. She therefore trained them from their infancy in all holy and pious practices suited to their age, and she offered them up to Jesus to live and die in His service, in whatever way it might be His will to make use of them. Our Lord accepted the offering, and gave her and them the high honor of suffering martyrdom for His sake.

Felicitas was so good and holy, that the women of her own rank thought very highly of whatever she said or did, and many of them, who were pagans, were converted by her example and influence. This displeased the heathen priests, and they complained to the emperor, and

St. Felicitas and Her Sons

persuaded him that the gods were very angry, and would not be pacified till Felicitas and her children would offer sacrifice to them. She and her sons were accordingly made prisoners, and taken before Publius, the prefect of the city. Publius was unwilling to use violence with a lady of such high rank and character as Felicitas; so he first took her aside, and tried gently to persuade her to sacrifice to the gods. But Felicitas answered: "Do not hope, O Publius! to win me with fair words, or to terrify me with threats; for I have within me the Spirit of God, who will not let me be overcome by Satan; and therefore I am sure I shall be too hard for you, who are the servant of Satan." Publius seeing that she had no fear for herself, thought he would move her by speaking to her of her children, and he therefore said to her: "Unhappy woman, is it possible that you are so tired of life that you will not even let your children live, but will force me to destroy them by bitter and cruel torments?" "My children," replied Felicitas, "would die an everlasting death if they offered sacrifice to your gods. But now, since they acknowledge and worship Jesus Christ, they will live with Him forever." After making this first attempt Publius dismissed her, thinking it would be best to let her consider coolly and quietly what he had said, and what tortures she was bringing on herself and her children, hoping that when she did so, she would come to a better mind.

The next day, as he was sitting in the temple of Man he sent once more for Felicitas and her sons. When they came before him he turned to her, and appealing to her feelings as a mother, he said: "Oh! Felicitas! take pity on your children, who are now in the prime of youth, and who are of such noble birth, and are so good and clever that they may look to the highest honors in the State. But Felicitas answered: "Your pity is cruel, and your advice is impious and deceitful." Then turning to her children, she said: "My sons, look up to heaven, where Christ expects you with all His saints. Fight manfully for the good of your souls, and show yourselves faithful and constant in the love of the true God, Christ Jesus." These words exasperated Publius, who looked upon it as an intolerable affront that this woman should defy him to his very face, and so he commanded that she should be cruelly beaten about the face and head. Then he turned to her sons, and, beginning with Januarius, the eldest, he tried to induce him by promises and threats to adore the gods. But the boy was not unworthy of his brave and saintly mother, and he answered: "You wish to persuade me to do a foolish thing, contrary to all reason: but I trust in my Lord Jesus Christ that He will preserve me from so great an impiety." On hearing these words, Publius gave orders that he should be stripped and very severely scourged; after which he was thrown into prison. All the other brothers were brought up in turn, and every art was used to conquer them, and induce them to obey the emperor. But it was all to no purpose; for they were supported and guided by the Holy Spirit, and they all made Publius the same answer, though in different words, as Januarius had done. They were therefore scourged so severely that their whole bodies were a mass of wounds, and in this state they were thrown into prison, till the emperor's further pleasure should be known.

During all the time that her sons were being thus tortured, Felicitas was forced to stand by and witness their sufferings. This holy mother remained firm and unmoved, while she gazed at the torments of her children; she did not shed a tear as the noise of the blows resounded in her ears; she did not shrink at the sight of their streaming blood, their quivering flesh, and their involuntary writhings of agony. The only words she spoke were to exhort them to stand firm, and to inflame their hearts with love for Jesus. It seems strange how a mother could act in this way. It was not because she did not love her children, or because she had not the natural feelings of a mother; for, on the contrary, every torture they endured pierced her to her very heart, and gave her even more pain than it did them. But it was because the supernatural character of her love for them gave her strength to conquer the weakness and tenderness of a mother's natural feelings. Looking on them with the eyes of faith, she saw in their temporal death only their gain of eternal life, in their present wounds the jewels of their future crown, and in the severity of their torments the greater blessedness prepared them in glory. She would have feared to leave them behind her on earth, lest any one of them should fall short of heaven, and, therefore, she rejoiced as much in the death of her sons, as other mothers weep when theirs are taken from them.

Marcus Aurelius was so hardened by his Stoic philosophy, that he could not feel the least compassion for Felicitas, and he ordered that all her sons should be put to death in various ways before her eyes. The three eldest underwent a very horrible and lingering death, being slowly beaten till they expired. Januarius was first torn with whips, and then with thick cords, loaded with lead, till he died; and Felix and Philip were bruised and broken with cudgels, until every bone being fractured, and their bodies being reduced to a shapeless mass, they at last expired. A milder fate awaited the others; for, Silvanus was thrown from a rock, while Alexander, Vitalis, and Martialis were beheaded. To have put their bereaved mother to death would now have been a deed of mercy; but the persecutors of the Christians did not know what mercy was. The emperor ordered her to be thrown into a dark and cold dungeon, where she was kept four months, in hopes that her patience being worn out, and her spirits broken by her sorrow, she would at last be willing to do anything to escape from solitude and torture. But there was now less chance than ever of St. Felicitas giving up her religion, for the loss of her children had only strengthened her to bear whatever might be inflicted on her. She had now no temptation to save her life by denying Jesus; for this world was become a blank to her, and nothing in it could give her the least happiness. She would have wept had her sons not died for Christ; but now that she had as many bright and glorious saints in heaven as she had once had children on earth, her only hope and longing was to be with them in the presence of Him, to whom she had offered them, and for love of whom they had laid down their lives. At last, when it was plain that she would never consent to adore the heathen gods, the emperor ordered her to be beheaded. Thus did this blessed saint suffer eight martyrdoms, being martyred in each of her children, and ceasing to suffer only when she ceased to breathe. A father of the Church, in speaking of her, says, "she is not a true mother, who knows not how to love her children as St. Felicitas loved hers."

St. Felicitas and her sons suffered martyrdom about A.D. 164. The Church keeps her feast on the 23rd November, and that of her sons on the 10th July.

CHAPTER XXII

ST. POLYCARP

IT was now above a hundred and thirty years since our Lord's death, and all His apostles and all the other people who had seen Him on earth were long since dead. Most of those, too, who had seen the apostles, were also dead. But there was still alive one person, who had been the intimate friend of several of the apostles. This was St. Polycarp. We have heard of him before when he went to visit St. Ignatius, and when he wept to think that St. Ignatius was going so soon to have the pleasure of dying for Jesus, while he was to be left behind. St. Ignatius comforted him by telling him that his turn would come at last, but that, in the meantime, our Lord had work for him to do in the Church on earth. St. Polycarp waited patiently for more than fifty years, and during all this time he found work to do which no one but himself could have done; but, at last, in the reign of Marcus Aurelius his turn came.

Polycarp had known several of our Lord's first disciples, and he had been particularly intimate with St. John, who had ordained him Bishop of Smyrna. To talk to Polycarp was then the next thing to talking to the apostles themselves; and now that the apostles were dead, holy persons who were younger than Polycarp loved to visit him, for the very purpose of hearing what be alone could tell them about the apostles. On these occasions he was in the habit of telling them all about his own familiar intercourse with St. John, and with others who had seen Jesus; and he used to repeat all that they had said to him, and what they had told him about our Lord, and His miracles, and His doctrine. This sort of conversation with Polycarp was not only a great pleasure to those who heard him, but it was also of great use to them. For the Devil had begun a new sort of attack on the Church. Finding that there was no hope of conquering it by persecuting it, he determined to try what he could do by corrupting it. He therefore tempted some of the Christians themselves to become his servants, and he made them proud, and put it into their heads to pretend to know more than anyone else, and to invent new and false doctrines which they taught as true ones, declaring that the Catholic bishops and priests were deceiving the people. Heretics always talk very boldly and proudly about their own superior knowledge; and so it was with the heretics in the time of Polycarp. They spoke so confidently that good, simple people sometimes became puzzled, and began to fancy that perhaps, after all, the heretics were right and the Catholics were wrong; and then it was a great comfort to them to go to Polycarp, and to ask him what the apostles had told him about these things. Even the Pope thought much of what Polycarp said. For, on one occasion, when some Churches in Asia Minor refused to keep Easter at the same time as the other Christians did, Pope Anicetus spoke to Polycarp on the subject, and, when he heard from him that St. John used to keep it at that time, out of the fulness of his apostolic power he gave these Churches leave to follow their own old custom. As to Polycarp, he had such a horror of heretics, that when he was told of the wicked things they said, be used to stop his ears and to exclaim, "O good God! unto what times hast thou reserved me that I should

St. Polycarp

tolerate these things?" Once he happened to meet in the streets of Rome a celebrated heretic called Marcion, but he turned away his face, and would not salute him. Marcion felt what a discredit it would be to him if this holy old man did not acknowledge him, and he therefore went impudently up to him, and said to him, "Dost thou not know who I am?" "Yes," answered Polycarp, "I know thee very well." Acknowledge me, then," rejoined Marcion. Whereupon Polycarp answered, "I do acknowledge thee for the first-born of Satan," and, turning quickly away, he left the heretic in the greatest confusion.

This venerable saint was one of the martyrs in the reign of Marcus Aurelius. The persecution was carried on very furiously in Asia, and especially in the city of Smyrna: for the emperor's ministers vied with each other to see who should spill the most Christian blood, and who could invent the most cruel tortures to inflict on the Christians. They were so torn with scourges that their bones and arteries were laid bare, and the inside of their bodies was exposed to view; they were placed on prickly sea-shells and on the sharp heads and point of spears; and, after passing through every kind of punishment and torment, they were at last thrown as food to the wild beats. They bore these tortures with such wonderful fortitude, that those who stood round were struck with amazement.

During these troubles Polycarp, who, as we have said, was Bishop of Smyrna, watched over his flock, comforting the afflicted, encouraging the faint-hearted, and helping all to the best of his power. In the midst of this storm he was perfectly calm, his hope and trust being fixed upon God, to whom he never ceased to pray, beseeching Him to take pity on His Church, and either to put a stop to the persecution, or to give His children strength to endure it. The pagans know what a support he was to his people, for they used to call him the master of the Christians of Asia, and they now fancied that if he were put to death, all the others would give up their religion. So, instead of being converted by the wonderful constancy of the first martyrs, they only became more furious, and thirsted for St. Polycarp's blood, crying out, "Away with these wicked fellows. Let Polycarp be sought for."

When Polycarp heard that they wanted to get hold of him, he was not the least distressed or frightened; he continued his usual occupations, and took no precautions to save his life. His flock, however, entreated him so earnestly to leave the city, that he was at last persuaded to go to a house in the country, where he lay hid for a short time. Three days before he was taken prisoner, God revealed to him what sort of death he should die. He dreamt that the pillow under his head took fire, and was entirely burnt; and understanding that this dream was from God, and what was its meaning, he said to his friends, "Be assured, my brethren, that within a few days I shall be burnt alive. Praised and glorified be my most sweet Lord Jesus Christ, who will vouchsafe me the crown of martyrdom." But though Polycarp was so joyful at the thought of death, his friends could not make up their minds to part with him, and they insisted on his removing from house to house, so as to avoid his pursuers. However, after three days, when the time appointed by God was come, his enemies found him out by means of two Christian boys whom they happened to meet in the street, and one of whom they beat cruelly till he consented to show them where Polycarp was hid. When they entered the house in which he was, he might easily have escaped, but he knew by his vision that it was God's will he should die, and therefore he would not He only said, "Lord, thy will be done," and then going down to meet those who

St. Polycarp 151

were come to make him prisoner, he received them with a calm and happy countenance, just as if they had been his best friends. He ordered dinner to be prepared for them, and he very courteously invited them to refresh themselves after their journey, begging that meanwhile they would let him pray undisturbed for one hour. They granted his request; whereupon he stood up and prayed without stopping for two hours, recommending the Universal Church to God, and mentioning by name every one, whether small or great, noble or simple, with whom he had ever been connected. His prayer was so full of the grace of God, that all who heard him were astonished. Even the pagan officers were so touched with the sweetness of his words and his venerable air, that they were sorry they had ever come to seize him, and they said one to another, "Is it possible that it was for this venerable old man that so much search has been made? Have so many soldiers and spies been sent to catch him, and so many snares been laid to entrap him?" But they had no choice except to obey their orders; and so, when he was ready, they put him on an ass, and set off with him to the city of Smyrna.

As they were going along they met Nicetas, a man of high rank, and his son Herod, the Irenarch, one of the magistrates, whose business it was to keep the peace. When Nicetas and Herod saw Polycarp's silvery hair and his venerable countenance, they thought it a pity that such an aged man should come to so cruel an end. Perhaps, too, they thought that as old blood is not so hot as young, he would have none of that foolish enthusiasm, which had made the younger men so obstinate about a mere matter of religion, a set of opinions which they might easily have kept in their own hearts, without making such a fuss about them. So they took him into their chariot, and thinking to do him a kindness, they began to persuade him to look better to hist own interest than to lose his life, when, by only saying a few words and putting a grain of incense into the fire, he might spend the rest of his days in peace. "For what harm, said they, "can there be in saying 'Lord Caesar,' and in sacrificing so as to save your life?" At first Polycarp made them no answer, which encouraged them to hope that he was beginning to waver, and so they continued to urge him. But at length he said to them, "You lose your time, for I will never do as you advise me." Then they became very angry with him, and using the most shocking language, they pushed him out of their carriage with so much violence, that he sprained his thigh. The saint, however, took no notice of their rudeness, or of the pain which he was now suffering, but, as if nothing had happened, he walked on eagerly to the place called the stadium, where public games and shows were being exhibited.

It was during the public games that the greatest violence was most frequently done to the Christians. The pagans were assembled on these occasions, to amuse themselves by seeing men fight with each other or with wild beasts, and they used to laugh and shout for joy, while the place was covered with blood, and sometimes even hundreds of their fellow-creatures were dying before their eyes. The sight of these games made the people so ferocious, that they seemed to become like lions and tigers, and actually to thirst for blood; and then, the least trifle, even the voice of a boy in the crowd, would be enough to make the whole multitude cry out, "The Christians to the lions."

The people of Smyrna were now all assembled in the stadium, looking more like demons than like men, tossing their arms savagely in the air, jostling each other,

St. Polycarp

screaming, shouting, yelling, singing, while ever and anon there rose above all the other wicked sounds, that most wicked of all cries, "Away with the Christians, Polycarp to the lions."

In the midst of the savage crowd stood the cause of all this uproar, a meek old man above a hundred years of age, whose silvery locks and calm grey eye cried shame upon those who were thirsting for his blood. He entered the stadium with an unmoved air, for a voice still and small, but yet louder than the roar of the multitude, sounded in his ears, saying, "Be strong, Polycarp, and contend manfully." No one saw who it was that spoke; but many of the brethren heard the voice, and it filled the heart of the martyr with fresh joy and courage. As he advanced, and it came to be generally known that Polycarp was at last taken prisoner, the uproar increased, so that there was some difficulty in taking him up to the proconsul.

At length, however, he got through the crowd, and stood before the Roman governor, who asked him, "Are you Polycarp, the bishop?" And he answered, "Yes, I am Polycarp." The proconsul was struck with his venerable appearance, and thought, like Herod and Nicetas, that it was a pity that the old man's few remaining years should be cruelly cut off. So he determined not to be very hard upon him, and, doubtless, he thought it would be no difficult matter to get him to do some little thing to satisfy the clamors of the people. He did not know that in such a case there is no difference between great and little things, for it was a simple question of whether he would confess Christ or deny Him, whether he would serve God, or serve the devil.

The proconsul, however, used many arguments to "persuade Polycarp to renounce Christ, begging him to have pity on his own great age, and when he found that he had success, trying to get him at least to do as others had done, saying to him, "Swear by the genius of Caesar. Repent, and say, "Away with the atheists," meaning by this word "atheists," the Christians, who were called atheists by the pagans, because they did not believe in the heathen gods. Whereupon, Polycarp, looking down with a calm and grave countenance on the great multitude in the stadium, beckoned with his hand to them, and casting up his eyes to heaven, heaved a deep sigh and said, "Away with the atheists," showing plainly by his manner that he meant to call the pagans, and not the Christians, atheists. The proconsul, however, still urged him, saying, "Swear, and I will dismiss you. Revile Christ." But Polycarp answered, "Eighty and six years have I served Him, and He never did me any wrong. How then shall I blaspheme my King, who has saved me?" The proconsul said, "Swear at least by the genius of Caesar." Polycarp replied, "If you pretend not to know who I am, or if you are so foolish as to think I could swear by the genius of Caesar, hear my free confession. I am a Christian. But if you wish to learn what the doctrine of Christianity is, grant me a day, and listen to me." The proconsul rejoined, "Speak to the people, and get them to listen to you." "I have thought it right," replied Polycarp, "to reason with you, for we have been taught to give magistrates, who are appointed by God, the honor that is due to them; but I do not consider the people the proper persons before whom I should defend myself."

The proconsul now thought of trying what threats and fear would do; so he said, "I have wild beasts at hand; I will throw you to them unless you change your mind."

"Call them," answered Polycarp, "for we have no reason to change from the better to the worse, though it is always good to change from wickedness to virtue." "If you despise the beasts," rejoined the proconsul, "and will not

St. Polycarp

change your mind, I will have you burnt to death." Polycarp answered, "You threaten to burn me in the fire that is soon extinguished, but you know nothing of the judgment to come, and of the fire of eternal punishment reserved for the wicked. But why do you delay so long? Bring out the wild beasts, and the fire, and whatever else you will." While Polycarp was speaking thus, he was filled with joy, and his countenance shone brightly with the grace that dwelt in his soul.

The governor was astonished at the strange obstinacy of this old man, whom nothing could move or frighten, and who would do not even the smallest thing to deny his religion. He therefore gave up his endeavors to save his life, and sent a herald to proclaim in the middle of the stadium, "Polycarp confesses that he is a Christian." On hearing this, a great shout rose from all the multitude, and both Jews and Gentiles cried out, "This is that teacher of Asia, the father of the Christians, the destroyer of our gods; he that teaches multitudes not to sacrifice, and not to worship. the gods." They clamored that he should be thrown to the wild beasts, and they called to Philip the Asiarch, whose office it was to regulate the public shows, to let loose a lion upon him. But Philip replied that he could not do so, because the games of wild beasts were ended, and it was contrary to law for him to begin them again. Then they cried out all together, "Let Polycarp be burned alive." All this was thus ordered by God, that the vision which He had sent three days before to Polycarp might be fulfilled.

The crowd had scarcely uttered their savage cry than they began to carry it into execution; and the Jews, as usual, were very zealous in assisting. Wood and shavings were collected from the neighboring shops and baths and a funeral pile was quickly raised. Meanwhile the saint calmly prepared to offer himself a burnt sacrifice to God. He laid aside his clothes, loosed his girdle, and attempted to take off his shoes, which he had not been in the habit of doing for himself, since on account of his age and the great respect in which he was held, he had long been waited on by one or other of the brethren, who vied with each other in serving him. When all was ready the executioners were about to nail him to the stake, but he said: "Let me be thus; for He that gives me strength to bear the fire, will also give me the power to remain unmoved in it, even though I be not secured." They, therefore, did not nail him, but only tied him to the stake. And now he stood with his hands behind him, bound to the stake like a victim chosen out of the Lord's great flock, and about to be offered an acceptable sacrifice to him. Raising his eyes and voice to heaven, he prayed aloud: "Father of thy well-beloved and blessed Son Jesus Christ through whom we have received the knowledge of Thee, the God of all angels, and powers, and all created things, and of all the family of the righteous that live before Thee, I bless Thee that Thou hast thought me worthy of this day and hour, and hast granted me to have a share in the number of the martyrs, and in the cup of Christ, unto the resurrection of eternal life both of the soul and body, in the incorruptible felicity of the Holy Spirit; among whom may I be this day received in Thy sight, as a rich and acceptable sacrifice, as Thou, the faithful and true God, hast prepared and revealed. Wherefore, on this account and for all things, I praise Thee, I bless Thee, I glorify Thee, through the eternal High priest, Jesus Christ, Thy well-beloved Son; through whom be glory to Thee, with Him in the Holy Ghost, both now and forever. Amen."

As soon as Polycarp had finished his prayer, the executioners lighted the fire. And then there appeared a miraculous sight. For as the flames arose on every side, they seemed to swell out in a curve, as when the sail of a ship is filled with wind, so that they did not touch the body of the martyr, but formed a wall around him, and an arch over his head. And he was seen in the middle of them, not like burning flesh, but like gold and silver, purified in the furnace; while those who stood around perceived a fragrant smell like the fumes of incense or some precious aromatic drug. At length his enemies, seeing that his body could not be consumed by the fire, ordered the executioner to go up to him and plunge a sword into him; and when this was done such a quantity of blood gushed out, that the fire was extinguished, and the multitude were filled with wonder, asking each other how it came to pass that Christians were so different from other men.

The Christians were now very anxious to get possession of the body of their martyred bishop, and to bury it under the altar where the daily Sacrifice was offered up. But the Devil, whose malice could not be satisfied even by the death of this servant of God, urged on the Jews to represent to the governor, that the Christians ought not to be allowed to have the body, lest they should give up worshiping Jesus and should begin to worship Polycarp. It was all in vain that the Christians said, "We can never abandon Christ, who suffered for the salvation of all mankind, or worship any other. For Him we worship as the son of God; but the martyrs we deservedly love as the disciples and imitators of our Lord, on account of their exceeding love to their King and Master." But the pagans did not know how very much the Christians loved Jesus, and therefore, they could not understand that the reverence which they paid to the martyrs was quite different from the love and adoration which were given to Jesus. They, therefore, believed all that the Jews said, and a centurion threw St. Polycarp's body into the middle of the fire, and burnt it according to the custom of the Gentiles. At last, however the Christians were allowed to take possession of the saint's bones, which they prized as relics, more valuable than precious stones and more tried than gold, and they buried them in the church of Smyrna, where they assembled every year to celebrate joyfully the day of his death, which they used to call the birthday of his martyrdom. The martyrdom of St. Polycarp took place at two o'clock in the afternoon of the 23rd January, A.D. 166, and the Church keeps his feast on the 26th of the same month.

CHAPTER XXIII

Fifth Persecution

SEPTIMIUS SEVERUS

THE history of the Church is, in many respects, like the life of individuals. Things do not continue always in the same state; there are constant changes; and neither joy nor sorrow lasts very long. The reason why this is ordered by God seems to be the same in both cases. For if a man were to be always happy, he would probably forget God, and if he were to be always miserable, he might fall into despair. Thus also if the Church were always at peace Christians would become careless, and would forget that they were Christ's soldier's, hired to fight for Him against the world, the flesh, and the devil; and if persecution were always going on, the Gospel could not be preached, and the number of Christians would become smaller and smaller, till at last there would be none remaining.

Marcus Aurelius died after a reign of nearly twenty years; and, after his death, the trials of the Church ceased for a time. His son and successor, Commodus, was a very wicked and tyrannical prince; but, for some reason which we do not know, he was kind to the Christians. After his death the government was in a very unsettled state, and people were thinking too much of other matters to trouble themselves about the Christians. So for rather many years the Church was at peace and, during this the Christians had many opportunities of associating with pagans and speaking to them about the things of God, and a great many conversions took place.

After some years, Septimius Severus was quietly settled on the imperial throne. He was a very clever prince; and, finding the empire in great disorder, he set himself to put everything to rights. He made a great many new laws, and reformed the senate, and restored discipline to the army; and at last he turned his attention to the Christians. In the beginning of his reign Severus was very kind to the Christians. It is said that he was well disposed to them, because he had once been cured of a painful disease by some holy oil, which was given him by Proclus, a Christian. But after he had been a few years on the throne, he changed his conduct towards them, and began to persecute them. The immediate cause of this persecution is not known, but it seems probable that he thought the Christian religion interfered with the discipline of the army, and made people disobedient to the emperor. Tertullian mentions[10] that once, on the emperor's birthday, all the Roman army was drawn out, and a crown being given as a reward to each soldier, one of the soldiers refused to take his crown. His reason was, that certain idolatrous ceremonies were observed in the distribution of these crowns; and he being a Christian, felt that he would be guilty of idolatry if he had anything to do with them. No one cared much about his religion, but his refusal of the offered reward was looked upon as an act of mutiny, and he was put to death. Severus was very strict in requiring all his subjects, and especially his soldiers, obey him; and

---

[10] De Corona, 1.

it is probable that he thought this Chris soldier's example a very dangerous one, and that passing one thing to another, he fancied that the Christian religion taught people to disobey the emperor, and he therefore determined to root it out of his empire. Each persecution that fell on the Church was more severe than the preceding ones. This was no more than might have been expected; for, as the contest between the pagans and the Christians was not merely a struggle between two religions on earth, but a desperate battle between: our Lord Jesus and the Devil, it was only natural that the more ground our Lord's kingdom gained, the more angry the Devil would become, and the more violently he would stir up his servants against the Christians.

The persecution under Severus was so dreadful that people began to think that the end of the world was come, and Antichrist would soon appear. St. Alexander, Bishop of Jerusalem, was thrown into prison, and kept there seven years. St. Irenaeus, a disciple of St. Polycarp's, who had succeeded Pothinus as Bishop of Lyons, was put to death. He was a very great saint, and had written several very learned books against the heretics of those days, and had spread the Gospel in different parts of Gaul and Spain, by sending several of his disciples to preach there. What made his martyrdom more glorious was, that almost all his flock were martyred with him. The slaughter of the Christians of Lyons was so great that streams of blood ran down the streets and squares; and an old writer says, that the number of martyrs amounted to 19,000 men, besides women and children.

But the persecution was most severe in Africa, and especially in Alexandria, where the emperor happened to go just after he had published his edict against the Christians. A great many inhabitants of Alexandria were put to death and a still greater number of persons from all parts were brought there, as to a great theater wherein they exhibited a glorious spectacle of invincible courage and love for Jesus, and after enduring all sorts of dreadful tortures, were rewarded with bright crowns of martyrdom.

Among those who distinguished themselves at Alexandria during this persecution, was a youth called Origen, who afterwards became one of the most learned men and greatest writers of the age. Some of his writings unhappily contained unsound doctrine, and have therefore been condemned by the Church, so that one cannot reverence him as one would a great saint. Still he displayed at this time such an ardent desire for martyrdom, that he is a striking instance of the wonderful power which the love of Jesus exerts on a heart in which it burns brightly, consuming, as it were, all other feelings and affections, and causing even a youth to long passionately for what he would otherwise naturally dread, and make every effort to avoid. Origen's father, Leonidas, was a very good Christian, and was among the martyrs in this persecution. When Origen was still very young, Leonidas[11] perceived that God had given him very great talents, and he therefore took the greatest care to educate him well. He began by teaching him Christian doctrine and the Holy Scriptures; and when he was quite familiar with these, he had him instructed in Greek and philosophy, and the other things which clever men then learned. Origen took with great eagerness to the study of the Scriptures; and when he was still very young he gave signs of deep piety and devotion, so that it is said that when he was asleep, his father would often come to his bedside, and standing over

---

[11] Euseb. *Hist. Eccles.*, 1. 6, c. 2.

him, would uncover his breast, and kissing it reverently, as being a shrine inhabited by the Spirit, would thank Almighty God who had given him the honor of being the father of such a child.

Origen was not seventeen years of age when is father was thrown into prison. Though he was so young, he longed so ardently for martyrdom that he exposed himself in every way in hopes of being seized; and was ready even to give himself up to the persecutors. His mother did all she could to moderate his ardor: she implored him not to deprive her at once of her husband and her eldest son; she entreated him to think of his six younger brothers, the charge and support of whom would now be thrown on him; but finding that her words had no effect on him, and that he was bent on being a martyr, she hid his clothes, so that he was forced to lie in bed, and could not run himself into danger. Still, however, he could not be quiet; for, when he was unable to go out, he wrote to his father to encourage him to be firm, and fearful that the thought of his wife and seven sons might tempt him to waver, he said: "Take heed, father, not to change thy mind on account of us."

Soon after this his father was beheaded, and all his property being seized by the emperor, the family was thrown on the charity of other Christians, and on what Origen could gain as a teacher of philosophy. He soon became very celebrated, on account both of his learning and the austere life he led. He slept on the bare ground, and passed the greater part of the night in meditation on the Bible, the whole of which he had learned by heart. He never drank wine, he ate scarcely enough for his health, and he made long and frequent fasts. Even in winter he went barefooted, and wore only one garment. But while his own life was so austere, his behavior to others was so gentle, that everyone was drawn to him, and even the pagans loved to listen to him. His zeal and his affect the martyrs knew no bounds. He visited them and he encouraged them when they stood before the judge and he accompanied them to the place of execution, speaking boldly to them and giving them the kiss of peace. His conduct threw on him the fury of the mob, and it was only by miracle that he escaped being stoned. Ambushes were laid for him; persons were hired to assassinate him secretly; and he was obliged to be constantly moving from house to house, till at last the city of Alexandria did not seem large enough to conceal him. He was often seized and dragged through the town, and several times he was put to the torture. On one occasion he was shaved like the heathen priests, and placed on the steps of the temple of Serapis, where he was ordered to distribute palms to those who were going in. He made no difficulty about taking the palms, but as soon as he had got them, he cried out with a loud voice, "Come receive these palms, not in honor of your idols, but in honor of Jesus Christ." Notwithstanding, it was not our Lord's will that he should be martyred, and so he always escaped, and lived for about fifty years after this time.

Among the martyrs of Alexandria was Basilides, whose conversion was brought about in a very remarkable way. There was a slave called Potamiana,[12] who was very beautiful. Her master, who was a pagan, fell in love with her, and wished her to live with him as his wife; but Potamiana was a Christian, and would not consent to do such a wicked thing. Her master, accordingly, gave her up to the prefect Aquila, accusing her of being a Christian,

---

[12] Euseb. *Hist. Eccles.* L. 6, c. 5.

and of having spoken against the emperor. At the same time he gave Aquila a sum of money, and he begged him not to hurt Potamiana if she would agree to do as he wished; but to put death if she continued to refuse. Aquila did all he could to persuade Potamiana to go and live with her master as his wife, and finding words were of no use, he made her suffer several horrible tortures. But Potamiana knew what sin was; she knew what an offence against God sin is, what pain each sin has given to the loving heart of Jesus, and what torments, infinitely worse than any Aquila could inflict on her, would await her in hell, if she consented to commit the sin they wished. She therefore continued firm in her resolution, and did not care for anything they did to her. At last Aquila ordered a great fire to be prepared, and a large cauldron of pitch to be placed on it; and as soon as the pitch was boiling, he said to her, "Now obey your master, or if not, I will have you thrown into that cauldron of boiling pitch." "God forbid," answered Potamiana, "that there should be found a judge, who could be so unjust as to condemn me for not doing what is wicked." Finding that the sight of the boiling pitch and the prospect of such a dreadful death, did not in the least move her, the prefect ordered her to be stripped and thrown in. Though Potamiana did not fear the pain which she was about to suffer, yet she cared very much for being stripped of her clothes, and exposed naked before the crowds, who thronged to witness her trial and execution. She would rather suffer any amount of pain than submit to such a violation of modesty, and she therefore said, "I have only one request to make. I entreat you by the life of the emperor not to cause me to be exposed naked; but let me be put in gradually with my clothes on, and then you will see what fortitude and patience will be given me by that Lord Jesus, whom you do not know." Now this way of being put into the cauldron would make Potamiana suffer much more than she would otherwise have done, for if she were stripped and thrown in head foremost, she would die almost instantaneously; but if she were put in with her clothes on, her feet would be put in first, and she would sink gradually, and the pitch would rise slowly round her, and would burn her all over, so that she would suffer the most excruciating and lingering tortures, before her head would be covered, and death would come to her relief. Aquila did not feel disposed to show Potamiana any favor, but as what she asked would only increase her torments, he granted her request, and passed sentence accordingly on her. She was then given in charge to a soldier called Basilides, who was to see the sentence executed.

Though Basilides was only a rough Roman soldier, he had a generous nature. He had been struck with the beauty of Potamiana, and while she was being tortured he had watched her with great interest, for it seemed wonderful to him how a young woman, who was so gentle and delicate, could bear more than the bravest man he had ever met with; and he looked on her as one would look upon an angel, and treated her with the reverence due to a being of a superior order. As she was being led along the streets, he kept off the crowd who pressed upon her, and protected her from their insults; and when she was being put into the frightful cauldron, he took care that her modesty should not be outraged by the slightest exposure of her person. She thanked him warmly for his gentleness and humanity, and she promised him that as soon as she should have departed this life, she would intercede for him with her Lord, and it would not be long before he would feel the effects of her gratitude. She was then put into the boiling pitch, which gradually penetrated through her clothes, and rose slowly from her feet to the crown of her head; but she bore the excruciating pain heroically, and after a very lingering time expired.

Not long after this Basilides was required by his fellow soldiers to swear by the false gods, and refused to do so; and on being further pressed, he said that he was a Christian, and that it was not lawful for him to swear at all. At first his companions thought he was joking; but when he persisted in saying that he was a Christian, they took him before the prefect, who, after having heard him confess his faith, sent him to prison. When the Christians of Alexandria heard what had befallen Basilides, they came to visit him in the prison, and asked him how he happened to have been so suddenly converted; and he answered, "Potamiana appeared to me three nights after her martyrdom, and as she stood before me she told me that she had interceded for me with the Lord Jesus, and that He had granted her request, and would soon receive me into His glory." He was then baptized, and very soon after he was beheaded, continuing firm in his confession to the last.

CHAPTER XXIV

ST. PERPETUA AND ST. FELICITAS

THE memory of St. Perpetua and St. Felicitas is celebrated every day in the Canon of the Mass. They suffered in Africa in the reign of Severus.

Vivia Perpetua was a lady of noble family, brought up in the greatest luxury, and married to a man of high rank. She had everything to make her cling to this world, for she had not only her husband, but also a father, a mother, and two brothers of whom she was very fond, and a little baby whom she was nursing. She was only twenty-two years of age, and was of an affectionate and timid disposition, so that she did not seem naturally well fitted to endure martyrdom with courage, or to bear the separation from her little baby and her aged parents, whom she loved so much. But the heroic virtue of the martyrs does not depend on natural courage and strength, and the grace of God has often shone out most brightly in the midst of natural weakness; and so this weak and delicate Roman lady, though she had none of the stern fortitude of St. Symphorosa and St. Felicitas, was enabled by the grace of God to act as bravely as they had done, and to merit as glorious a crown. The imprisonment of a lady of Perpetua's rank made no little stir, and as soon as her father heard of it he hurried to her, and did all he could by the most affectionate words and caresses to make her give up her faith. But pointing to a vase which was on the ground, she said, "My father, do you see that vase on the ground?" "Yes, my dearest child," he answered. "Can you call it by any other name than its own?" asked she. "No," replied he. "Well, then," rejoined Perpetua, "no more can I call myself anything except what I am, namely, a Christian." Her father, on hearing her speak thus, was almost out of his mind with grief, and he fell upon her, and would have done her some injury, if the bystanders had not forced him away. After this heart-rending scene she did not see him for some days, and she thanked God that he did not come; for she loved him very much, and nothing less than the much stronger love which she felt for Jesus could have given her strength to bear the idea of making her dear father so unhappy.

But though Perpetua loved Jesus, she could not help trembling at the thought of the tortures which she would have to suffer. When she was first thrown into prison she was very much frightened at the darkness of the dungeon, she was half suffocated with the heat and bad air, and she was shocked at the rudeness of the soldiers, who pushed her and the other prisoners about; for she had always lived in a splendid palace surrounded with every luxury, and had been accustomed from her childhood to be treated with respect. If, then, she shrank from these little trials, what should she do when she was put to the torture, or when she had to face wild beasts in the Amphitheater? She was conscious of her own weakness and at first she trembled, but she knew that if she prayed to Jesus, He would give her strength to bear everything. A few days after she was put into prison, she and some of the other prisoners who were catechumens, were baptized; and as she came out of the water, the Holy Spirit inspired her to ask for patience in all the bodily sufferings which she might be called to endure, and from this time she became so calm and so joyful that in spite of all her own sufferings she was able to cheer and comfort her fellow-sufferers.

At first she was not allowed to have her baby with her, and this was a great grief to her, because she knew that, as she was nursing him, the little fellow must be half starved. But after a few days she gave a present to the jailer, and he allowed her to send for the baby, and from that time the dark and gloomy dungeon seemed to her to be a palace, and she said she would rather be there than in any other place in the world. Her mother and her brothers, too, came to see her. She recommended her infant to her mother's care, and said all she could to comfort and strengthen her brothers, one of whom was a catechumen. But their visits were a great trial to her, for they were so overwhelmed with grief on her account that it almost broke her heart to see them, and nothing less than the grace of God could have enabled her to bear the double pain of parting from those she loved, and of making them so miserable.

There were in the prison with her three men called Satur, Saturninus, and Secundulus; and two slaves, called Revocatus, and Felicitas. Though Revocatus and Felicitas were only slaves, and it was not the custom of noble Roman ladies to associate with slaves, yet Perpetua treated them with the greatest humility and kindness, as if they had been her own brother and sister; and when Felicitas was ill, she waited on her and nursed her, as a servant would have done.

During her imprisonment she had the following beautiful vision, which was a great consolation to her and her fellow prisoners. She saw a ladder of gold which reached from earth to heaven, but it was so narrow that only one person at a time could go up it. On each side were swords and lances, and scythes, and daggers, so that anyone who went up carelessly would be dreadfully cut;

and at the bottom there lay an enormous dragon, which tried to frighten those who wished to go up. It seemed to her that the first who went up with Satur, and when he got to the top, he turned to Perpetua and said: "Perpetua, I am waiting for you. But take care that the dragon does not bite you." And Perpetua answered: "In the name of the Lord Jesus, it will not hurt me." When she came to the foot of the ladder, the dragon moved slowly away, as if it were afraid of her, and she stepped on its head, and went safely up the ladder. When she arrived at the top she saw a large garden, and seated in it a tall man with white hair, dressed like a shepherd, and milking his flocks; round him were many thousands of people, all dressed in white robes. He looked up at Perpetua, and said: "Welcome, my daughter," and he gave her some of the milk that he had just drawn from his flocks and she took it reverently, with her hands joined as if in prayer; and all who stood round him said, "Amen." Then she awoke with a very sweet taste in her mouth. She told this vision to her companions, and they all understood from it, that they were to suffer martyrdom, and that Satur would be the first who would die. So from this time they gave up thinking of or caring for the things of this world, and thought only of preparing for death.

A few days after it was said that they were to be examined again, and Perpetua's father hastened to the prison to try once more to move her constancy. "My daughter," said he, "have pity on my grey hairs! have pity on your father, if indeed I am worthy to be called your father. Look at these hands which nursed you, and have reared you to your present age; look at your mother and your brothers; look at your baby which cannot survive you. I have always loved you better than your brothers; do not now make me a reproach among men. Give up this proud obstinacy of yours, and do not ruin us all, for none of us will dare to show our faces if any misfortune should happen to you." The old man spoke in a tone of touching tenderness, he kissed her hands, he threw himself at her feet, and bathed in tears he called her not his daughter, but the mistress of his life. His wild grief was a sad trial to poor Perpetua. She wept over his gray hairs, and did all she could to comfort him. But the only answer she could give to his entreaties was, "On the scaffold the will of God will be done, for we are all in God's power and not in our own." At last the poor old man went away heart-broken.

The next day the martyrs were taken before the judge, and an immense crowd was assembled to witness their trial. They went singly up to the tribunal, and all the others were examined and confessed their faith before Perpetua. When at last it came to her turn, her father appeared with her infant in his arms, and going up to her, he said in a supplicating tone, "Have pity on your child." At the same time the judge said, "Spare the gray hairs of your father; spare the tender years of your son; sacrifice to the prosperity of the emperor !" "I shall do no such thing," answered Perpetua. "Are you a Christian ?" asked the judge. "I am," replied she. As her father was still pressing her, and urging her to yield, the judge ordered that he should be driven away, and one of the officers struck him with a stick. Though Perpetua had been enabled to bear up against her father's grief, yet she was unprepared for this insult to his old age; and this blow given to him caused her much more pain than anything she herself had to endure. The judge then sentenced them all to be thrown to the wild beasts; after which they were taken back to the prison, rejoicing at the glorious combat and the bright crowns that awaited them. Perpetua was spared the pain of parting from her child, for her father, who had taken it away, would not let her have it again; and wonderful to say, the

Sts. Perpetua and Felicitas

child did not cry for the loss of its nurse, but took other food without appearing to notice the change.

After their condemnation the martyrs spent their whole time in prayer and thanksgiving. The soldier who had charge of them, and whose name was Pudens, was converted by them while they were in prison, and treated them very kindly. He allowed them to see their friends, and their prison was constantly thronged with the Christians who came to console them, and who were themselves greatly edified at the sight of the joy with which they looked forward to martyrdom. They were particularly struck to see how cheerfully Perpetua, a noble and delicate young lady, gave up every comfort and luxury for the sake of Jesus, and how, though she felt deeply the separation from her husband, her father, her mother, her brothers, and her little baby, all of whom she loved very dearly, yet she would rather suffer all this, and make those who loved her miserable, than part from Jesus, or do Him the outrage of denying His religion. Only one word, one little word, would have set her free and made her relations happy, but she would not say that one word, because it would have been sin, and she knew that each sin a Christian commits has pierced and wounded the loving Heart of Jesus.

While they were waiting for the games at which they were to be thrown to the wild beasts, Secundulus died in prison. Felicitas was expecting in about a month to have a little baby, and it was therefore arranged that she was not to suffer with the others, but to wait till after the birth of her child. They were all very sorry for this, and, especially, Felicitas, who was afraid that she might have to suffer with common malefactors, thieves, or murderers, instead of with these holy martyrs; while they could not bear the thought of leaving behind them one, who had been such a good companion to them in all their trials. Accordingly, three days before the games they joined together in prayer to God, entreating Him that if it were His will, Felicitas' child might be born in time for her to go to martyrdom with them. Their prayer was heard and granted, and very soon after the child was born. She happened at the time to be in great pain, and being scarcely able to bear it, she screamed very loud; whereupon, one of the jailers laughed at her, saying, "If you complain so much about this little pain, what will you do when you come to be exposed to the wild beasts?" But she answered, "Now it is I alone who suffer, but then the Lord Jesus will be in me, and He will suffer for me, because I shall be suffering for Him." Felicitas' baby was a little girl, and very soon after it was born she was obliged to part with it. She gave it up joyfully for Jesus' sake, and committed it to the charge of her sister, who promised to take care of it.

During this time our Lord sent the martyrs several visions to comfort and strengthen them. Satur, who was naturally very much afraid of wild beasts, had a beautiful vision, in which he saw himself and his fellow-martyrs taken into heaven by the angels, and when they arrived there they were led to a place which was so glorious and shining that the very walls seemed to be made of light. At the gate were four angels, who gave white robes to all who were going in, and inside there was an immense multitude of people who never ceased to cry, "Holy Holy Holy!" He saw Jesus seated on a throne, looking more glorious than words can tell, and yet so loving and so tender that he could not feel afraid of Him; and four angels lifted him and his companions up to the throne, and Jesus kissed them, and passed his hand over their faces. After this, all those who stood round gave them the kiss of peace, and Satur noticed among them many of his friends who had already been martyred for Jesus' sake. He was so filled with joy that he seemed in the vision to say to Perpetua, "You have now all that you wish for," and she seemed to answer, "God be praised! I was very happy on earth, but here I am much, much happier!"

Perpetua also had a vision the day before the games. It appeared to her that while she was waiting for the wild beasts, a horribly ugly man, an Egyptian, came up to fight with her, but that there stood at her side another men, young and very tall, who encouraged her to fight well, and promised to give her a palm branch if she conquered the Egyptian. Then she began to fight, and after a hard struggle she got the better of this horrible looking Egyptian, and trampled him under her feet. Upon this the people seemed to shout, and her companions began to sing, and she went up to the tall young man, who kissed her and gave her the palm branch, saying, "Peace be with you, my daughter." Then Perpetua awoke from the vision, and she understood it to mean that the fight next day would not be against wild beasts merely, but against the devil himself, but that she would be sure to gain the victory.

That day the prisoners took their last meal in public, as was then the custom with persons who were condemned to die. Great crowds came to see them, for everyone had heard about their courage and holiness. The martyrs spoke boldly to them, threatening them with the anger of God, if they would not leave their sins, and believe in Him; and telling them how happy they themselves were in the midst of their sufferings, because they loved Jesus, and He was with them. Satur, too, reproved the people for their idle curiosity in coming to stare at them, saying, "Will you not have time enough tomorrow to look at those you hate. Look well at our faces, so that you may know us when we meet again before God's throne on the great Day of

Judgment." Hereupon those who had come only from curiosity were ashamed of themselves, and went away confused; but great many of those, who had come from better motives, were converted.

At last the day for the games arrived. The martyrs set out from the prison to the Amphitheater with great joy; for they knew that they were setting out on their way to heaven. Perpetua walked the last; her countenance was calm, her look was abstracted, as if she was in an ecstasy, and she kept her eyes bent on the ground, so as to conceal the excessive joy which beamed in them. Felicitas, too, was overjoyed that she was sufficiently recovered from her illness to be martyred with her friends. When they came to the gate of the Amphitheater their guards wished to dress the men as priests of Saturn, and the women as priestesses of Ceres; but they refused most firmly to submit to this, saying, "We are come here of our own free will only in order to keep our liberty. We have sacrificed our lives to avoid doing such things. This was our agreement with you." What they said was so just, that the officers could not help giving them their own way. As they went along through the streets, Revocatus, Saturninus, and Satur pronounced the judgments of God on the people; and as they passed before Hilarion, the judge, they said, "Thou hast judged us; but God will judge thee."

Their sufferings began with a very cruel scourging. They were stripped naked, and made to pass before a long line of the officers of the Amphitheater, each of whom struck them with whips armed with balls of lead or iron, so that when they reached the end of the line their whole bodies were torn and bleeding. But the martyrs rejoiced at this pain, because it gave them the opportunity of imitating the Passion of their Lord. After being scourged, they were led into the Amphitheater to be exposed to the

Sts. Perpetua and Felicitas

wild beasts. Our Lord has said, "Ask and it shall be given you;" and He now fulfilled this promise to the martyrs, giving to each of them the kind of death which each had particularly wished for. Saturninus and Revocatus had expressed wish to be exposed to several kinds of beasts, so as to win a more glorious crown; and accordingly they were first attacked by a leopard, and afterwards by a bear, but without being mortally wounded by either. Satur feared nothing so much as a bear, and hoped that the leopard would kill him with a single bite. He was first exposed to a wild boar, which attacked the keeper, and gave him a wound of which he died some days after, while it only dragged Satur along the ground. He was then tied near the den of a bear; but their good friend, Pudens, had taken care to place some putrid meat at the door of the den, so that the bear would not come out. Thus Satur remained uninjured, and was put aside for a second combat.

Perpetua and Felicitas were now stripped, and put into nets, to be exposed to a furious wild cow. But the people, savage as they were, were shocked to see a lady of Perpetua's rank, and a woman like Felicitas, who was just recovering from illness, exposed naked before such an immense crowd of people; and, accordingly, they were taken away, and covered with some light garments, after which they were again placed before the wild cow. Perpetua was the first to be attacked. She was tossed in the air, and fell on her side, but she soon came to herself, and perceiving that her dress was torn, thought only of covering herself, without caring for any pain she might be suffering: she then got up, and seeing that Felicitas was lying bruised, she went to help her up. Both of them then stood erect, waiting for another wild beast. But the people, whose pity had been excited for them, would not allow them to be exposed again; and they were accordingly led away by the gate called the Sana Vivaria. When Perpetua got outside of the Amphitheater she seemed to waken from an ecstasy, and looking about her, she asked, to the great wonder of every one round her, "When are we to be exposed to that cow?" In fact all the time she had been in the Amphitheater she had been so filled with the love of Jesus, hearing heavenly sounds, and seeing heavenly sights, that she had not noticed the cow which tossed her, and had not felt the least pain. Her friends told her what had happened; but she would not believe their words, till she saw on her body and on her dress the marks of what she had undergone. Then calling her brother and Rusticus, a catechumen, who was a great friend of hers, she said, "Stand firm in the faith, love one another, and do not be frightened at our sufferings."

Meanwhile, Satur, at another gate, was saying to Pudens: "Well, you see it is as I foretold; no beast has yet touched me. Believe, then, with your whole heart. I shall soon be again called for, and then I shall be dispatched by a single bite from a leopard." At the end of the games he was led out again, and was exposed to a leopard, which bit him so severely that he was covered with blood. The people cried out, "He is well washed! he is saved!" alluding in mockery, to baptism. But Satur, turning to Pudens, said, "Farewell! remember my faith. Do not be troubled by this, but let it strengthen you." He then asked Pudens to give him the ring off his finger, and, after dipping it in his blood, returned it to him as a pledge of his friendship and a memorial of his martyrdom. After this he fell down dead on the spot, called the Spoliarium, where those who survived the attacks of the wild beasts were generally dispatched. Thus Satur was the first to die, as had been foretold in Perpetua's vision.

Sts. Perpetua and Felicitas

The people now called for the other martyrs to be led into the middle of the Amphitheater, in order that they might have the pleasure of seeing their death-blow inflicted on them. The martyrs willingly obeyed; and, after giving each other the kiss of peace, walked firmly forward of their own accord. Revocatus, Saturninus, and Felicitas suffered first, and expired immovable and in silence. Perpetua was the last; and happening to fall to the lot of an unskillful executioner, who wounded her between the bones of her neck without killing her, she could not help crying out with the pain; but instantly recovering herself, she calmly guided the man's trembling hand, and thus, with her own assistance, her martyrdom was completed.

The martyrdom of these saints took place on the 7th March, on which day the Church makes a commemoration of them. The precise year is not known, but it was between A.D. 203 and A.D. 206.

CHAPTER XXV

ST. CECILIA

WHEN Our Lord Jesus Christ was on earth, He said that the kingdom of heaven is like to a grain of mustard seed, which is the least indeed of all seeds, but when it is grown up it becomes a tree, so that the birds of the air come and dwell in the branches thereof. Two hundred years from our Lord's birth had passed away when the Emperor Severus began to persecute the Church. During all this time, the kingdom of heaven, which had been founded by the little Babe who lay, apparently poor and helpless, in the manger of Bethlehem, had been growing, and growing without people's noticing it, or being able to say how or when it grew. Now, however, it was so great a kingdom that, as Tertullian says,[13] the Christians filled the cities, the islands, the castles, the towns, the assemblies, the camps, the palace, the senate, and the forum, and left to the pagans only the temples. They were so numerous that, if they had joined the enemies of Rome, the empire would have been overthrown; or if they had even emigrated, and left the pagans alone to inhabit the cities, the empire would have seemed to be deserted, and there would not have been men enough left in it to defend it against its enemies.

---

[13] *Apologeticus* 1, 36.

St. Cecilia

It is natural to suppose that when there were so many Christians, it was not such a disgrace to be a Christian as it had been when the only Christians were a few fishermen and other poor, ignorant men of Galilee. Now the most celebrated philosophers were Christians, and the most learned books were written by Christians, and numbers of rich and noble persons openly called themselves Christians. The consequence was, that pagans mixed much more with Christians than they had formerly done; pagan philosophers visited Christian philosophers, and argued with them, and books were written on both sides; and there was a great deal of public talk about Christians, their doctrines, and their way of life; and pagans had no longer any excuse for hating Christianity, or being ignorant of the true and only way of salvation. All this was ordered by God with a view to preparing the whole Roman Empire for becoming Christian, as it actually did in the course of the next century. It is very curious and interesting to notice, in reading the history of Rome at this time, how the laws which the pagan emperors made of their own will, and the wars which the neighboring barbarian nations carried into the Roman territory, and the revolts of rebellious soldiers, and many other things which seemed to happen naturally, were all overruled by God, so as to bring about the supernatural object of setting up the kingdom of Christ and overthrowing that of the devil.

But Satan did not let all this go on quietly without making some resistance. Every now and then, when things seemed to be going on smoothly with the Church, he would stir up a persecution, more fierce and bloody than any of the preceding ones. And even in times of peace he was not idle; for when many of the pagans would begin to think that the Christian religion was better than their own idolatry, he would persuade them that though it was better on the whole, yet that only some of its doctrines were true and so, instead of submitting to the Church and receiving the whole truth, they would pick out a little bit of the truth here, and a little bit there, much as Protestants do now-a-days, and so they would make up a patch-work sort of religion of their own, which they fancied was very superior to the Catholic faith. This kind of half Christianity had indeed one recommendation, which was a great one to these persons, namely, that it did not get them into trouble; whereas, if they had become real Christians, they would have had to suffer persecution, and to give up everything they loved to follow Christ. Some of these half Christians went even further, for they professed to believe the whole Catholic faith, and were baptized; but as they did not really submit to the Church, and did not give themselves up to love and serve Jesus with their whole hearts, they soon fell into heresy, and were in even a worse condition than the poor pagans who had not received the grace of the sacraments.

One of these pagans who admired the Christian religion very much, and believed such of the Christian doctrines as pleased his own fancy, was the Emperor Alexander Severus. His mother, the Empress Mammaea, who educated him, had such reverence for God, and thought so much about religion, that some persons have believed she was a Christian. When she was at Antioch she sent for Origen to come from Alexandria to see her, and she treated him with great honor; but it is to be feared that she cared more about listening to his clever conversation than about learning from him what she must do to be saved, and that therefore she never was really converted. Her son, the Emperor Alexander Severus, was a very amiable prince; and, though he was a pagan, he thought a great deal about religion, and spent some time in prayer.

He even placed a statue of our Lord in a private oratory of his; but he put beside it the statues of the heathen gods and of several good men who had lived at various times, which showed that he was not a Christian, since he thought that these heathen gods and good men were all equal to Jesus, and did not believe that there is only one true God of heaven and earth.

Though Alexander Severus was so well inclined to the Christian religion, yet he was a weak prince; and many of his officers, who hated the Christians, relying on his easy temper for impunity, put into force against them the old laws which the emperor had not cared to repeal. One of these was Turcius Almachius, Prefect of Rome, who took advantage of the emperor's temporary absence to begin a persecution, in which five thousand persons are said to have perished. Among them was Pope St. Urban, St. Cecilia, the most glorious of the Virgin Martyrs, her husband, St. Valerian, and her brother-in-law, St. Tiburtius.

St. Cecilia was born in Rome.[14] Her parents were rich and of a noble family, but they were pagans; she, however, was brought up from her earliest childhood as a Christian. How this happened, whether it was through the influence of some of her other relatives who were Christians, or of a Christian nurse, we cannot tell; we only know the fact that she was educated as a Christian, and that her parents did not object to her practicing her religion freely. As soon as Cecilia was old enough to reflect at all, she became aware of the great difference there was between herself and those by whom she was surrounded, and at last it burst upon her with a feeling of awe and dread, that she

---

[14] This account of St. Cecilia is chiefly taken from the Acts of her martyrdom as given in Gueranger's "Histoire de S. Cecile."

stood alone in that great household. This thought made her very miserable, and there crept over her a wretched sensation of solitariness, for there was no one in her family, not even her dear, fond mother, who could understand her feelings, or would listen to anything she might wish to say about God, and her soul, and eternity, and the other subjects about which she was always thinking. She would often slip away from her young companions, and shut herself up in her own room, and weep in secret at her lonely fate. At last, the Holy Spirit, who had been stirring up these thoughts and feelings in her young heart, began to comfort her, for He led her to ask herself how it had come to pass that she was not like those around her. Was it not because God had loved her, and had chosen her to be His own child, and had been pleased to reveal Himself to her alone, while He had left the rest of the family in pagan darkness? With this thought there came upon her a gush of love and joy, such as she had never known before, and a sweet voice within her seemed to whisper that there was One, who loved her more warmly and more tenderly than any earthly mother could love her, and that He was inviting her to throw herself into His everlasting arms, and to lay her head upon His loving Bosom, and to confide to Him all the joys and sorrows of her inmost heart.

From this time Cecilia was an altered being. She shunned the society of her young and happy companions, she did not care for being praised by her parents, or flattered by their friends, and she did not lay plans about what she would like to do, or what she would wish to have, as most people are always doing. She had now but one thought, which was, to know the will of God; she had but one wish, which was, to love and serve Jesus more and more each day. She spent her time in the church, kneeling

St. Cecilia

before the silver dove in which the Blessed Sacrament was kept hanging over the altar, or feeding and clothing and visiting the Lord Jesus in His sick and poor, or studying the Holy Gospels which told her about Him, and when she would be called away by her parents, and obliged to leave her devotions, she would lay this precious book in the folds of her dress and press it lovingly to her heart, in token of her adoration of His life-giving words, and of her ardent desire to be penetrated with His spirit and transformed by the power of His grace.

The Christians of those days had always the thought of martyrdom before them, for most of them had had friends or relatives who had been martyred, and on the feasts of the martyrs it was the custom to celebrate Mass over their graves; and none could tell how soon a persecution might break out again, nor how soon it would come to their own turn to confess their faith and shed their blood as these same martyrs had done. This was a grave and anxious thought to most Christians, and a solemn one to all; but to Cecilia it was a thought of simple hope and joy given her whole heart to her dearest Lord Jesus? Was it not her most passionate desire to see Him in His beauty, and to gaze and gaze on Him forever? Did not every day that she was detained on earth away from Him, appear to her a long, dark night of weary waiting? She was still young, and might have to wait for many and many a long year; but if there were to be a persecution, she would perhaps be put to death, and then she would have the happiness of going to Him at once. Besides, was she not always thinking of how to please Him, and how to show her lover to Him? And what more could she do for Him than to lay down her life for him, or what more precious gift could she offer Him than her own heart's blood?

But while Cecilia loved to think and read about Jesus,

and to pray to Him, and to do His sweet will, and while the longed to shed her blood for Him, there was still one thing which she loved and longed for even more than all these. She had read in the Scriptures that St. John saw in heaven a band of virgins, who sing a new song which none but themselves can learn, and who follow the Lamb whithersoever He goeth. O! that she could be one of that chosen band! That she could be one of those who dwell closest to His Sacred Heart! That she could be instructed in those divine secrets which He reveals to the pure and chaste alone. And then she vowed by His boundless love for her, and her own poor love for Him, that, come what might, she would never marry earthly man, but would remain forever the chaste, unspotted virgin spouse of Him, who had wounded her heart with His love, and who was more lovely than all the sons of men.

But Cecilia's parents had very different views for her. As she was very beautiful, and they were persons of station, their great ambition was to see her well married in her own rank of life; and, therefore, contrary to her will, they engaged her to Valerian, a young nobleman, who was quite equal to her in rank, and wealth, and amiable qualities, but who was a heathen. Cecilia told her parents that she could not marry Valerian, because she had made a vow not to have any other husband than Jesus Christ; but they would not listen to her, telling her that her vow was only a silly girlish fancy, that when she came to be older and wiser she would think very differently about it, and that in the meantime it was her duty to obey them. Poor Cecilia was very unhappy. She loved her parents, and did not wish to disobey them, but she loved Jesus more, and she could not break the vow which He had led her to make to Him. While the preparations for the wedding were going on, and everyone in the house was happy and joyful, she alone was sad, and remained solitary in her own room. Her only hope now was in God. She threw herself entirely on our Lord's protection; she humbly and earnestly besought Him to preserve her pure and spotless as His own spouse; she called on our Blessed Lady, the Queen of Virgins, to come to the assistance of her unworthy child; and she begged all the angels, the apostles, the martyrs, and all the saints, to intercede for her, and to be her guard and defense in the dreadful trial which awaited her. She fasted for two, and sometimes for three days in succession; she mortified her flesh with hair shirts and disciplines; she prayed, night and day, almost incessantly; and the nearer the wedding day approached, the more she increased her devotions and penances. God is always near those who call on Him, and He could not leave His loving child alone and comfortless. In the moments when her sorrow was deepest and her heart seemed to sink within her, He breathed sweet and secret comfort into her soul, revealing to her that He had accepted her vow, and had taken her to be His own chaste spouse, in token of which He had sent an angel to guard her; but He also told her that she must not hope to win her crown without a struggle, and that if she would be His virgin bride, she must throw off all fear of man, and be prepared to fight boldly, even to the shedding of her blood.

At length the wedding day arrived, and Cecilia was dressed in beautiful robes of silk and gold, adorned with precious stones. The marriage ceremony was performed with great pomp and magnificence, according to the usual pagan custom, and in the evening a splendid procession, accompanied by torches and bands of music, escorted the bride to the house of her husband. But though Cecilia was forced to take a part in the ceremonial, her heart had no share in it. Under her costly wedding robe she wore a hair shirt covered with sharp iron points, which wounded her at every step she took; when the pagan rites were being performed, she turned away her head and renewed her vow to her Heavenly Bridegroom; and amid the songs of the musicians who were taking her home, she sang in her heart, joining her voice with those of the angelic choirs, and constantly repeating to herself, "Preserve me pure and undefiled in body and soul. In thee, O Lord, I have hoped; let me never be put to confusion."

At length the wedding party broke up, and Cecilia was left alone with Valerian. The moment was now arrived when she must brave the anger of her pagan husband, if she would remain faithful to her Heavenly Spouse. For a minute she stood silent, as if absorbed in thought; then, filled with Divine grace, the crimson blood rushing to her cheek and her bright eyes sparkling, she turned quickly to Valerian, and said in a sweet and gentle tone: My dearest husband, I have a secret which I wish very much to tell you, if I could be certain you would keep it for me." Valerian promised most solemnly that he would not betray her secret to anyone, and then she said to him: "Know, then, that there is an angel of my God, who always accompanies me, and takes care of me, and especially guards my virginity. If you in any way attempt to injure it, he will kill you; but if you will love me with a pure and chaste love, he will love you as he loves me, and will do you the same great favors he does to me." These words sounded strangely in the ears of a heathen, and Valerian was very much troubled at them. But though he could not understand Cecilia he felt that there was something supernatural in her words. There was a struggle in his mind between anger and jealousy, and the grace of God which was working unconsciously within him; but his better feelings conquered, and he answered her kindly, saying, "Dearest Cecilia, if you wish me to believe you, let me see this angel who, you say, guards you. When I see him, if I find that he is indeed an angel of God, I shall grant your request; but if I find that he is only some man with whom you are in love, I shall kill both him and you on the spot." Cecilia replied, "Valerian, if you will follow my directions, and believe in the one only true and living God, and will be baptized in that font which washes away all sin, you may yet see the angel who watches over me." "But who will wash away my sins?" rejoined Valerian. "I know an old man who will do so, and will make you worthy to see the angels of God," answered Cecilia. Where is this old man to be found?" cried Valerian, eagerly. "Go out of the city by the Appian Road," replied Cecilia, "and when you reach the third milestone, you will find there a poor man who lives on my alms. Bless him in my name, and say to him, 'Cecilia sends me to you, and desires you to take me to the Holy Father, for I am charged with a secret message to him.' The poor man will take you to Pope Urban, who is he of whom I just now spoke to you; and if you will do as he desires you, on your return to this room you will see my angel."

We have already said that at this time Turcius Almachius, the governor of Rome, was persecuting the Christians during the emperor's absence. He had put a great many of them to death, and was very anxious to get hold of Pope Urban. The Holy Father, therefore, had been obliged to leave Rome, and he was now lying hid in a wild and solitary place three miles from the city. The Christians knew where he was, and they used to go by night to visit him; but as there were a great many spies on the lookout, watching to find out where he was concealed, they were obliged to use a great many precautions in their intercourse with him, and consequently the persons who took charge of him would not let anyone see him or speak to him, except those who could tell the secret signs and watchwords which were known only to Christians. Cecilia knew these secret signs and how to get at the Pope; and as she saw that Valerian was sincere in his wish to be instructed, she was not afraid to trust him with the secret. She therefore told him where to go, and what signs to use so as to get at Pope Urban, and she bade him tell the Holy Father that Cecilia had sent him to him to be instructed and baptized.

Valerian set off at once in the middle of the night, and after walking three miles he arrived at the wild and solitary spot, which Cecilia had told him about. It seemed the most unlikely place in the world for anyone to live in, for there was no house to be seen, only brambles and brushwood, with here and there a heap of stones and ruined buildings, showing that at some former time it had been used as a burying place. Valerian, however, continued to walk on, carefully following the directions which Cecilia had given him. After he had gone a short way off the road, groping his way in the dark through the brushwood, and stumbling among the ruins, he saw a man lying apparently asleep on a large stone. He went up to him, and made the secret sign which Cecilia had confided to him; whereupon the man jumped up, and receiving him cordially as a friend and brother, led him down some steps into an old catacomb where the Pope was hid.

Valerian told the Holy Father all that had passed between him and Cecilia, and that he was come to be instructed in the Christian religion. The old man, transported with joy, fell on his knees, and raising his eyes to heaven, cried out, "Lord Jesus Christ, the source of all chaste desires, receive the fruit of the holy seed which Thou Thyself hast sowed in the heart of Cecilia. Good

St. Cecilia

Shepherd of the sheep, thy servant Cecilia has fulfilled the mission which Thou gavest her, and the husband who came to her with the fierce spirit of a roaring lion, she has led back to Thee, O Lord ! gentle as the gentlest of lambs. If Valerian did not already believe, he would not have come hither. Open his heart, O Lord! that he may believe more perfectly in Thee, and may renounce the devil and all his works." Urban prayed for a long time, and Valerian was moved to his inmost soul. Suddenly there stood before them a venerable old man, clothed in dazzling white robes, and holding in his hand a book written in letters of gold. At this sight Valerian fell on the ground as if he were dead; but the old man raised him gently, and said to him, "Read the words of this book and believe." Valerian raised his eyes and read aloud, "One Lord, one faith, one baptism, one God and Father of all, who is above all, and through all, and in us all." When he had done reading, the old man said, "Believest thou this, or dost thou still doubt?" Valerian cried out in a loud and firm voice, "I believe that there is nothing more true in heaven or earth." Hereupon the old man disappeared, and Valerian remained alone with Pope Urban. The Holy Father no longer delayed, but baptized him at once, and clothed him in the white robe which newly baptized persons used then to wear; after which he sent him back to Cecilia.

While Valerian had been away Cecilia had remained in the room in which he had left her, and had never ceased to pray that God would complete the work of his conversion. As soon as he reached home he hurried to this room, and there he beheld her on her knees in prayer, by her side a beautiful angel clothed in brightness, and his face shining with extraordinary splendor. Valerian was wonderstruck, and could not take his eyes off the beautiful sight; and while he gazed, he perceived that the angel had in his hand two garlands of the choicest roses and lilies, one of which he placed on his head and the other on that of Cecilia, saying to them, "I have brought these garlands from heaven, and Jesus Christ sends them to you, that you may henceforth love one another with a pure and chaste love. These flowers will never wither nor lose their sweet smell, but no one can see them except those who love chastity as you love it. And, Valerian, because you have granted the request of your wife, God has sent me to tell you that He loves you very tenderly, and is ready to grant you whatsoever you will ask of Him." Valerian, filled with joy and surprise, prostrated himself on the ground, and giving fervent thanks to God, said to the angel, "There is nothing in this life which I wish for more, than to see my brother Tiburtius converted to the faith of our Lord Jesus Christ. For I love him as my own life, and I long to see him a partaker of the same grace which I now enjoy." On hearing these words, the angel's face beamed with that joy which those pure spirits feel at the conversion of a sinner, and he replied, "Thou hast asked for what our Lord Jesus is more willing to grant than thou art to ask, and accordingly, in like manner as thy heart has been won for Him by His servant Cecilia, so wilt thou win the heart of thy brother, and before very long both of you will suffer martyrdom." The angel then disappeared, and left Cecilia and Valerian alone.

Soon after Tiburtius came in, and though he could not see the garlands which the angel had brought from heaven, yet he smelt them. He was very much surprised to smell roses and lilies at that season of the year, when these flowers were not in blow, and he asked where the sweet smell came from. Then Valerian and Cecilia told him what a great favor they had received from God; and they went on to tell him how the gods whom the pagans adored were only devils, and not gods, and how the only true God was He whom the Christians worshiped, and they said everything they could think of to persuade him also to become a Christian. Before very long, Tiburtius seemed to be convinced, and he asked to be led to the man who was to baptize him but as soon as he heard that it was no other than Pope Urban to whom he was to be taken, he cried out: "What, is not he the leader of the Christians, who is obliged to hide himself to escape the officers of justice. If he is discovered he will be put to death, and if we are found with him we shall share his fate; and so, in our wild search for a God, who hides Himself in heaven, we shall be exposing ourselves to certain death on earth." "If there were no other life than this on earth," rejoined Cecilia, "what you say would be most just. But this life which we are now living is one of sorrow and suffering, and soon comes to an end, but after it is ended, there will be another never-ending life, in which the just will be admitted to unspeakable joys, and sinners will be punished with eternal torments. How then should we fear to lose this short and passing life, when by so doing we secure to ourselves the life of heavenly joys which never end?" It was very hard to persuade Tiburtius of the truth of this; he had no difficulty in giving up the worship of idols of wood and stone, for his reason told him they could not be gods, but it was quite another matter to be willing to lose his life for the Christian religion. But Cecilia seemed to be filled with the spirit of an apostle, and she pressed argument after argument on him with such supernatural grace and fervor, that at last he gave in, and once more asked to be led to Pope Urban. Now he really was converted, and he received baptism in the best of all frames of mind, for he not only gave up all his former sins and unbelief, but he looked forward to shedding his blood for the new faith, to which he had been so graciously called.

From this time the two brothers laid aside their worldly rank, and gave themselves up to those works of charity which distinguished the Christians of those days. They distributed their wealth among the poor, they visited and comforted the Christians who were in prison and under persecution, and they buried with their own hands those who had been martyred for the love of Jesus. Their new mode of life naturally attracted notice, and it soon reached the ears of Turcius Almachius. He sent for them and rebuked them, telling them that it was a disgrace to young men of their noble birth to associate with low and contemptible persons like the Christians, and to squander away their money among poor people, as they did, instead of spending it in a way suited to their position in society; and he advised them to give up their folly and to live as their forefathers had done, and to worship the immortal gods who defended the Roman Empire, as the emperor had ordered everyone to do. But the two brothers answered, "We think it a much greater honor to be Christians than to be nobles or senators of Rome, and we prefer the favor of the King of Heaven to that of an earthly emperor; and therefore we are resolved to keep the laws of the true God, without caring for any laws of men which are opposed to them." Almachius was at a loss to know how to deal with them. He knew that the emperor was friendly to the Christians, and though he had not hesitated to put to death many thousands of persons of the lower class, yet he was afraid to touch these two young noblemen, lest he should get himself into trouble. He had sent for them in hopes of frightening them by angry words; and he now reasoned with them, and used every argument he could think of to persuade them to submit to him. But his pagan arguments only drew from them stronger and warmer expressions of their devotion to the Christian religion, till at last he was obliged, in support of his own authority, to order them to be scourged. This only made the matter worse, for while they were being scourged, and a herald was proclaiming, "Beware how you blaspheme the gods," Valerian cried out in a voice which drowned all other sounds, "Citizens of Rome, let not the sight of our sufferings prevent your confessing the faith of the Christians. Stand firm, and believe in the only true God. Trample underfoot the idols of wood and stone which Almachius worships; burn them to ashes; for be assured that all who bow down to them will be punished in eternal flames." Almachius could not endure such open contempt of himself and his gods, and, carried away by rage, he ordered that the two brothers should be beheaded at a temple of Jupiter, four miles from Rome.

The execution of this sentence was entrusted to Maximus, a kind-hearted man, who was really sorry that these two rich young noblemen should throw away their lives in the way they were doing; and when he saw them walk cheerfully to execution, it appeared to him that they were thoughtless youths, who had never seriously reflected on what they were about to do. He was therefore filled with compassion for them, and began to remonstrate with them on their folly. But when he came to talk to them he soon changed his opinion; for they spoke to him with such fervor about the joy of laying down their lives for Jesus, and gave him such good reasons for despising this life and trying only to gain eternal glory, that he soon began to see that it was he, and not they, who was foolish and thoughtless. "Ah!" cried he, "if I could only be quite sure that what you tell me about this future life is true!" Whereupon, Valerian, moved by a sudden inspiration from the Holy Spirit, exclaimed, "If you will only repent and be baptized, at the same moment in which I and my brother quit this mortal body, your eyes will be opened, and you will see our souls ascend to eternal glory." This assurance completed Maximus' conversion. The brothers asked of him only one favor, which was that he would delay their execution till the next day. He did not hesitate a moment to grant it, and instead of leading them to death, he took them to his own house, where he and his whole family were instructed by them, and converted to the Christian faith. In the dead of night Cecilia came to visit them, and she brought with her a priest, who baptized Maximus and the other converts.

The next morning Valerian and Tiburtius were led out to the temple of Jupiter to be beheaded. The sentence was executed, and just at the moment when their heads were struck off, Maximus cried out aloud that he saw two angels brighter than the sun carrying their blessed souls up into heaven. Several pagans, who were standing by, were so struck with his words and the miraculous sight he had seen, that they were converted and became Christians. But Almachius was only more and more enraged, and he ordered Maximus to be put to a cruel death. He was therefore beaten to death with whips loaded with plummets of lead.

By the Roman law the property of all persons who were put to death as criminals was confiscated to the imperial treasury; and therefore Almachius' next thought was how to get possession of the property of the two brothers, who, he knew, had been very rich. He went therefore to Cecilia, and demanded from her the property of her husband and her brother-in-law. She answered, "You need not trouble yourself about it, for it is quite safe and beyond your reach." He bade her explain what she meant, for he did not understand her. So she said: "I have laid up

St. Cecilia

all my husband's and my brother's treasures in heaven, where neither rust nor moth can hurt them, and where you cannot enter in to seize them." Almachius was provoked at being put off with words which he could not understand, and he therefore angrily ordered Cecilia to have done with this foolish trifling, and to tell him at once where the money was. Then she told him, that Jesus had said that all that Christians gave to their poor brethren was given to Himself, and He would repay it; and so she had distributed the property of the martyrs among the poor, in order that they might be repaid it a hundredfold by Jesus, in whose presence they now were. Almachius was very angry when he found that he had been thus outwitted, as he thought it, by a weak and silly woman; but he thought it more prudent to dissimulate and to take no notice of what she had done.

Almachius had already been carried much farther than he had intended or wished, and he would now have been very glad to have stopped in his career of crime. But there is nothing in the world so hard as to stop in the midst of a course of wickedness, for pride and a thousand wicked passions conspire with the devil to urge on the miserable sinner. Cecilia was a person of such high rank, and the deaths of her husband and brother-in-law had made such a sensation that all eyes were fixed on her; and as she made a very open profession of her religion, and went about publicly visiting the Christians who were in prison, and burying those who were put to death, she soon became the talk of the town, and people began to wonder how Almachius could allow her to do what he punished so cruelly in everyone else. He was, therefore, forced to notice her conduct, and being very anxious not to make any great stir about her, he did not summon her before his tribunal, but sent some of his officers to her house to call on her to sacrifice to the gods.

When these officers saw Cecilia they were struck with her youth and beauty, and above all with the pure and heavenly air which breathed in her every look. They felt the same pity for her which Maximus had felt for Valerian and Tiburtius, and they tried, as he had done, to convince her of the folly of sacrificing her youth, her beauty, her wealth, and all the pleasures of this life, for what they called a vain superstition, when, by only saying a few words, or by throwing into the fire on the altar a single grain of incense, she might secure the enjoyment of the greatest happiness this world could offer. But Cecilia's heart was in heaven, and her eyes were opened by divine grace to see the things of earth and of heaven in their true light, and not as they appear to men to be; so, turning to them, she thanked them sweetly for their mistaken kindness, and said to them, "But do not think, my good friends, that dying for Jesus will be any loss to me; so far from it, it will be an inestimable gain. For I have placed my trust in my Lord, and I am confident that in exchange for all that I lose in this poor and passing life, I shall gain infinitely more in the next. Do you not think it is wise to give up a worthless thing in order to gain what is of inestimable value-to give up dirt for gold, sickness for health, death for life, and that which soon comes to an end for what will last forever? Why, then, do you not wish me to give my body to tortures which no sooner pass away, and to death itself, since by suffering these things, I shall enter into the palace of my dearest Spouse, who is Lord and Master of the universe, and who will bestow on me a happiness which has no end?" Cecilia's words penetrated into the hearts of those who heard them, so that they could not conceal their emotion. Seizing the happy moment, and transported with a sudden movement of apostolic zeal, she jumped up upon a block of marble which happened to be close to her, and turning to the troop of officers and soldiers, she cried out, "Do you believe in that Lord Jesus of whom I have been speaking to you?" Whereupon they all called out, as if with one voice, "Yes, we believe that Christ the Son of God, whose servant you are, is the only true God" "Return, then," said she, "to Almachius, and tell him that I am prepared to die, and ask only for a short delay; after which come back to me, that you may receive the blessings of eternal life." The officers did as she bade them. They carried her answer to Almachius, and then returned to her house, where they found Pope Urban, to whom Cecilia had sent the news of what had happened. He instructed and baptized them all, their number being no less than four hundred, among whom were many persons of rank.

The noise which these conversions made now left Almachius no alternative but to summon Cecilia before his tribunal. It is impossible to say with what joy she appeared before him. The happy hour was at last come; she had preserved her virgin's robe pure and unsullied, and she hoped soon to present it to her Heavenly Spouse, dripping and sparkling with her blood.

Almachius questioned her at great length, and casting off human fear, as her Lord had bade her do, she answered him fearlessly and boldly, now rebuking him for his sins, now holding up to scorn the gods whom he worshiped, and now, again, exalting and praising Him whose love was her only joy, and for whom she hoped soon to shed her blood. In every word she spoke she seemed to triumph, till at last Almachius, feeling himself fairly beaten and put to shame by this young woman, could no longer hesitate to pass sentence on her.

Still, fearing the emperor's anger, he did not dare to

have her publicly executed, but sentenced her to a death at once secret and cruel. He ordered her to be shut up in a dry bath in her own house, and fire to be placed under the bath, so that she might be scorched by the intense heat, and at the same time choked by breathing the close and hot air. Here she remained one whole day and night, at the end of which time the executioners opened the bath, expecting to find not only that she was dead, but that her body was shriveled and dried up by the heat. To their great wonder they found her as cool as if she had been lying in a pleasant garden, with fresh breezes blowing round her; not a drop of moisture was on her face or body; and she moved as briskly as if she had waked out of a refreshing sleep. While she had been shut up in this place of torment her dearest Lord had been with her, as He had formerly been with the three children in the fiery furnace, and He had protected her, so that the fire had not had any power over her.

Almachius did not dare to leave his bloody work unfinished, and hardening himself to the miracle which had just been wrought, he sent one of his lictors to strike off her head. But the executioner's sword had scarcely more power over the spouse of Christ than the burning heat. Cecilia had prayed to Jesus to prolong her life for three days. It was her last request on earth-and He not only granted it, but gave her more than she had ever asked or hoped for. She stretched out her neck to receive the blow of the executioner's sword, and he struck with all his force; but, though he made a deep gash, he did not accomplish his bloody task. Bracing his arm to its utmost strength, he struck a second time, and then a third, but still the head was not severed from the body; the law forbade his making any further attempt, and he fled in terror, feeling assured that nothing but a supernatural power could have thus resisted the weight of his powerful arm. For three days Cecilia lay on the marble floor of the bath, her head half severed from her body, the blood trickling slowly forth, and kept alive only by a miracle. She had often prayed to shed her blood for Jesus, and she had hoped to shed it once, and once for all. She had never thought of such a death as this she had never dreamt of shedding her blood as often as there were drops of blood in her veins. There she lay for three days, pouring out her blood, drop by drop, in one long blissful martyrdom, and sighing out her soul in one sweet ecstasy of love. The Christians flocked to visit the dying saint. The poor, who had lived on her charity, came to bathe with their tears the hands which had so often ministered to their wants; the old came to learn from the lips of the youthful virgin the most sublime lessons of heavenly wisdom; and even little children were brought to receive the blessing of one who was their superior in purity and childlike love. Among the rest came the Holy Father, who hesitated not to quit his hiding place, that he might have the consolation of seeing once more his favorite child, and ministering to her in her dying hour. When he approached her she turned to him with a sweet and joyful look, and said: "Father, I asked our Lord to grant me these three days in order that I might place my last treasures in the hands of your Holiness. I commit to your charge the poor whom I have hitherto fed, and I bequeath to you this house. When I am gone, consecrate it for a church." Even the wicked Almachius seemed to be awe-struck by the supernatural atmosphere which surrounded the dying saint, for he made no further attempt to touch her, and did no; hinder the visits of her friends. During these three days the persecution was stayed, and the Christians passed freely to and fro, as if it had been a time of peace.

At last the three days drew to a close, and Cecilia knew that her last hour was come, and that she was about to pass into the ravishing presence of God. She composed herself for this last passage as if she were laying herself down for a long night's sleep. Turning herself on her right side, she placed her feet together, and drew her knees slightly up; she then laid her hands on each other, three fingers of the right hand being extended, according to primitive custom, in token of the three Persons of the Holy Trinity, and the fore finger of the left stretched out, to represent the unity of the Godhead; and finally, as if retiring from mortal view into the presence of her Beloved, she turned her face round against the ground, so that none could witness the last secret communings of her passing soul, and in this position she expired. Those who were present shrank from altering any of the circumstances attending her death. They laid her in a cypress coffin, in the same attitude in which she had composed herself for her last sleep, wearing the rich robe of silk and gold in which the executioner had found her; and they placed at her feet the linen cloths, which had been used to collect the blood which oozed from her wound. The following night Pope Urban buried her in the catacomb of Prætextatus, close to the spot in which she had herself buried Valerian, Tiburtius, and Maximus. According to her last request, her house was turned into a church, which bears her name to the present day. Soon after her martyrdom Pope Urban himself was martyred, and was buried near the place where St. Cecilia lay.

Nearly six hundred years passed away, and the Church of Christ had triumphed over the pagan idolatry, and Pope Paschal reigned in Rome in peace. One day, A.D. 821, he happened to be praying in the church of St. Cecilia, to whom he had a great devotion, when, being struck with the dilapidated state of the building, he made a resolution to restore it. He lost no time in setting workmen to repair the stone-work and the roof, and to adorn it in a style of magnificence, even far surpassing its original splendor, when it was the dwelling of a Roman noble. But he felt that after art should have done its best, it would want its principal ornament, so long as it did not contain the relics of the virgin martyr to whom it was dedicated. He therefore instituted a search for her body, in the catacomb of Prætextatus, near the spot where the bodies of St. Valerian, St. Tiburtius and St. Maximus were known to lie. But all in vain, no traces of St. Cecilia could be discovered; and Paschal was about to give up the search in despair, being convinced that the Lombards must have carried away her body, as common report said. One day, however, when he was assisting at the recital of the Divine Office in St. Peter's, he seemed to fall asleep, when suddenly there stood before him the virgin martyr herself, who, thanking him for the trouble he had taken to do her honor, encouraged him to proceed, assuring him that he had often been close to the spot where she lay, and if he persevered, he would certainly find her. Reanimated by this vision, Paschal set once more to work. After some further search he discovered the cypress coffin, on opening which, there appeared the saint, lying on her side in the modest posture in which she had composed herself to die, the knees joined and slightly bent, the fingers extended in symbol of her faith, and the face turned away from mortal view, as if she were still in secret converse with God. There was the rich antique robe of silk and gold in which she had been martyred, and which was sprinkled with her blood; and at her feet there were the linen cloths which had been used to stanch the bleeding from her half severed throat. There she lay, calm and beautiful, as if asleep, untouched by the finger of time and death, a striking and visible proof of the tender love with which our Lord had watched over even the mortal body of His pure and virgin spouse. The beholders gazed with reverence and silent awe, and they seemed to hear our Lord saying to them, "I adjure you that you wake not My beloved till she please." It is impossible to describe the joy of Pope Paschal at this sight. He had the body reverently moved, and not daring to touch that on which our Lord had set the seal of His love, he left her in the cypress coffin just as he had found her, merely satisfying his devotion by throwing over her body a light silken veil, and lining her coffin with the richest damask; and finally, he deposited the whole in a marble sarcophagus, under the altar of her own church. He also removed and placed in another marble tomb beside her, the bodies of St. Valerian, St. Tiburtius, and St. Maximus, while in a third, he deposited those of St. Urban, and St. Lucius, another pope who was martyred in this century.

Time went on-nearly eight centuries rolled away; and the Church which had seemed to reign supreme over the civilized world was shaken to her very center. The Protestant heresy had broken out, and men had arisen who had not feared to blaspheme the saints of God. St. Ignatius and St. Philip Neri had been raised up to stem the flood of Infidelity; but they were dead; and it might have appeared to those who knew not the Church's supernatural life, that evil times were setting in, and that the virtues of the saints would soon die out of men's memory. This was the moment when St. Cecilia was once more to come out of her grave, and to proclaim in the silent but thrilling accents of the tomb, the virtues and the glories of the saints.

There lived at Rome at this time a Cardinal, Paul Emilius Sfondrato, who emulated Pope Paschal in his devotion for St. Cecilia, and who resolved, like him, to renovate her church. In the course of their labors, the workmen penetrated to the spot where St. Cecilia lay, and once more, on the 20th October, 1599, the light of day shone on that cypress coffin. With trembling hands, Sfondrato removed the lid, and his eyes rested on the sleeping virgin. There she lay, all unchanged-the same modest posture, the bent knees, the extended fingers, the averted face-the same blood-stained antique robe, the bloody linen at her feet, and the thin veil which Pope Paschal had thrown over her. The marks of decay appeared only on the damask with which Paschal had lined her coffin. She seemed to smile on her loving children, and to say "See how our dearest Lord loves chastity-see how He honors virginity; for He keepeth the bones of his virgin spouse-not one of them shall be broken."

Rome was in a tumult of joy at this second appearance of their favorite saint. The Pope, the Cardinals, the nobles, priests and laity, rich and poor, all thronged to look upon the precious relic, and to behold this wonderful trophy of the glorious immortality of the saints. Portions of the linen cloths soaked with her blood, which were found at her feet, were distributed as precious relics to her most illustrious devotees; but the rest was left untouched, till the sound of the Archangel's trumpet should waken that saintly body from its sleep. The cypress coffin was enclosed in a silver case, lined with the richest purple silk embroidered in gold, and on the 22nd November Pope Clement VIII deposited St. Cecilia once more in the ancient crypt, under the altar. A beautiful marble statue, reclining in the same attitude as that in which the saint lies in her coffin, was carved by Stephen Maderno, the first sculptor in Rome, and is placed under the high altar, where it may be seen at the present day.

The martyrdoms of St. Cecilia, St. Valerian, St. Tiburtius, and St. Maximus, took place A.D. 230.[15] Her feast is kept by the Church on the 22nd November, and that of the other martyrs on the 14th April.

---

[15] Tillemont, places their martyrdom A.D. 178.

CHAPTER XXVI

Sixth and Seventh Persecutions

MAXIMIN & DECIUS: ST. GREGORY THAUMATURGUS. ST. FELLI

ALEXANDER SEVERUS was murdered about five years after the martyrdom of St. Cecilia. He was succeeded by Maximin, a barbarian soldier, who was remarkable for his great strength of body, and was more fit to be a gladiator, or a keeper of wild beasts, than Emperor of Rome. He hated the memory of his predecessor, and finding the palace filled with Christians, he began to persecute them, not so much from hatred to their religion as because Alexander Severus had favored them. This has been called the sixth persecution of the Church, but it was by no means general; and the Christians do not seem to have been the only victims of Maximin's cruelty; for he was a savage monster, and his death was desired by all classes of persons in the empire. His reign was happily a very short one, and after his death there was another season of peace for the Church; so that it may be said that for thirty-eight years, from the reign of Septimius Severus to that of Decius, no general persecution took place. During this time the number of Christians went on increasing rapidly, and beautiful churches were built in most of the principal towns of the empire. But while everything looked so prosperous without, there was much evil going on within. The devil was not less busy now than he had been before, though he had begun to work more secretly against Christ's kingdom. He made use of this long peace to tempt the Christians to forget that they were Christ's soldiers, and that they ought never to stop fighting against the devil and the world. Finding that no one troubled them, they began to busy themselves with worldly affairs,[16] and to live more like common worldly people than they had formerly done. They thought about getting rich, about living in a style suited to their worldly rank, about dressing handsomely, and about getting on in the world; and some of them even intermarried with pagans and heretics. In proportion as they thought more about the world they thought less about Jesus. They did not love Jesus as they had done formerly; they gave less to the poor; they were not so zealous in preaching the Gospel, and Christians were no longer so much remarked for their pure lives and their love to each other. Swearing and perjury, angry words and bitter quarrels, selfishness, and disobedience to superiors, became common; and while some of the brethren were left to die of hunger, others were living in luxury, and thought only of heaping up riches for themselves and their children.

It was well for the Church that this peace did not last longer, and that persecution came to revive the faith and love of Christians. At the time of which we are now speaking, which was in the middle of the third century after Christ, the Roman Empire was in a very wretched state. The Goths and other barbarian nations from the north and east were pouring into the richest provinces; the people had been so long without seeing an enemy that

---

[16] St. Cyprian, *De Lapsis*, 4.

they did not know how to defend themselves; and the armies who ought to have defended them were so mutinous, and so busy choosing new emperors and murdering old ones, that they were of little use against the barbarians. It seemed as if the Roman Empire must be overthrown, when Decius was made emperor. He was a very brave, soldier-like man: he did not spend much time in talking and reasoning, but he set resolutely to work, trusting in his good sword and his energy to conquer all his enemies. When people are in trouble, they naturally think of God; and so in this time of danger the Romans turned to their false gods. They began to think why the gods had sent them all these misfortunes; but instead of looking into their own hearts and repenting of their sins, they found it easier to lay the blame on others; and so they said it was the Christians who had drawn down on them the anger of the gods. Decius then thought that the first enemies he had to conquer were the Goths and the Christians; and while he himself set out to fight bravely against the Goths, he left orders behind him for beginning a great persecution of the Christians, as being the enemies of the gods, and the cause of the public misfortunes.

The persecution[17] broke out with terrible violence. The magistrates thought of nothing but finding out the Christians, and punishing them; and a frightful array of tortures, fire and sword, wild beasts and iron chairs, racks and scourges, and all sorts of cruel machines, were placed before each tribunal, so as to strike terror into the hearts of those who were brought before the magistrates. Everyone tried to surpass his neighbor in cruelty. Some turned informers; others pursued those who fled, or hunted out

---

[17] Rhorbacher, *Hist. Eg. Cath.* 1. 29.

those who were hid; while others, again, seized the goods of the Christians, Friends and relations betrayed each other; fathers accused their sons, and sons their fathers; brothers gave up each other to torture and death; so that no one knew whom to trust. So many people fled and hid themselves that many of the towns seemed to be deserted, and in others so many people were imprisoned that the prisons could not hold them, and the public buildings had to be used as prisons.

The storm fell first on the bishops; for the emperor, thinking that the sheep could not stand long without their shepherds, had given orders that the bishops should be the first to be seized. The Pope, St. Fabian, ended a holy life by a glorious martyrdom. St. Alexander of Jerusalem, and St. Babylas of Antioch were put to the torture, and afterwards thrown into prison, where they both died. St. Dionysius of Alexandria also was seized, but he happily made his escape into the desert, where he remained till the persecution was over. Alexander of Comanus was burned to death. St. Cyprian of Carthage owned his safety only to flight; and so also did St. Gregory Thaumaturgus, Bishop of Neocæsarea, and Maximus, Bishop of Nola.

The persecution soon spread to all classes of Christians, and then the bad effects of the long peace appeared. It was not to be expected that people who had been trying in time of peace to serve two masters, God and the world, would be willing now, in the time of trial, to give up everything for God. In Alexandria great numbers were found ready to renounce their religion at once, in order to keep their money or the public offices which they held. It was the custom to take those who were accused of being Christians, before a magistrate, when they were publicly called by their names, and desired to make their choice between being tortured and sacrificing to the gods. Some of the Christians were so terrified at the sight of the horrible tortures that surrounded the tribunals, that they ran eagerly forward to the altar of sacrifice, crying out that they had never been Christians; others, overcome by terror, were dragged forward by their friends, pale and trembling, fearing to offer sacrifice, and yet not daring to refuse. Many, when they were first seized, stood up boldly for their faith, but gave it up as soon as they felt the weight of their chains and the hardships of imprisonment; while others, who endured the first tortures with constancy, gave way under the second or third.

In Carthage[18] it was, if possible, even worse. Many of the Christians in Carthage did not wait to be seized or questioned, but ran of their own accord to offer sacrifice, just as if they had long been waiting for the opportunity to do so. They went in such crowds that they could not all be received on the same day, and when it grew late the magistrates wished to put them off to the morrow; but they earnestly entreated to be allowed to renounce Christianity at once, and without any delay. Many were not content with losing their own souls, but persuaded others to share their ruin; and even mothers were seen to carry their young children to the altar, and, as far as in them lay, to rob them of their faith, by putting the pagan incense into their little hands. The number of those who fell away was so great, that people thought they saw in it the fulfilment of that terrible prophecy of our Lord, that if it were possible even the elect should be deceived.

But though so many forsook Jesus, many remained constant to Him; and the number of the martyrs who suffered at this time was very great. On the whole, the

---

[18] St. Cyprian, *De Lapsis*, 6, 7.

Church gained by the persecution; for many of those who fell away had been among the half-Christians who were mentioned in the last chapter, and they were no real loss; while others of the apostates repented, and became more earnest Christians than they had ever been before. These last had really loved Jesus, but had been unconsciously drawn away by the world, so that when they came to be tried, they had not the courage to give up their worldly goods and to suffer for Him. But as soon as they had denied their religion, they felt so wretched that they could have no peace till they had confessed their sin, and had got leave from their bishops to do penance for it, in hopes that after many long years they might be forgiven and re-admitted to Church communion. Thus in every way the Church gained by the persecution, being purified by it as gold is in the furnace, and coming out of it free from dross and brighter than before. Thus it is that our Lord never fails to bring good to His own people out of what appears evil, and to turn to their profit whatever the devil does to injure them.

Two of the Bishops whose names have been mentioned as having escaped death by flight, owed their safety to the miracles which God worked in their behalf. They were St. Gregory Thaumaturgus, and Maximus of Nola.

St. Gregory, Bishop of Neocæsarea in Pontus, was called Thaumaturgus, or the Wonder-worker, on account of the great number of miracles he worked. He labored so hard in preaching the Gospel, and was so successful in making converts, that at the time of his death there were only seventeen pagans in his diocese, in which, when he first went there, there had been only seventeen Christians.

When this persecution began,[19] he advised his people to save themselves by flight, and he himself set them the example. He took with him his deacon, who had formerly been a heathen priest and had been converted by his miracles, and they went together to a barren and rocky mountain. The persecutors searched very eagerly for him, and having heard where he was hid, they followed him thither. Some of them guarded all the paths from the mountain, so as to prevent his getting away, while the others set to work to hunt him out. As soon as Gregory saw them coming, he desired the deacon to join him in prayer, and to have the greatest confidence in God. He then began to pray, with his eyes and his hands raised to heaven. Meanwhile, the pagans ran all over the mountain, and looked into every cave and every cleft in the rocks, but nowhere could they find Gregory. They came close to him, they touched him, but they passed on, for God had blinded their eyes so that they could not see that it was he. At last they returned to the town, saying that Gregory was not on the mountain, for they had seen nothing there except two trees growing very near each other. When they were gone, a pagan, who had been their guide, returned to the spot where they had seen the two trees, and there, to his great surprise, he found, instead of two trees, Gregory and his deacon standing and praying. He threw himself at Gregory's feet, and being converted, became the companion of his flight.

The history of Maximus and of one of his priests, St. Felix of Nola, is still more interesting. The father of St. Felix was a native of Syria, who came to Italy and settled with his family at Nola, a town about fifteen miles from

---

[19] Rohrbacher Hist. Eg. Cath. 1. 29.

Naples. He had two sons called Hermias and Felix. Hermias became a soldier, and followed the Roman emperor to the wars against the barbarians; but Felix resolved to be a soldier in a better service, and to follow Jesus Christ, the King of kings, in the great war against the world, the flesh, and the devil. He therefore gave all his worldly goods to the poor, and devoted himself to the service of the Church He was made reader and exorcist, and in this last office had so much power over evil spirits, that he never failed to cast the devils out of the persons whom they were tormenting. At last he was ordained priest, and was much respected on account of his great talents, and the sanctity of his life.

When the persecution broke out, the emperor's officers came to Nola for the purpose of making Maximus, the bishop, prisoner. Maximus had notice of their coming, and he was in doubt whether it would be best for him to wait for them and be put to death, or to fly and hide himself in the mountains. He was an old and a holy man, and he longed to end his life by the glorious martyrdom which would certainly befall him if he remained in Nola, whereas, if he fled, though he would save his life, he would suffer a great deal; for he would be forced to hide in caves and solitary places, among wild beasts, and exposed to the greatest hardships and privations, and after all he would not have the pleasure of dying for Jesus. But he said to himself, "Though it is more for my own interest to stay and suffer martyrdom, yet it will be most for the interest of my flock that I should fly and save my life. Ought I then to look most after my own good or that of my children? Our Lord said to His apostles, 'When they shall persecute you in this city, flee into another;' and so, since it is lawful for me to fly, and it seems good for my people that I should do so, I will give up my own interest for theirs. Though I desire to die for Christ, I will live for the love of Christ, hoping that He will give me some other opportunity of dying for Him." There are many ways of giving up all for Christ; and so while some were giving up their lives and those they loved best, this good bishop resolved to give up even his crown of martyrdom for Christ's sake. He therefore recommended his flock to the care of Felix, and set off to hide himself in the wildest and most solitary part of the neighboring mountains.

When the persecutors arrived at Nola, their first inquiry was for Maximus, who they soon learned was beyond their reach. They therefore turned their fury against Felix, who was now the principal person in the church of Nola. They seized him, and being unable to move him by threats, they loaded him with very heavy chains, and threw him into a dark and damp dungeon, the floor of which was strewed with bits of glass and broken tiles, so that he could not sit down, or sleep, or take any rest whatsoever. Meanwhile the poor bishop was not better off than his priest. Though he was at liberty, yet he felt like a prisoner while he was shut out from his flock. His love for his people was so great that no prison, or torture, or death, seemed half so bad as being away from them; and though he had the greatest confidence in Felix, he feared they might be suffering from his own absence, and he often thought of returning to the city to die with them. Another trial too came on him. He had nothing to eat except the berries which he found on the bushes, and these were not enough to keep-up his strength; besides which, the season being winter and the ground being covered with snow, he was half frozen with cold. In this way the old man was soon brought to death's door, and lay on the ground benumbed with cold and famishing with hunger. Thus, at the same moment, both the bishop and the priest stood in need of help, and God, who never forsakes those who trust in Him, did not forget them.

In the dead of night, when the jailers and prisoners were asleep, a dazzling brightness suddenly lighted up the dark dungeon in which Felix was a prisoner. He saw before him an angel so beautiful and glorious that he scarcely dared to look at him; and he heard a sweet voice bidding him arise and follow. He obeyed, and rising, followed the angel; and as soon as he began to move, his chains dropped off him, and the doors of the prison opened of their own accord, and the soldiers who kept guard at the prison gates seemed not to see them, and took no notice of them as they passed. As they walked along, the glory from the angel shed a heavenly light around; but no one could see it except Felix. They passed along the streets, and through the city gates, and through many an open field, and many a rough by-road, till at last they came to the mountain; and as soon as they reached the place where Maximus was hid, the angel vanished, and left Felix alone. Felix at first wondered why the angel of God had brought him to this wild place on such a cold, dreary night; but by the light of the twinkling stars he soon saw the good old bishop lying on the snow, looking more like a corpse than a living man. He went up to him, and embraced him; but he was quite stiff and insensible; so then he laid himself down quite close by him, and began to breathe on him, hoping to revive him by giving him some of the warmth from his own body. But the old man was exhausted and dying as much from want of food as from cold, and therefore all Felix's efforts to revive him were useless. Felix was very much troubled to see his bishop in such an extremity, and not to be able to help him; but he felt sure that God had sent him there for some other purpose than merely to see the old man die. So he prayed to God, and asked Him to look down on their necessities, and to tell him how to relieve Maximus. As he prayed, he cast his eyes on a bramble which grew close by, and on it he spied a bunch of grapes, which he took joyfully and reverently, as having been sent from heaven, since he knew that grapes did not grow at that cold season, or in so wild a place. Then, opening Maxima mouth, he squeezed into it some of the juice of the grapes, and as soon as the good bishop had tasted the juice, he began to revive; he opened his eyes, and moved his lips, and at last he sat up, and began to praise God. He soon saw Felix, and he asked him why he had been so long in coming; for that he had prayed in his distress to God, and God had promised to succor and visit him. Felix then told him all the wonderful things that had happened, and how God had sent an angel to take him out of the prison, and bring him here, and how he had found the bunch of grapes hanging on the bramble. Then these holy men were filled with excessive joy to think of the love of Jesus, and the tender care he took of them in their trials, sending His angel to them, and working great wonders to relieve even their little bodily wants. They consulted together as to what it would be best for them to do; and after praying for God's guidance, they resolved to return to the city. And now a fresh difficulty presented itself. The good old bishop was still so weak and infirm that he could not walk; and though Felix was young and active, yet he had suffered greatly in his imprisonment, and was not strong enough to carry the old man all the way from the mountain to the city. But Felix had learned that nothing is impossible to those who are doing God's holy will, and therefore he did not doubt that, as it was God's will that Maximus should return to Nola, he would give him the strength to carry him there. He therefore took up the old man confidently on his shoulders, and being supported by the love of Jesus, the heavy burden seemed as nothing to him, and he was enabled to carry him all the way without difficulty, and to get into the city secretly before the morning dawned. Felix gave Maximus in charge to an old woman who was taking care of his house, and he also managed to hide himself till the persecution subsided.

After a short time, the emperor's officers left Nola and went to some of the neighboring towns and villages. Then Maximus and Felix came out of their hiding-places and went about among the Christians, who stood in great want of them. Some had lost friends in the late persecution, and needed to be consoled; others were so much depressed by all they had gone through, that they seemed to have scarcely any faith or love remaining, and they required to be encouraged and strengthened, lest they should fall into despair; while others again had been tempted to deny their religion, and these wandering sheep had to be sought out by their good shepherd and brought back to repentance. So the holy bishop and his priest had enough to do in looking after them all, and it was well for the church of Nola that God had been pleased to save the lives of these two saintly men. But this calm did not last long.

The emperor's officers soon returned to Nola, and then the Christians did not dare to show themselves in public, or to assemble for prayer and Communion, except secretly by night. The persecutors heard, however, what Felix had been doing during their absence, and they made search for him, as being the leader of the Christians and a greater support to them than even the bishop himself. Felix had not yet hid himself, and when the search for him began, he happened to be in the market-place. Everyone in Nola knew him well, so that there seemed to be no chance of his escaping through the crowd that was in pursuit of him. They, however, came up to him, and they asked him if he knew Felix the priest, for though he was before their eyes, God had so blinded their minds that they did not know him. Felix answered that he had never seen Felix's face, which was quite true, since no one can see his own face. Then the pursuers passed on, and Felix took the opportunity to step into a chink in a wall, which, though it was so shallow that he could easily be seen in it, was the best hiding-place he could find at that moment. After the pursuers had gone a little way, someone told them what a blunder they had made, and that the very man they had spoken to was Felix himself. So they came back in a great hurry, and finding that Felix was no longer standing there, they began to search all round for him, knowing that he had not had time to go very far. Then it appeared in what a wonderful way God makes use of the veriest trifles and the meanest creatures, to assist and defend those whom He loves; for after Felix had got into the chink in the wall, a spider wove a close web all over the entrance, and when the pursuers came up to it, they saw nothing but an old wall thickly covered with cobwebs. They knew that Felix could not have passed through the cobwebs without breaking them; and as the cobwebs were so thick, they naturally supposed that they had been there a long time. They therefore were sure that Felix was not in the chink, and they went away very much disappointed not to find him, and puzzled to think how he could have escaped them. Then Felix saw that when God is with us, spiders' webs are strong walls, and when He is not, the thickest walls are of no more use to defend us than spiders' webs; and he praised God in the words of the psalm: "Though I should walk in the midst of the shadow of death, I will fear no evils, for Thou art with me."

After his pursuers were gone, Felix came out of his hole, and since he could not venture into any house in the city, he looked out for a better hiding-place among some ruined buildings. Here God again interposed miraculously to supply all his wants. As no one, not even his friends, knew where he was, he must soon have died for want of food, had not God inspired a devout woman who lived close by, to provide for him. This woman every day, after she had baked the bread for her own family's use, was moved by the Spirit of God to place a portion of it near the spot where Felix lay hid, but without knowing what she was doing. Every day she put it there, and yet she never remembered that she had done so; and thus, without being aware of it, she had the merit of feeding one of our Lord's saints. Still, however, Felix had nothing to drink. But God caused so much dew to fall every night into a broken trough, which chanced to be there, that he had quite enough of water to quench his thirst. In this way Felix lived for six months without seeing or speaking to any human being, but he was comforted by visits from the angels, and even from our Lord Himself. At the end of that time the storm of persecution passed away, and he came out of his solitude and began to preach and teach as he had formerly done. The people had thought that he was dead or gone into some distant land, and when he appeared so unexpectedly among them, and told them how his life had been preserved, they were filled with gratitude to God, and revered Felix as a great saint. About this time the old bishop Maximus died, and the Christians of Nola wished Felix to be his successor. But Felix was so humble that he could not bear to be raised to so high a dignity, and therefore he persuaded them to choose in his stead Quintus, a very good man, who had been ordained priest a few days before himself, and who he said ought on that account to be preferred to him. Quintus was accordingly made bishop, while Felix continued to preach and to have all the labor, without caring to enjoy any of the honor belonging to the office of a bishop.

Felix's love of poverty was as great as his humility and his confidence in God. His father left him a good fortune, but he distributed it among the poor, keeping barely enough to support himself. He lived as sparingly as he could, and at the end of each year, if anything remained out of his little pittance, he gave it to the poor. During the persecution, his goods were seized by the emperor's officers and were publicly sold, so that when he came out of his hiding-place in the ruins, he had nothing to live on. When everything was quiet some of his friends advised him to do as many others had done, and to apply to have his goods restored. But Felix wished to have no treasures except in heaven, and he answered, "God forbid that I should again possess those goods which I once left for Jesus Christ's sake, or that I should covet those riches of the earth, which I have forsaken in order to make more sure of the treasures of heaven." He was content to pass the rest of his days in holy poverty, supporting himself on the herbs which grew in a little garden, in which he labored with his own hands without anyone to help him. When God blessed his crop and sent him more than he himself wanted, all that was over was for the poor; and if any one made him a present of clothes, he at once gave them to some beggar who was in want of them, never keeping for himself more than the one suit which he wore. Thus he lived a very holy life for many years, and at last he died in peace on the 14th January, on which day the Church celebrates his feast. A great many miracles were wrought at his tomb; and people used to come from all parts, even from beyond the sea, to obtain favors from God through his intercession.

CHAPTER XXVII

ST. AGATHA

ONE of the martyrs in this persecution was St. Agatha, whose memory is held in great honor throughout the Church. She was born of rich and noble parents in the city of Palermo in Sicily, and was remarkable for her extraordinary beauty and her great virtue. When she was very young she was filled with a great love of chastity and an ardent desire for martyrdom, so that she was always praying to our Lord to protect her as His pure and spotless bride, and to give her an opportunity of shedding her blood for His sake. When the emperor's edict reached Palermo, and it was publicly proclaimed that all the Christians were to be seized and put to death, the city was filled with grief and terror. People began to hide themselves or to fly into the country, or if they ventured into the streets, they slank stealthily along, afraid to look up, and trembling lest every one they met should be an enemy about to seize them. But Agatha was not the least frightened; on the contrary, she was very glad, for she hoped that the time she had long wished for was now come, and that she should very soon obtain the martyr's crown, and rest for ever in the loving arms of her dearest Spouse Jesus Christ. Agatha made no secret of her religion, but went on visiting the sick and trying to convert sinners to Christ, just as she used to do before the emperor's edict arrived, she was soon seized and taken

St. Agatha

before Quintianus, the Roman governor. As soon as Quintianus saw her, he was so struck with her great beauty that he fell desperately in love with her. He forgot the orders of the emperor, and his duty as a judge. He did not consider what a bad example he was setting to those under him, or what disgrace he would get into if his conduct came to the emperor's ears; but he thought only of how to gratify his love for Agatha, and how to persuade her to live with him as his wife. He saw plainly that she was too pure and holy to agree to do as he wished, and that his only chance of succeeding was to make her as bad a himself; he therefore resolved to use every means to corrupt her innocent mind, and to put into her head all sorts of wickedness of which she was now ignorant. Instead, therefore, of treating her severely on account of her religion, he spoke very kindly and gently to her, and told her he was very sorry the emperor's edict prevented his setting her at liberty, as he pretended that he wished to do; but he promised to write to the emperor in her favor, and he said, that till the answer to his letter arrived he would not keep her in the common prison, but would put her under the charge of an old woman, the mother of a family, who would be very kind to her, and would protect her from every sort of danger. His words sounded very fair, and though Agatha had a secret misgiving that he was not quite sincere, she thanked him for his kindness, and went home with the old woman.

This old woman, whose name was Aphrodisia, was quite a different person from what Quintianus had represented her to be. She was a very wicked old woman, and she had five handsome daughters, whom she had trained in every sort of vice, and with whose assistance she now made it her business to corrupt young men and women, and to entice them into leading sinful lives.

Quintianus knew her very well, and he offered her a large sum of money if she would draw Agatha away from her love of chastity, and make her consent to live with him as his wife.

Aphrodisia determined, therefore, to do her best to make Agatha as wicked as herself; but as she perceived what an innocent and pure-minded girl she was, she thought it necessary to set about her diabolical task in a very cunning and round-about way. She made her associate with her own wicked daughters, and she hoped that after being for some time in their company, she would learn to care for very different things from those which she now loved. The daughters of Aphrodisia were silly, conceited girls; they had no regular useful occupation, but spent their whole time in idleness or foolish conversation. They cared for nothing but gossiping about their neighbors, or repeating the compliments that were paid them, and other kinds of vanity. They were careful not to say any anything very wicked which would shock Agatha, and so it might have seemed that, after all, there was no great harm in their way of life. Many a soul, however, has been lost by beginning to do things in which there seemed to be "no great harm." But this was not the case with Agatha; for she knew that little sins lead to great ones, and that those who love the things of the world, with which Aphrodisia and her daughters tried to tempt her, cannot love God also. She turned with disgust from what pleased them, because her heart and her thoughts were fixed on what was so much more beautiful and charming. She did not care for laughter and merriment, because she was always longing to hear the sweet music of Paradise, and the joyful songs of the angels. She was not flattered with the praises they lavished on her beauty, because her only wish was to please Jesus, and she knew that He would look at her heart, and not at her face. The pleasures of the world seemed cold and dull to her, because she enjoyed constant communion with Jesus. And when Aphrodisia would praise Quintianus to her, and tell her how noble and generous he was, and how much be loved her, she would think how much more noble and generous was Jesus, who was the Lord of heaven and earth, and had given every drop of his precious Blood for her, and that Quintianus could not love her one quarter so much as Jesus, who had laid down His very life for love of her. Thus, the thought of Jesus, and the love of Jesus, never for a moment left her, and they were a sure protection against all the arts of Aphrodisia, and the temptations of the world.

Though Aphrodisia and her daughters saw that they did not succeed in corrupting Agatha, yet they still went on idling, and gossiping, and chattering, and doing all they could to make her join in their vain and silly pursuits, hoping that she would be gradually drawn to take pleasure in them, and would at last lay aside her queer, stiff notions, and not set up to be better than other people. Agatha got so tired of their foolish conversation, which was a constant interruption to her own holy thoughts, that, after bearing a long time with it, she determined to silence them, by letting them know that she saw through their wicked plan, and would never consent to it. So one day, after she had been a month with them, she said boldly to Aphrodisia: "Aphrodisia, I see plainly that you are trying to corrupt me, and to make me deny my religion and bring dishonor on myself and my family. But do not think that you will ever succeed. I look on your tongue, not as the tongue of a woman, but as that of the devil himself, who is talking in you; and since I hate him, I do not listen to any of your wicked words. As a Christian, I am bound to do good even to my enemies, and therefore I entreat you to look to your own interest, and to give up your infamous occupation of enticing simple girls to sin and ruin. Though the governor allows you to go unpunished, believe me, the God of heaven will not do so. You are old, and must soon die; look then to your soul, repent of your wicked life, do penance for your sins, and believe in the true God, lest He visit you in His anger, and cast you into hell fire for ever and ever. But even if you do not care for your character, or for your soul, it is not worth your while to lose your time as you are now doing; for I tell you plainly I have given my whole heart to Jesus, and I am so resolved to keep the vow of virginity which I have made to Him, that, through His grace assisting me, the sun shall lose its light, the fire its heat, and the snow its whiteness, sooner than I shall change my mind, and break my vow. Let Quintianus, then, do his worst; let him get ready all his tortures; let him sharpen his swords, prepare his lions, heap together fuel for fires; let him set open the gates of hell if he can, and stir up all the devils against me I will die a virgin and a Christian; and I do not fear his violence, because I know that the Almighty God, to whom I have given my body and my soul, will protect me."

These words opened the eyes of Aphrodisia, and made her see that she was losing her time and trouble. She was very sorry to give up the money that Quintianus had promised her, but there was not the least chance of her succeeding in her wicked plot; so she went to Quintianus, and said to him, "I have taken the greatest trouble with the young lady you placed under my charge, and I have done everything I could to tempt and corrupt her. I have offered her fine clothes and precious jewels, and all sorts of worldly pleasures that other girls are so fond of but she cares for none of these things; and the only wish she has night or day, is to die for Jesus. In fact, she is so firm in her

St. Agatha

religion, and so determined to preserve her virginity, that it will be easier for you to melt iron and to soften the hardest diamond, than to make her change her mind."

This was a great disappointment to Quintianus, who had made quite sure of Agatha. His love now turned to rage, and he determined either to force her to do as he wished, or to revenge himself most cruelly on her. He therefore had her brought before him, and he asked her to what family she belonged. She answered, "I am of an ancient and noble family, which is well known throughout Sicily, as my friends can tell you." "Why then," said Quintianus, "do you disgrace your noble birth by following the custom of vile and contemptible people ?" "Because," replied the saint, "though I am born a lady, yet I am the slave and bondwoman of Jesus Christ my Lord, and I am not proud of my noble birth, because the only true nobility is to serve Christ with a pure heart." "And we, who despise your crucified God," inquired Quintianus, with a sneer, "are we degraded from our nobility?" Agatha replied, "If you be such slaves to the devil as to adore wood and stone, where is your nobility or your liberty?" The wicked judge was so provoked at her cool firmness, that he desired an officer to strike her on the face, in order, as he said, that she might learn not to answer her lord so impertinently. The officer struck her with such violence, that her face was bruised, and her fair and delicate skin became black and blue; but though she was so disfigured in the sight of men, she looked only the more beautiful in the eyes of God and the holy angels. She did not take the least notice of the officer's rudeness, or of the pain that the blow gave her, but she continued to answer Quintianus boldly about her faith and hope in Jesus, and her great love for Him. Quintianus at last found that he could make nothing of her, and he ordered her off to prison, bidding her consider well whether it would be easier to die in torments, or to deny Christ.

Agatha was overjoyed to hear that she was to be put into prison, and she entered the gloomy dungeon with a light step and a bright smiling face, as if it had been the most charming place in the world. She thanked God for having allowed her the honor of suffering for Him, and she begged Him to give her the victory over the devil, and to crown her with the crown of martyrdom. The next day she was again taken up before Quintianus, who tried both by persuasion and threats to make her give up her religion and her love to Jesus. But she answered him with the game firmness as before, saying, "Quintianus you promise me life, comfort, and happiness, if I will forsake Christ, but I tell you that I will not have any other life, comfort, or happiness than Jesus Christ Himself. Do not think to frighten me by your threats, for I assure you that no stag, when it is hunted and almost dead with thirst, ever longed for the water of a clear spring, as I long to suffer your tortures, in order that I may be the sooner and the more closely united to Jesus. Wheat is not stored up in the granary till it has been winnowed of the chaff, and neither is the soul received into heaven till the body is dead on earth. If you wish to use the sword against me, I am ready to stretch out my neck; if you will have me whipped, here are my shoulders; if you will burn me with fire, here is my body; if you will give me to be torn by wild beasts, my flesh, my feet, my hands, my head, all my limbs, are ready for whatever torment you will inflict on me. You may torture, burn, flay, bruise, break down, and kill this poor body of mine; but the more cruelly you treat me, the more will you please me, and the greater favor shall I have from my sweet Spouse Jesus Christ. What then are you doing, and what are you waiting for? Why do you linger and lose time?" The governor was so enraged at her words, and at the resolute tone in which she spoke, that he ordered one of the executioners to wring and twist one of her breasts in a very barbarous manner, and then to cut it quite off. Agatha was not the least moved by this cruel order, but said gravely and calmly to her wicked judge: "Are you not ashamed, you cruel tyrant, to torment a woman in her breasts, since it was from your mother's breast that you received your first nourishment?" But Quintianus did not listen to what she was saying, for he was like a young tiger which becomes more ferocious after it has first tasted blood, and having now tasted, as it were, the pure blood of this innocent virgin, he was only thirsting the more savagely to drink it to the last drop.

After her breast had been cut off he sent her back to prison, and ordered that she should be given nothing to eat. or drink, and that no surgeon should be allowed to dress her wound, hoping that she would die from pain and exhaustion. Agatha laid herself down on the damp dungeon floor, exhausted by the loss of blood, and aching all over with the extreme suffering she had undergone, for there is perhaps no pain greater than that of having a breast cut off. Her head was throbbing with fever, but she had no other pillow than the hard stones; in the place where her breast had once been, there was a horrible ghastly wound, which was still bleeding and smarting from exposure to the air, but she had no kind friend to bind it up or to cool its burning heat; she was parched with thirst and faint with hunger, but the jailer refused to give her one drop of water or the least morsel of food. Still she was happier than the happiest of human beings, for she remembered that in suffering all this pain she was imitating her dearest Lord in His Passion, and this thought turned her pain into pleasure. Instead of feeling that her suffering was more than she could bear patiently, it seemed to her only too little, and she longed to suffer more. The aching of her head seemed very slight when she thought of Jesus' head crowned with thorns; the pain in her one breast was not to be compared to what he had suffered, when his whole body was scourged and bruised from head to foot; her bed of stones was easier than His bed of agony on the cross, and the feverish thirst she was suffering was as nothing to that burning thirst with which His loving Heart had thirsted for the salvation of sinners. Then, too, she thought how soon all this would pass away, and what joys awaited her, the white robe washed in Jesus' blood, the virgin's crown He would place on her head, the martyr's palm He would put into her hand, and best and sweetest of all, the loving arms in which He would receive her, and hold her to His sacred Heart, not for a short passing moment, but forever and forever, still closer and closer to all eternity.

While she lay thus in great bodily torture, but comforted and supported by the love of Jesus, a venerable old man, attended by a youth who carried a torch, came into the dungeon and stood before her. The old man appeared to be a surgeon, for he had in his hand all sorts of salves and dressings for wounds, and looking at her with a kind, smiling countenance, he said gently to her: "My daughter, the tyrant has gained nothing by all the tortures he has inflicted on you, and he shall pay dearly in everlasting flames for the pain he has put you to. I was present when your breast was cut off, and I saw that it could be healed; and I am therefore come to cure you, and to restore you to perfect health." But Agatha answered, "I have never in all my life used any medicine for my body, and I will not now be gin to do so. My only and entire trust is in my Lord Jesus, and I know that if it were His holy will, He could heal me with only a single word." The old man still pressed her to let him dress her wound, but she would not consent; for she felt confident that our Lord would help her, and she would not put herself under the care of any one else. When the old man found how she trusted in Jesus, and in no one but Him, he smiled sweetly on her, and said that she was quite right in feeling and acting as she did; and then he went on to tell her that he was the apostle St. Peter, and that he had been sent by our Lord to heal her wound, and to restore her breast which had been cut off, and that as a sign of the truth of what he said, she should instantly be perfectly whole and sound. As soon as he had spoken these words, he disappeared. Then Agatha looked down at herself, and to her great joy and surprise she found that the wound was quite healed, and that her breast was restored to its place; whereupon she cried out with a loud voice, saying, "I thank Thee, my Lord Jesus Christ, that Thou hast been pleased to be mindful of me, and to send Thy apostle to heal my wounds and to restore my body to its former condition." She had scarcely finished this thanksgiving when a heavenly light shone through the dark prison, and illuminated it so brightly, that the soldiers who guarded it ran away and left the doors open. Many of the prisoners took advantage of the opportunity to make their escape, and they advised Agatha to do the same, but she answered, "God forbid that I should fly from the field of battle till I have completely conquered my enemy."

Quintianus expected every day to hear of Agatha's death, but when he inquired about her he was told that she was quite well. He could not believe this, and thought that they were deceiving him, so after four days he ordered her to be brought again before him. Then indeed he saw that what he had been told was true, and that she was really quite cured. He was very much confounded and awestruck, for it was plain that the hand of God only could have worked such a miracle. For a few minutes he trembled, and thought of repentance; but the devil, whose slave he had been for so many years, soon put such thoughts out of his head, and worked him up into a greater rage than before. He now ordered the floor to be strewed with red hot coals and sharp bits of broken tiles and earthenware, and he commanded Agatha to be stripped naked and rolled on the floor, so that the coals burned her, and the tiles and earthenware at the same time cut her. But while this torture was being inflicted on her, our Lord sent a violent earthquake, which shook the city and killed two friends of the governor's. Then all the people in the city, being in a great fright, cried out that the earthquake was a just punishment from God for the cruelty with which Agatha had been treated; and they raised a great tumult, and ran in crowds to the governor's house, insisting that she should be set at liberty. Quintianus was now afraid lest they should carry her off by force; and so he sent her back to prison, and had her laid on the cold hard stones, all burnt and cut and a mass of sores, and he locked her up close, so that no one should take her out of his hands. But One mightier than any earthly governor, One whom neither bolts nor bars can shut out, was at hand to set her free. When the holy virgin was laid on the prison floor she lifted her hands to heaven and prayed, "My eternal God, who of Thy pure goodness hast armed me with Thy grace to fight for Thy faith, and hast enabled me, who am so young and weak, to overcome so many torments, open, O Lord! the hands of Thy mercy, and receive my soul that thirsteth after Thee with the greatest desire and love." And Jesus heard her prayer and came quickly to her rescue. She had now suffered as much as it was His will that she should suffer for Him; and so He allowed her body to die, while at the same time He carried her blessed soul out of that dark and miserable dungeon, and took it up to heaven, and placed it amid that beauteous band of virgins, who always see His face and follow Him whithersoever he goeth.

The martyrdom of St. Agatha took place A.D. 251, on the 5th February, on which day the Church celebrates her feast.

CHAPTER XXVIII

GALLUS: ST. CORNELIUS. ST. LUCIUS

THE EMPEROR DECIUS died after a reign of two years, and his death was a great relief to the Church. He had such a jealous dread of the kingdom of Christ, which he saw growing up in the center of his empire, that after the martyrdom of St. Fabian he would not allow a successor to him to be chosen, saying that he would as soon see a rival emperor on the imperial throne as a Pope in the city of Rome. The consequence was, that for above sixteen months there was no Bishop of Rome, and the Church remained without a visible head. This was a great affliction not only to the Christians at Rome, but to the Church at large; for many difficult cases had arisen out of the persecution, and these could not be settled without the Pope's authority. As soon, then, as Decius was dead, the Roman clergy hastened to elect Cornelius Pope. It required a great deal of courage for anyone to consent to be the Pope at such a time as this; for the persecution was not yet over, and the Pope was always one of the first to be seized and thrown into prison. There was not a single Pope, from St. Peter down to Cornelius, and even for many years after, who did not end his life by martyrdom.

It was not very long before Cornelius was called on to prove that he was ready to suffer for Christ's sake The new emperor, whose name was Gallus, gave orders to continue the persecution, and the first blow fell, as usual, on the Bishop of Rome. Cornelius was banished to Centum Cellae, a city of Italy, with a view of removing him from the care of his Church. But as Centum Cellae was not at any very great distance from Rome, the Christians went to visit him there, and he managed to write letters to the bishops who wanted his advice; and so his banishment was not so great a loss to the Church as might have been expected. When the Emperor Gallus heard how busy Cornelius was, he was very angry, and had him brought prisoner to Rome. He spoke to him in private, but finding that he answered him with great courage, and was not likely to give up his religion, he condemned him to be beaten about the mouth with balls of lead, and then to be taken to a temple of Mars, where, if he would not sacrifice, his head was to be cut off.

As they went along the road to the temple, Cerealis, the soldier who had the charge of Cornelius, and who had heard what miracles the Christians often worked, asked him to go to his house to see his wife Salustia, who had been confined to her bed for fifteen years with palsy. Cornelius consented, and when they arrived at the house of Cerealis, he went up to Salustia, and taking her by the hand said to her, "In the name of Jesus Christ of Nazareth arise and stand upon thy feet." Then Salustia rose up and said, "In very truth Christ is God, and the Son of God." Then she and Cerealis, and all the soldiers that were with him, being converted by the sight of the miracle, threw themselves at the feet of Cornelius, and begged him to baptize them; and when he had instructed them, he baptized them all, to the number of twenty-one persons.

It was not long before the news of what had passed in Cerealis' house reached the emperor. He was very angry, and he immediately gave orders that Cerealis and Salustia, and all the soldiers who had been baptized, should be led together with Cornelius to the temple of Mars, where, if they would not offer sacrifice, they were to be beheaded. This was accordingly done; but Cornelius and his little band of converts stood firm, and so far from consenting to offer sacrifice to the idols, they spat at them and reviled them. So they and their holy father Cornelius were all beheaded together.

After the death of St. Cornelius, Lucius was elected Pope. He had gone into banishment with St. Cornelius, and had returned with him to Rome. He did not long hold his bishopric in peace, for he had scarcely been elected when he was banished. A few months after he was allowed to return again to Rome, where his presence was a great comfort and support to the Church, which was still suffering persecution; but before many more months had passed over his head, he also was called to receive the crown of martyrdom. He was beheaded after he had been Pope for only eight months, or as some say only five months. As he was on his way to execution he recommended the Church and his flock to the care of his archdeacon, Stephen, who was accordingly elected to succeed him as Pope.

CHAPTER XXIX

Eighth Persecution

VALERIAN: STS. STEPHEN, SIXTUS, LAWRENCE, AND HIPPOLYTUS

THE Emperor Gallus reigned scarcely two years, and his death brought peace to the Church. He was succeeded by Valerian, who was very kind to the Christians during the first four years of his reign. This interval of calm was a very great blessing. It has been already mentioned that many persons who had denied the faith at first, had afterwards repented and begged hard for absolution. While the persecution lasted many of the bishops were obliged to leave their flocks and hide themselves, so that it was not possible for them to meet in synod, and to consult together and decide how all these penitents should be treated; and hence great disputes and divisions had arisen. But during these few years of quiet after the accession of Valerian, the bishops held councils, and wrote letters to the Pope to ask his opinion, and so all these quarrels were looked into, and peace and order were gradually restored.

After Valerian had reigned between four and five years he changed his conduct towards the Christians. It is not known with any certainty what was his reason for the change, but it is probable that he was influenced by a favorite of his called Macrianus. Macrianus was a very wicked man and a true servant of the devil. He was given to all sorts of magic and sorcery, and when he wanted any very particular favor from the devils whom he used to consult, he would not hesitate to sacrifice to them young children, and even new-born babes. It is easy to believe that the devil made use of such a man to stir up a very severe persecution against the Church.

This persecution was carried on with quite as much cruelty as that under Decius had been. But the Christians bore it much better; for instead of being frightened as they had been in the reign of Decius, they now suffered tortures and death with fortitude, and often with great joy. The persons who behaved the best, and were the most joyful on account of the persecution, were the unhappy apostates, who, though they had at first denied their faith, had afterwards repented, and asked for pardon and penance. The rules of the Church at that time were much more severe than they are now; and persons who had fallen into open mortal sin were not allowed to receive holy Communion till after they had done penance, sometimes for ten, twenty, or thirty years, and in a few cases, not till they were on their death-beds. During these long years of penance they were, at first, not allowed to pray inside the church, but were obliged to kneel at the door, dressed in sackcloth, weeping for their sins, and begging the prayers of their brethren. After the persecution of Decius the number of these penitents was very great; and now when another persecution was on the point of breaking out, it seemed hard that these poor creatures should be called to stand another great trial without being strengthened by the Body and Blood of Christ. The bishops, therefore, determined to pardon all who had given signs of true repentance, and to receive them at once to Communion. The persecution, therefore, brought great joy. They did not forget their sins because they were forgiven, but after they had received our Lord in holy Communion, they felt only the more sorry for them, and they longed to wash out their stains in their own blood. They were so happy to have an opportunity of recovering the martyr's crown which they had formerly lost, that they took no care to escape, or to hide their religion, but acted boldly so as to attract notice to it.

The persecution again fell first on the bishops. St. Dionysius of Alexandria was taken from his flock, and banished into Libya. Nine other bishops from different towns in Africa were seized, and after being scourged, were sent to work in the copper mines. St. Cyprian, Bishop of Carthage, was banished to Curubis, a place not far from the city, and after he had been kept a prisoner there for a year, he was brought back to Carthage and beheaded. Besides these bishops a great number of priests, deacons, and men and women of all ranks, were either banished or put to death.

In Rome a great many people were martyred; and among them a number of persons who had been converted by the Pope, St. Stephen, and were encouraged by him to suffer for Christ. One of them was Lucilla, a lady who had formerly been blind, but had been restored to sight by Stephen's prayers, in consequence of which, she and all her family had become Christians, and now suffered martyrdom with great constancy.

This naturally drew on Stephen the anger of the emperor, who ordered that he and his clergy should be seized and put to death. Twelve priests were beheaded at once, without any trial. Tertullian, servant to one of the martyrs, had the charity, though he was a pagan, to bury these martyred priests; and this good action having reached the ears of Stephen, he sent for him, and instructed and baptized him, recommending him particularly to look after and bury the bodies of the martyrs. At that time, people were often martyred very soon after they were baptized; and so it was with Tertullian, who was seized two days after his baptism, and after being tortured, was beheaded.

The next day Stephen himself was made prisoner, and led before the emperor. Valerian asked him, "Are you he who tries to upset the republic, and persuades the people to forsake the worship of the gods?" Stephen answered, "I do not upset the republic, but I exhort the people to give up the service of the devils whom they worship in their idols; and to adore the only true God, Jesus Christ." Valerian then ordered him to be led to the temple of Mars, to offer sacrifice; and if he should refuse to do so, he was to be beheaded. When the holy Father was brought into the temple, he lifted up his eyes to heaven, and with his face bathed in tears, and his heart glowing with the love of God, he cried out, "Lord God, Father of my Lord Jesus Christ, who didst destroy the tower of Babel, I humbly beseech Thee to destroy this place where the devil deceives the people, and persuades them to worship him as God." He had scarcely uttered the last word, when loud thunder was heard, and bright flashes of lightning were seen, and a thunderbolt fell on the temple, and threw a great part of it to the ground. The soldiers were so terrified, that they thought of nothing but saving themselves, and they ran away, and left Stephen and the other Christians to themselves.

As soon as Stephen found himself thus unexpectedly set at liberty, he went down into the catacomb called the cemetery of Lucina. There, with the graves of the martyrs around him, he made an address to his flock, exhorting them to be firm in their faith, and not to fear the threats and torments of tyrants, who could only kill their bodies but could not touch their souls; and in order to encourage them the more, he began immediately to offer up the Holy Sacrifice of the Mass.

While he was celebrating it, a band of soldiers entered, whom the emperor had sent to seize and kill him; but though he heard them coming, and knew for what purpose they came, he was not the least troubled, but went on without the slightest change of countenance, or any faltering of his voice, and he finished the Sacred Mysteries as quietly and devoutly as if death had not been awaiting him. Then sitting down on his pontifical chair, he looked calmly on the soldiers who had tracked him even into that underground church.

They came up to him and cut off his head, as he still sat in the chair, and his body was buried in the same spot.

After an interval of three weeks, Sixtus was chosen to succeed St. Stephen. He was a man of great holiness, and did good service to the Church in this time of trial; for he made a great many converts by his preaching and his good example, and he was a great support to those who were tortured and imprisoned, exhorting them to die courageously for their faith, and showing them by his own fearless conduct that he spoke no more than he was prepared to practice. After he had been Pope about a year he was seized and led before the Emperor Valerian, who tried to persuade him to give up his religion; but Sixtus spoke out boldly in its defense, and said there was nothing he wished for so much as to suffer all sorts of torments for the love of Jesus. Valerian, therefore, had him thrown into the Mamertine prison, where St. Peter and St. Paul had been con fined; and after some days, finding that he still continued firm, he ordered him to be taken to the temple of Mars, where he was to be beheaded unless he would sacrifice to the gods. As he went along his archdeacon Lawrence met him. Lawrence was accustomed to serve the Holy Father's Mass, and now he was so anxious to suffer and die for Jesus that he could not bear to see Sixtus going to execution without him; so he cried out after him, "My father, where are you going without your son? Where are you going, holy Pontiff, without your deacon? Are you going alone to offer yourself a sacrifice to God? Why do you not take your minister with you as usual? What have I done to displease you, that you now cast me off? Have you ever seen any cowardice in me? You have entrusted to me the charge of distributing the Blood of Christ to the faithful; and do you now think me unworthy to be your companion, when you are about to shed your blood for Christ?" While Lawrence spoke thus, his heart was burning with the most intense love of God, and the hot tears were running down his cheeks. But Sixtus turned to him, and said by way of comforting him, "It is not I who leave you, my son; but Our Lord reserves you for a sharper battle. I am old and feeble and am to be dispatched after a slight skirmish, but you, who are young and strong, shall triumph more gloriously. Dry up your tears, fear not, within three days you shall follow me." The Holy Father then gave Lawrence directions to distribute the treasures of the Church among the poor, and took leave of him; after which he was brought to the temple of Mars, where, as he would not sacrifice, he was beheaded.

 The officers who led St. Sixtus to execution having heard him speak of treasures, repeated his words to the governor, who sent for Lawrence and said to him, "You Christians complain that you are treated with cruelty; but now there is no question of tortures. I ask only for what you can easily give me. I am told that your priests offer up libations in vases of gold, and receive the blood of the victims in chalices of gold, and that at your midnight meetings the wax lights are placed in golden candlesticks. Bring me then all your gold plate and other hidden treasures for the emperor wants money to pay his soldiers. I am told that your religion teaches you to give to everyone what belongs to him; the emperor has a right to the money, which is coined with his image, whereas your god never coined money, nor brought anything but good words into the world. Render then to Caesar that which is Caesar's; give the emperor the money, and keep the good words to yourself." Lawrence was not disturbed by what the governor said, but answered calmly :-" I confess that our Church is very rich, and that the emperor does not possess such treasures as we do. I shall willingly lay them all before you, only I beg of you to give me three days to put them into good order, and to take a proper account of them." The governor was very much pleased with this answer, and gladly granted Lawrence the three days he asked for.

During these three days Lawrence ran about here and there, seeking out in the by-lanes and worst streets of the town the poor who were supported by the alms of the Church, and among whom, in obedience to St. Sixtus' dying command, he distributed all the Church's treasures. He assembled them, wrote down all their names, and on the appointed day arranged them in rows in the court before the church. Then he went to the governor and said, "Come and see the treasures of our God, which I have collected and arranged. You will see the whole court full of vessels of gold and heaps of money." The governor followed him joyfully, for this was more than even his covetous heart had imagined. Fancy, then, what was his disappointment and rage, when on reaching the church he saw, instead of glittering gold chalices and bright silver coin, rows of old people, blind, lame, crippled, or covered with sores. He looked very fiercely at Lawrence, but the saint calmly said, "Why are you angry? Behold the treasures I promised you! I have added to them the pearls and precious stones, which are the virgins and widows who form the Church's crown. Take these riches, and use them for the benefit of Rome, of the emperor, and of yourself."

The governor was in such a rage at being disappointed in this way of all the money he had been expecting to get, that he thought he never could be revenged on Lawrence. He ordered him to be stripped, and torn with a kind of whips called scorpions, while at the same time he sent for all kinds of other tortures, by way of showing Lawrence that the whipping was only a small part of what he would have to endure. But Lawrence's heart was so inflamed with the love of Jesus, that every torture seemed nothing in comparison to what he wished to suffer. So instead of being dismayed, he said, "Do you expect, wicked wretch, to frighten me with these tortures? They are tortures for you, but comforts for me, for I have long been wishing for them; and I have longed to sit at this board and to feast on such dainties as these."

After Lawrence had been severely scourged, plates of red-hot iron were placed on his bleeding sides; but still he mocked at the governor, telling him that he did not feel his torments. Then turning to God he thanked Him, and prayed thus :-"My Lord Jesus Christ, true God, and Son of the living God, have mercy on Thy poor servant, who has not denied Thee, but has confessed Thee boldly before men." But the more patient and joyful Lawrence was, the more furious the governor became. He could not understand how any human being could bear joyfully all that he had inflicted on Lawrence; he thought that his supernatural fortitude could come only from some power of magic; and he therefore accused him of being a magician, and threatened, unless he would at once sacrifice to the gods, to put him to worse tortures than any one before had ever suffered. But Lawrence replied, "Your torments will have an end, and I do not fear them. Do what you will to me, I am prepared for the worst." The governor accordingly ordered him to be beaten with leaden plummets till his whole body was buried and torn. Lawrence then prayed to God to receive his soul; upon which there came a voice from heaven which told him that he had yet much more to suffer. The voice was heard by all who stood round, and by the governor himself, who turning to the people cried out, "Romans, do you not see how the devils help and encourage this fellow, who derides both the gods and the emperor, and has no respect for their sovereign power nor any fear of torments."

Lawrence was next placed on the rack, and his body was stretched out so that every limb was disjointed, while at the same time his flesh was torn with hooks. He still continued as calm and cheerful as before, and his heart overflowed with love and confidence, while he said aloud:- "Blessed be Thou, my God, the Father of my Lord Jesus Christ, for Thy great mercy towards me who so little deserve it; grant us, O Lord! Thy grace, that all here present may know that Thou dost not abandon Thy servants, but dost give them comfort and strength in their sufferings." Then there came from heaven an angel, who wiped his face and bleeding shoulders, and eased the pain he was suffering. The angel was seen by several persons; and one of the soldiers, called Romanus, who saw him, was converted, and going up to Lawrence, asked to be baptized, and not long after this same Romanus was martyred.

The governor was now quite mad with rage. He sent

for all the various kinds of torture that could be invented, and had them laid at his feet, declaring that he would spend the whole night in tearing and torturing the body of Lawrence. But the blessed martyr only answered, "If it be so, then will this night be the brightest and happiest of my life, full of joy and gladness, and free from all darkness or sadness."

At last, when the governor had nearly done his worst, and scarcely knew what more he could do, he ordered the executioners to prepare a large gridiron, just the size of Lawrence's body, and to place him on it with a slow fire underneath, so that he might gradually burn and waste away, and die a very lingering and painful death. His orders were quickly executed, the gridiron was soon ready, and glowing coals were put under it. Then Lawrence was stripped, and his body was seen to be all bloody and torn, covered with wide gaping wounds, and so mangled that it scarce hung together. He lay down and stretched himself upon the gridiron, where meekly and humbly resigning himself to the will of his Lord, he said, "Receive, O God! this sacrifice of mine, and may it be acceptable to Thee." The executioners busied themselves to rake the fire and make it burn up more fiercely, and the spectators stood amazed at the constancy of the martyr, while the angels rejoiced to behold such a miracle of virtue and fortitude. No one who looked at Lawrence's countenance would have thought that he was lying on a bed of iron, and broiling over a slow fire, for the grace of God endowed him with such supernatural strength and patience, that he triumphed over the weakness of the flesh and the powers of hell, so that one would rather have thought that he was lying on a bed of down in a state of the greatest luxury. For, as St. Augustine has said, he was burning with the love of Jesus Christ, and therefore he did not feel the torments of the persecutor, and though the fire burned his body, the love of our Savior, which was burning in his heart, held him up against the fury of the flames. In spite of the fire and the pain, he still retained his wonderful courage and magnanimity, and turning his eyes on the governor he said to him, "Come, miserable man, look and see, I am roasted on this side, turn me now to the other; and when they had turned him he added, "Eat now of my flesh, for it is done enough."

At length the hour came when it was our Lord's will to give Lawrence the glorious crown, which He Himself had given him grace to win. Lawrence then began once more to praise God, saying, "I give Thee thanks, my Lord and my God, that Thou hast made me worthy to enter the gates of eternal happiness." And when he had spoken these words, he ended his mortal life, and his blessed soul mounted victorious into heaven, to receive the reward which it had merited upon earth, and to be clothed with splendor more bright and glowing than the flames which had consumed his body.

When the governor saw that St. Lawrence was dead, he and the executioners went away, leaving the dead body on the gridiron. In the morning Hippolytus, a soldier, who had been appointed to guard St. Lawrence in prison, and had been converted by the sight of his wonderful constancy, came to the place and took away the body, and buried it in the Via Tiburtina. But when this reached the governor's ears, he sent to Hippolytus' house, and seized him and all the persons who were there with him. Among the prisoners was an old woman called Concordia, who had nursed Hippolytus, and when she was brought before the judge, she answered so boldly that he condemned her to be scourged to death. Hippolytus was obliged to stand by, and look on while this cruel punishment was inflicted on the old woman; but instead of being grieved or frightened to see her sufferings, he only thanked God that his nurse, who had fed him when he was a helpless infant, had died worthily for Christ's sake. He stood thus unmoved, while nineteen persons of his family, one after the other, were tortured and put to death; till at last, the governor finding that nothing could induce him to deny Christ, ordered him to be tied to the tail of a wild horse, which being let loose, galloped over stones and through rivers and woods, till the body of the saint was literally torn to pieces. God did not leave the wicked governor unpunished even in this world; for soon after, when he was sitting in the Amphitheater called the Coliseum, he was suddenly seized with the most horrible pains, and crying out to St. Lawrence and St. Hippolytus to have mercy on him, he expired in agony.

St. Lawrence was martyred on the 10th, and St. Hippolytus on the 13th August, A.D. 258, and the Church keeps their respective feasts on these days.

CHAPTER XXX

Ninth Persecution

DIOCLETIAN: ST. SEBASTIAN

THE EMPEROR VALERIAN reigned happily as long as he treated the Christians kindly, but from the time he began to persecute them his good fortune left him. He died in a very miserable way. He made war on the Persians, and was taken prisoner by them; and his son, Gallienus, to whom he had given a share in the empire, was so unnatural that he was glad to get rid of his old father, and did not try to get him at liberty. The consequence was that Valerian lied a prisoner in Persia; and it is said that, after his death, his skin was stuffed with straw and kept by the Persians, who were very proud to think that a great Roman emperor had died a prisoner in their hands.

Gallienus cared little for any religion whatsoever, whether Christian or pagan, but he thought it very unjust that the Christians should be persecuted merely for what they believed. He, therefore, passed several laws forbidding any one to molest them, and ordering that they should have the same justice as the pagans. This was a very great thing for the Church, for before this time, the emperors who had not persecuted the Christians had never taken any care to protect them as they did their other subjects. But now that there were laws in their favor, no one could venture to touch them; and as there was now no danger or disgrace in being a Christian, a great many conversions took place. This happy state of peace lasted in some places nearly thirty years, and in others above forty.

The great battle between our Lord and the devil for the possession of the Roman Empire was now nearly over. As year after year passed away it became more and more plain that the devil's power was becoming less and less, while the number of Christians was constantly increasing, so that, in a short time, the city of Rome, which was the capital city of the pagan idolatry, seemed about to become the queen and mistress of all Christian Churches. But it often happens at the end of a battle, that the general who is nearly beaten plucks up all his courage, and makes a desperate attack on his enemy. This was what the devil did now; for seeing that he had only one more chance left of keeping this great empire to himself, he set loose all the powers of hell, and stirred up a terrible persecution against the Church, the like of which was never seen either before or after, and probably will never be again till Antichrist appears.

This great persecution took place in the reign of the Emperors Diocletian and Maximian. The Romans had now so many enemies to fight against, that it had been found necessary to have more than one emperor, and Diocletian had, therefore, given Maximian a share in the empire. Maximian was a very cruel man, and a great enemy to the Christians; and though, at the beginning of this reign, there were still the laws of Gallienus to protect them, he paid no attention to these laws, but put to death a great many Christians in Rome and the other places which he governed. Diocletian, who had the chief power, had no particular dislike to the Christians, and, for many years of his reign, he thought it his best policy not to persecute a religion, which was professed by nearly one-half of his subjects. He had, however no better reason for being kind to the Christians than mere worldly wisdom, and so, after a time, Maximian and Galerius, whom he had appointed to be his successor, persuaded him that it would be wiser to persecute the Christians. So new laws were passed against them, and when Diocletian had once tasted their blood, he proved the most savage persecutor they ever had.

Christianity was now spread into every part of the empire, and Christians were to be found in every class of society; in the palace, in the army, in the courts of law, in the schools of philosophy, among rich and poor, old and young, in fact everywhere, from the emperor's own family down to the poor slave or peasant who worked for his daily bread. When the persecution was once begun, the only thing was to know where to stop; for the Christians were so numerous and so well known, that there was no difficulty in finding out whom to lay hands on. The number of martyrs in this persecution was greater than in all the others put together, and 70,000 are said to have perished in different parts of the empire in the course of only one month. Their very names are unknown on earth, though each is registered in heaven, and will be published on the great last day. Among those whose memory is celebrated by the Church, there are to be found persons of all ranks, classes, and ages; but as it is impossible to give the histories of all, or even of all which are very interesting, we must content ourselves with a few of those whose names are most known. One of these is St. Sebastian.

St. Sebastian was a young man of noble birth. He served in the Roman army, and was so distinguished for his bravery that he was made one of the captains of the emperor's guard. Diocletian thought very highly of his prudence and wisdom, and took such pleasure in his society that he had him always with him, talking constantly to him and consulting him in all affairs of importance. Sebastian, however, was a Christian, though he was careful to conceal his religion. He did not do this from fear, or want of love to God, for in fact his heart was burning with love, and there was nothing he longed for so much as to die for Jesus; but he did it because, so long as he was not suspected to be himself a Christian, he had better opportunities of encouraging and comforting those who were being persecuted. Still, he never denied his religion, but always held himself ready to confess it openly, and to die for it whenever God should call on him to do so; and meanwhile he went constantly about among the Christians, visiting those who were in prison, supplying their bodily wants, cheering those whose courage was sinking, bringing to repentance those who had fallen away, and thus saving many souls whom the devil was trying to ruin.

Among the persons to whom Sebastian was most useful, were Marcus and Marcellianus, twin sons of Tranquillinus and Marcia, who were rich and of noble birth. They had both been thrown into prison, and had been put several times to the torture, but they had been so supported by Sebastian, who was always encouraging them to fear neither death nor suffering for the love of Christ, that they bore their torments cheerfully. At last sentence of death was passed on them; but their execution was put off for thirty days, because their friends and relatives promised the prefect, that before the end of that time they would certainly persuade them to sacrifice to the gods. Meanwhile they were sent to the house of Nicostratus, one of the prefect's officers, who was ordered to keep them close prisoners, but to allow their pagan friends to come and see them whenever they liked.

The bodily pain which the twin-brothers had borne so manfully, was as nothing to what they had now to endure. They were of an amiable and affectionate temper, and had always loved their relations more than themselves. They were both married and had several children; their parents were still alive, their father being bed-ridden, and their mother old and infirm; and they had a large circle of friends and dependents, who were very fond of them, and looked to them for their happiness and support. First came the friends, who talked very gravely to them about their duties to their family, to their aged parents, their wives, and their little children, bidding them remember that the proof of a man's religion is the way in which he does his duty to those around him, and that it is quite a mistake to think of pleasing God by neglecting those whom He has entrusted to our care. They added that it was a disgrace to young men of their high character and noble birth, to be carried away, contrary to reason and common sense, by the folly of a set of low and wild enthusiasts like the Christians. Next came their aged mother, who besought them by the love with which she had nursed them, and by the tender care she had always taken of them, not to bring her grey hairs with sorrow to the grave. Then came their crippled father, carried in by two of his servants, and he literally reproached them for their folly in running after death as they were now doing, and he called on all, both young and old, to lament with him the ungrateful return which his own sons were making him in his old age for the kindness with which he had always treated them. But all that friends, and mother, and father said, was as nothing to the sorrow of their wives, who rushed into the prison almost distracted with grief, tearing their hair and uttering the wildest cries holding up their helpless babes before their eyes, and beseeching them not to be so cruel as to make them widows and their children orphans.

Marcus and Marcellianus tried to answer and console them all in turn. They told their friends of the duty above all other duties, of leaving father, and mother, and wife, and children for Christ's sake; they tried to comfort their mother by the example of our Blessed Lady, who had willingly offered up her only Son as a babe upon the altar, and had stood beside His cross to see Him die in agony; they spoke to their father of the love of Him who so loved the world that He gave His only Son to die for sinners; and they besought their wives to espouse themselves as holy widows to Jesus, who would be to them a more loving husband, and to their orphan babes a more tender father, than they themselves had ever been or could be. But it was all in vain-for their hearers were pagans, who knew not the love of God, and cared not for the sorrows of Jesus and Mary, and so all that they said to comfort them only made them more unhappy. Day after day their friends came to see them, and day after day the brothers had to go through the same heart-rending scene; till at last their courage began to fail, and it seemed as if they could not hold out much longer against the sight of the suffering, which they were inflicting on those whom they loved better than themselves.

Sebastian went very often to visit Marcus and Marcellianus, so that he saw how sorely they were tempted. One day when their relations had been weeping and wailing even more than usual, the poor brothers were so broken-hearted that it seemed as if they must give way. Then Sebastian saw that his own hour was come, and that it was the Lord's will that he should openly confess that he was a Christian, by way of encouraging Marcus and Marcellianus to stand firm.

St. Sebastian

Though the two brothers knew that Sebastian was a Christian, yet the rest of the party believed he was a pagan like themselves, and it would be very dangerous to let them know that he was a Christian. But Sebastian had long desired martyrdom, and he was not afraid of what might befall himself, if only he could save the two brothers from falling into mortal sin by denying their religion. He, therefore, spoke out boldly in the presence of all the party, saying, "Ah, brave soldiers of Jesus Christ, the King of kings, stand firm in this hard trial, and do not let yourselves be conquered. Tears may prevail with women, but they can have no force with brave men like yourselves. Teach your friends and relatives that the true soldier of Christ fears neither tortures nor death, and can easily trample under his feet all earthly affections, which would draw him away from the love of his Lord. You are now called to choose whether you will give up Jesus Christ, or these friends of yours. But what has hitherto made you confess Christ? What has kept you so long in this prison? What has given you strength to bear so many tortures? Was it not the love of Jesus Christ? Did you not always know that your death would be a great grief to your parents, your wives, and your children? Yet you went through all your former trials courageously, because of the hopes you had of enjoying Christ in His glory. And is it then possible that a few tears shall conquer you, who were not to be conquered by the greatest tortures? No, no; it cannot be. Do not let the love of your family deprive you of the glory which you have bought with your blood. Do not give up your arms when the victory is in your hand, and your foot is already on your enemy's throat. Ah! if they who weep now, knew all that you know about the glories which are prepared for Christians, and the torments which await the wicked, they would envy you instead of pitying you, and would follow you with joy instead of tears." Then turning to those who stood around, he besought them not to tempt these two young men to give up the eternal happiness, which was prepared for them in the palace of the King of Heaven, nor to dissuade them from enduring the greatest torments which could be inflicted on them, since, the greater were their present sufferings, the more glorious would be their immortal crown. "For," continued he, "the hopes of Christians are not idle fables, but solid truths. This is proved every day by the miracles which Christians work. They raise the dead, they give sight to the blind, they cure the worst diseases, only by calling on the name of Jesus; and it cannot be that they do these things by magic, as some of you say, because no one ever heard of a magician's raising the dead to life. And if these miracles which Christians work be true, most certainly the promises of Christ are also true, and it is reasonable that a man should die for them. But suppose they were not true, what greater miracle can there be, than to see the world converted without any miracle to the faith of Christ, in spite of the Roman emperors and all their power, and all the torments which have been inflicted on those who profess this religion. So dry up your tears, my friends, and joyfully accompany these holy martyrs to their triumph; and I hope, that by their merits, God will open your eyes also."

As Sebastian finished speaking, a bright light from heaven shone around, and in the midst of it were seen seven angels, and before them the King of angels-the Lord Jesus Christ-who, going up to Sebastian, gave him the kiss of peace, and said to him, "Thou shalt be always with me." All who were present saw this glorious vision, and were filled with amazement Among them was Zoe, the wife of Nicostratus, who had been dumb, but without being deaf,

St. Sebastian

for six years, so that she had heard all that Sebastian had said; and now, when she saw the glorious vision of our Lord and the bright angels round Him, she was converted, and throwing herself at Sebastian's feet, she made signs that she wished to become a Christian, and be baptized. When Sebastian understood what she meant to say, he answered:- " If I am the servant of Jesus, and if all I have said be true, the Lord Jesus heal thee, and loose thy tongue, and make thee speak." At the same time he made the sign of the cross on Zoe's mouth, and instantly she recovered her speech, and began to praise God, and to thank Sebastian for her cure. The sight of this miracle touched the heart of her husband, Nicostratus, so that he fell down at the feet of the two brothers, begging their pardon for having kept them prisoners, and bidding them return to their homes; for he was ready to be imprisoned and to be put to death rather than keep them prisoners any longer. Tranquillinus and Marcia also, with the wives and children of the martyrs, were converted. They began to cry once more; but it was for a very different reason from what had made them cry before; for now they wept to think that they should ever have tried to draw Marcus and Marcellianus away from their religion. The joy of the two brothers, when they saw all these wonderful conversions, was very great. They never ceased to thank and praise God, and to say to each other:- "Let us fight like soldiers of Christ; let us die for our Lord; and let us only try who shall be the first to die, and to show the other the way to suffer for Christ."

The new converts surrounded Sebastian, and earnestly begged him to let them be baptized. But he would not do so till he had made Nicostratus fetch up all the other prisoners who were in the house, so that they also might hear the word of God, and have an opportunity of becoming Christians. Nicostratus brought them all up, together with Claudius, the Registrar of the Court; and Sebastian preached to them; and the Spirit of God opened their hearts to receive the truth, so that they were all converted, and begged to be baptized. Sebastian then sent for a priest called Polycarp, who baptized them all, to the number of sixty-four persons, including Tranquillinus and his family, Nicostratus and Zoe with their family, Claudius and his family, and sixteen prisoners who had been confined in Nicostratus' house.

Several miracles were wrought at the time of their baptism. Tranquillinus had been a cripple for eleven years; but Sebastian promised him that if he had faith he would be cured by the water of baptism; and though he had to be carried by his servants, and placed in the water, yet no sooner did he touch it, than his bent and crippled joints became straight and strong, and he stood upright, and walked as actively as if he were a young man. Two sons of Claudius, also, had been very ill, the one with dropsy, the other with ulcers all over his body; and they were both restored to perfect health as soon as they were baptized.

The thirty days were now passed, and Chromatius, the governor of Rome, sent for Tranquillinus, to inquire what success he had had with his sons. Chromatius knew how long Tranquillinus had been a cripple, and he was therefore very much surprised to see him walk alone, and with a firm, active step. He said nothing, however, about his recovery, but went on to ask whether Marcus and Marcellianus were ready to sacrifice to the gods. Tranquillinus calmly answered "My sons are happy, and so am I; for God has taught me the truth of the Christian religion." "What!" cried the governor, greatly surprised, "and have you too lost your wits, and become a fool in your old age?" "He is a fool," replied Tranquillinus, "who

St. Sebastian 259

leaves the way of life to follow that of death." "What life, and what death?" inquired Chromatius. "If you will listen to me," answered Tranquillinus, "you and all your family shall be as happy as I am." Chromatius was very much astonished at the change, both in mind and body, which had come over Tranquillinus in the course of one short month, so he promised to give his whole attention to what he was about to say: "Only be sure," added he, "you tell me nothing which you cannot prove." Tranquillinus then related all that had happened in the house of Nicostratus; how our Lord had appeared to them; how Zoe had recovered her speech; how all who were present had been converted by these miracles and the preaching of Sebastian; and how he and the sons of Claudius, had been cured by the water of baptism. Chromatius listened very attentively to all that Tranquillinus said; for he too had lost the use of his limbs, and he could not help wishing that he could be cured as Tranquillinus had been. But he knew nothing about the Christian faith; and when Tranquillinus explained it to him, he had many doubts, and found it hard to believe such heavenly mysteries. Tranquillinus, therefore, sent for Sebastian, who instructed Chromatius and his family, as he had done those in the house of Nicostratus; and the Holy Spirit gave such wonderful power to his words, that all those who heard him were converted. Chromatius, however, hesitated for a long time; till Sebastian promised him that if he would believe, he should be cured by the water of baptism, as Tranquillinus had been. So, at last, he made up his mind to be baptized, and though his faith was very weak, and he doubted almost to the last, yet God cured him in answer to the fervent prayer of Sebastian. Chromatius was so thankful for the great favors that God had granted him, that he gave their liberty to fourteen hundred slaves of his, who were baptized at the same time as himself. "For," said he, "those who have God for their Father, ought not to be slaves to men."

It would at any time have been wonderful to see so many persons suddenly converted by the preaching of one man; but it was still more so at this time, because a severe persecution was going on, and the persons who were converted knew and saw every day what trials Christians had to undergo. Their love for Jesus must then have been very great, before they could have made up their minds to the certainty of torture and death, in order to gain the rewards of everlasting life, which Jesus had promised to His faithful and loving servants.

Soon after this the persecution became much more severe, and Chromatius found that he could not keep his office of governor of the city without openly declaring his religion. He therefore resigned it on pretense of his health, and by the advice of Caius, who was the Pope at that time, he went to live at a country-house, which he had at some distance from Rome. Here he was of very great use to the Christians; for all those whose faith was weak, or who did not feel themselves called by our Lord to suffer martyrdom, went out to stay with him, and as he was a very rich man and lived on his own estate, surrounded by his own slaves, they were quite safe under his protection. The rest of the Christians who were braver, and who longed to suffer for Jesus' sake, remained at Rome, like sheep waiting for slaughter. Among these were Sebastian, Marcus and Marcellianus, and Tiburtius, the son of Chromatius, a young man who led a very holy life, and had the gift of working miracles.

Marcus and Marcellianus were the first to suffer. Fabian the new governor, heard how they had formerly been condemned to death, and had been allowed thirty

St. Sebastian

days to change their minds; and so now, finding that they were determined not to sacrifice to the gods, he ordered the sentence to be executed on them. They were fastened to a pillar, and their feet were bored through with long nails; but while they were in this painful situation, they were so filled with spiritual joy, that they sang aloud in the words of the Psalmist, "Behold how good and how pleasant it is for brethren to dwell together in unity." Fabian advised them to give up their folly, and to save themselves from the greater torments that were prepared for them; but they answered: "We are very well off as we are, rooted in the love of Jesus Christ, and we desire nothing better than to remain in this posture, so long as our souls remain in our bodies." They were kept fast nailed in this way for a whole day and night, during which time they never ceased to praise God and sing psalms together, till at last, Fabian seeing there was no hope of conquering them, ordered them to be thrust through with a lance, which was accordingly done. Their father, Tranquillinus, and a great number of those who had been converted by St. Sebastian, suffered martyrdom about the same time.

As it was not publicly known that Chromatius and his family had been converted before they left Rome, it was some time before anyone suspected Tiburtius of being a Christian. This made it more easy for him to help those who were being persecuted. He led a very devout life, he gave all his money to the poor, and he went about secretly among the Christians, encouraging those who were tempted to deny their faith, persuading the careless to reform their lives, and setting a holy example to everyone. God was pleased to work many miracles by his means. We are told, that one day as he was passing through a street, he saw a crowd round a young man who had fallen down from a great height, and was so bruised that there was no hope of his life. Tiburtius joined them, and asked leave to speak a word or two in the young man's ear, as he thought he could do him good. The crowd made way for him, and he went up to the young man and said the Pater and the Creed over him, whereupon the young man immediately stood up quite cured, as if nothing had happened to him. Tiburtius took the opportunity to preach the Gospel, and a great many of those who heard him were converted and baptized.

At last, however, Tiburtius was betrayed by a man called Torquatus. Torquatus was a very wicked man, and though he was a Christian, he led the same sort of life as the pagans did. Tiburtius reproved him, and told him that if he did not repent, his being a Christian would do him no good, and that he would certainly go to hell. Torquatus was very angry to be spoken to so plainly; but he hid his anger, and pretended that he was very much obliged to Tiburtius, and promised to amend his life. He did this, however, only for the purpose of revenging himself the better. For a short time he was constantly with Tiburtius, and appeared to be very fond of him; but after he had artfully gained his confidence, he went to Fabian, the governor of the city, and accused Tiburtius of being a Christian. He carried his deceit so far that he even had himself seized at the same time; though, when they came before the governor, it soon became clear who was the true Christian, and who the false one, for Torquatus was ready to do everything he was ordered, while Tiburtius declared that he would die rather than do the least thing against the name of the Lord Jesus. The governor, therefore, desired that the floor should be strewed with burning coals, and he gave Tiburtius his choice either to sacrifice to the gods, or to walk barefooted over the red-hot cinders. Tiburtius did not hesitate a moment, but, making the sign of the cross, walked boldly over the coals just as if they had been roses under his feet. The governor looked on in amazement, not knowing what to think of him: but Tiburtius said :- "Away now with your obstinate infidelity, and confess Jesus Christ to be the true God whose commands all things obey. Or if you will not believe in Him, put your hands in a cauldron of boiling water, and call upon your god Jupiter, and you will then see whether for Jupiter's sake the water will not scald you. For my part, I do not feel the heat of this fire, and through the name of Jesus Christ, these red-hot coals seem to me like roses; for Jesus created both the fire and the roses, and all things obey their Creator." The governor was offended at the bold freedom with which Tiburtius spoke to him, and he answered, "Everyone knows that your Christ taught you magic, and that all Christians are sorcerers and magicians." Whereupon Tiburtius, who could not bear to hear such an insult offered to his Lord and Savior, cried out, "Hold thy peace, miserable man; and let not that accursed tongue of thine dare to utter such blasphemies against the sweet and holy Name of Jesus." These words put Fabian into such a rage, that he ordered Tiburtius to be instantly beheaded; and the sentence was executed without delay.

Last of all, after most of his spiritual children had won their crowns, Sebastian was called to suffer martyrdom. It came to the ears of the Emperor Diocletian that his favorite Sebastian, whom he had made captain of his guards, and had loaded with so many honors, had become a soldier of Jesus Christ, and was persuading men to forsake the gods of the Roman Empire, and to worship a man who had been crucified about three hundred years before. Diocletian was very angry when he heard this, for, as he was very superstitious, he was afraid that the Christians, by refusing to worship the heathen gods, would draw down some great judgment on the empire; and he thought it was very ungrateful of Sebastian, to whom he had been so kind, to join himself with a sect whom he looked on as his greatest enemies. He, therefore, sent for him, and said to him very angrily, "Sebastian, what is this that I hear? Is it possible, that after I have advanced you to such honor, and have placed you in this high command, you dare to live in my palace as a Christian, and are disloyal to me, and draw down on me the anger of the gods?" But Sebastian answered very meekly and humbly, "Sire, I have always been most loyal to you, and I have daily prayed for your safety and that of your empire, to the true God who is the Maker of heaven and earth; for it seems to me a great folly to worship stones, and to ask favors of those who cannot speak or move, and who have neither sense nor feeling." The emperor was so angry at these words, that he ordered Sebastian to be immediately taken out of his sight, and led into a field, where he was to be fastened to a tree and shot to death with arrows. No time was lost in executing the sentence, for Satan and his servants rejoiced to get hold of this great soldier of Christ. Sebastian was dragged out into the field, where the emperor's soldiers stripped him, bound him to a tree, and then shot their arrows at him till he was pierced all over. But, amidst these bodily sufferings, his soul was filled with peace and joy, and his heart burned so with love to Jesus, that he only longed to suffer more, and to be pierced with more arrows for His sake, till at last, when he was covered with wounds, he fainted from loss of blood, and the soldiers believing him to be dead, went away and left him lying there.

The following night Irene, the widow of a martyr, went to the place where Sebastian was lying, intending to take away his body and bury it; but to her great joy and surprise, she found that he was still warm and breathing. She therefore carried him to her house, where she dressed his wounds and nursed him very carefully, till, at the end of a few days, it pleased God to restore him to perfect health. The Christians, who had heard of his wonderful escape, came to visit him, and they begged him to go quietly into some distant place, so that he might not fall again into the hands of the cruel emperor. But this brave soldier had no thought of flying from the battle before he had conquered his great enemy, and won his crown. Therefore, instead of going way and hiding himself, he placed himself in a part of the city where he knew the emperor would be passing; and just as the emperor came up to him, he cried out in a loud voice: "The priests of your temples, O emperor! deceive you and tell you falsehoods against the Christians, making you believe that they are the enemies of your empire, while in reality it is they who protect it by the prayers which they daily offer for its preservation." The emperor was very much startled to hear these words spoken by a man whom he believed to be dead, and for a few minutes he was too much frightened to speak. But he soon recovered himself, and asked: "Are you Sebastian whom I ordered to be put to death? Did you not die? And if so, how did you come to life again?" And the saint answered: My Lord Jesus has been pleased to give me life, in order that here, before all the people, I may bear witness to the truth of His faith, and to your cruelty in persecuting the saints who have done you no harm. In His name, therefore, I command you, if you would preserve your life and your empire, to cease from your wickedness and to shed no more innocent blood." When the emperor found that he had to deal with a living man and not with a spirit as he had at first feared, he flew into a great rage, and ordered that Sebastian should be bound to a pillar and scourged to death. It was a great happiness to this brave martyr, as it had been to so many others, to be allowed to imitate the Passion of his dearest Lord, and, as the soldiers scourged him, and the blood flowed down his back, the smarting of his wounds and the tearing of his flesh seemed sweet to him, for he thought of the scourges that had fallen on the sacred Body of his Savior, and of the precious Blood which had streamed from Jesus' wounds to wash away his sins. They went on scourging him, till at last his body could bear no more, and he expired; and thus he won that glorious crown of martyrdom for which he had longed so ardently. After he was dead the executioners threw his body into the common sewer; but it was not our Lord's will that the relics of so great a saint should rest in such a place. Before very long, St. Sebastian appeared to a woman called Lucina, and told her where his body was; and he ordered her to go to a certain place where she would find it, and to take it away and bury it at the entrance into the catacombs, where the bodies of the apostles St. Peter and St. Paul were buried. Lucina did as St. Sebastian bade her; and she found his body where he had said, and she took it away and buried it in the catacombs, as he had ordered her to do.

St. Sebastian's martyrdom took place A.D. 288, and the Church keeps his feast on the 20th January.

CHAPTER XXXI

ST. MAURICE AND THE THEBAN LEGION

T. SEBASTIAN was not the only great soldier and saint who suffered in this persecution. The Church celebrates also the memory of St. Maurice and the brave Theban legion. Their martyrdom came about in the following way.

The Emperor Diocletian, after he had made Maximian his partner in the empire, and had given him the title of emperor, sent him into France with a large army. One of the regiments, or legions, as they were then called, had been originally levied at Thebes in Egypt, and was composed entirely of Christians. When the army had crossed the Alps, and was come in sight of the enemy, Maximian thought it would be well to review his troops, and to make them offer sacrifice to the gods, and take a vow that they would fight bravely. When Maurice, who was the captain of the Theban legion, heard what the emperor intended to do, he consulted with Exuperius, the standard-bearer, and Candidus, a senator; and they agreed that, as they and all the soldiers of the Theban legion were Christians, and could not sacrifice to the gods, the best thing they could do would be to separate themselves from the rest of the army, and to go to a place eight miles off, which was then called Agaunum.

When Maximian heard that the Theban legion was gone to Agaunum, and knew their reason for going, he was not at all pleased, and he sent them peremptory orders to return and sacrifice with the rest of the soldiers. Though Maximian said nothing about what he would do if they disobeyed him, yet everyone knew how he hated the Christians, and it was plain that the soldiers must either sacrifice to the gods, or make up their minds to suffer the worst that might befall them. But though the legion contained no less than 6,660 men, of different ages and characters, some old and others young, some very devout and others more thoughtless and fond of this world, yet all had now but one heart and one mind. When Maurice told them what were the emperor's orders, they cried out, as if with one voice, that they were ready to die for Jesus, but that no human power should ever force them to sacrifice to the gods; and they desired Maurice to go to the emperor and tell him that they were ready to fight for him bravely as they had ever done, and to obey him in all things which were not contrary to the law of God, but that being Christians, they could not worship the idols, which were devils and not true gods. This was a joyful message for Maurice to carry, so he went at once to the emperor and told him what the soldiers had said, giving him at the same time to understand that he himself, and all the other officers, were of the same mind.

Maximian was very much enraged to receive this answer, and he commanded the legion to be decimated, that is to say, every tenth man was chosen by lot and put to death. The soldiers rejoiced at this order of the emperor's, by which they would gain eternal life and a glorious crown; and their hearts being all on fire with the love of God and the desire for martyrdom, each man hoped the lot would fall on himself. In this way 666 soldiers were put to death.

Maximian thought that the rest of the legion would be

frightened by the terrible fate of their companions, and therefore, soon after the execution of the 666 soldiers, he again sent orders to them to join the army and offer sacrifice. But the glorious example of the 666 martyrs had had quite the contrary effect to what the emperor expected; for the rest of the legion, so far from being frightened by what had happened, were so inflamed with the love of martyrdom, that they joyfully prepared themselves for death.

Maurice was the foremost in this spiritual battle, as he had always been foremost in the battles with earthly enemies into which he had led his legion; and he spoke animating words to his men, encouraging them, by the hopes of eternal glory, to fight bravely to the last. Exuperius, the standard-bearer, also cheered them by his words. and his example, saying to them:- "You see, brothers, that I carry the colors of the emperor; but now I invite you not to an earthly war, but to a heavenly one. It requires great courage and constancy in us to pay God what we have promised Him. Let us, then, lay down our arms and die, that we may obtain the crown which He has prepared for us."

When the soldiers were brought before the emperor and were ordered to sacrifice, they with one voice refused to do so; and Maurice said to Maximian in their name:- "O Caesar we are thy soldiers, but we are also the soldiers of Jesus Christ. From thee we receive our pay, but from Him we have received eternal life. To thee we owe service, to Him obedience. We are ready to follow thee against the barbarians, but we are also ready to suffer death rather than renounce our faith."

The heroic virtue of these Christian soldiers seemed to the pagan emperor nothing but obstinacy and stubbornness, and so he became more and more angry, in proportion as be found that they were more and more resolved to die rather than deny their religion. He therefore commanded his whole army to be drawn out, and this Theban legion to be placed in the middle of it; and then he gave orders that the other soldiers should fall on this rebellious legion, and not leave a single man of it alive. The Christian soldiers had arms in their hands, they were brave men, in the full vigor of life, and they were well able to fight and to sell their lives dearly; but they were now about to fight a different battle from what they had ever done before; so hey laid down their earthly arms, and arming themselves with faith and the love of God, they prepared to gain a new kind of victory, Maurice was at their head, and encouraged by his example even more than by the words which he spoke, they all knelt known, and lifting up their hands and their hearts to Heaven, they offered up their lives a sacrifice to Jesus. In this attitude they waited for death, and in this way they conquered without fighting; and thus, without lifting a sword, they fought and gained the crown of martyrdom.

After these holy martyrs were all dead, the pagan soldiers who had killed them stripped their bodies, and sat down to feast and make merry, very well pleased with their day's work. It chanced that a soldier called Victor, who did not belong to that army, came by that way; and when he saw so many dead bodies on the field, he thought there had been a battle, and he asked those who were making merry to tell him all about it. But when he heard the story he broke out into lamentations, for he too was a Christian; and he cried out, "Oh, miserable man that I am! Why was not I in the company of these holy soldiers that I might have died with them!" The other soldiers knew by these words hat Victor was a Christian; and so they fell on him and cut him in pieces; and he had his wish, and obtained the same glorious crown as the brave Theban Legion.

St. Maurice and the Theban Legion suffered martyrdom on the 22nd September, A.D. 286, on which day their feast is celebrated by the Church. The place where all this happened is a few miles from the Lake of Geneva, and is now called St. Maurice, in honor of the martyr saint.

CHAPTER XXXII

ST. GEORGE

IT was an ancient custom among Christians to invoke St. Sebastian, St. Maurice, and St. George as the great champions of the Church against the enemies of the faith; besides which, St. George has always been more particularly the patron saint of England The history of St. George, then, seems naturally to follow those of St. Sebastian and St. Maurice.

It is very difficult to relate the history of St. George, because he was such a great saint and was so famous in the East, that heretics wrote untrue accounts of his life to serve their own wicked purpose, and published stories about him which were quite untrue. The consequence is, that no details are related of his life and martyrdom in the services of the Church; and out of all that is told of him, it is hard to say quite certainly what is true and what is false. The following history, however, is generally believed to be the true one.

St. George was born in Cappadocia of rich and noble parents, and was educated from his earliest infancy as a Christian. When he was very young he entered the army, where he distinguished himself by his bravery, and became a great favorite with the Emperor Diocletian. When Diocletian was thinking about persecuting the Christians, he assembled his principal officers, and consulted them whether it would be for the good of the empire to do so.

St. George

Those who live at the courts of great princes are often flatterers, and so it was with Diocletian's courtiers. When he asked them for their advice, they thought only of what would please him most; and therefore seeing that he wished to persecute the Christians, they said that it would be right for him to do so, and they praised him for wishing to stand up for the gods. St. George, however, expressed his true opinion, and he said that it would be very unjust to punish people who had not committed any crime, besides which it was contrary to the worship of the true God to do so.

The emperor and all who were present discovered by the way in which St. George spoke that he himself was a Christian. They therefore did all they could to persuade him to give up his religion, setting before him, on the one hand, his youth, his noble birth, his riches, the great favors he had already received from the emperor, and the still greater ones he might expect; and on the other hand, the loss of all these good things, and even of life itself, if he were so foolish as to be obstinate and refuse to sacrifice to the gods, as the emperor desired him to do. But St. George took little notice of all they said; for the love of Jesus was fixed so deep in his heart, that he was ready to lose his life rather than give up the least article of his religion. He was not troubled or frightened by anything they could say; but, on the contrary, fixing his eyes boldly on the emperor, he spoke thus:- "It is a pity, Sire, that you do not know and adore the true God; for if you did, He would give you a far better kingdom than the one you now possess. Your present kingdom must pass away, since whatsoever is in this world lasts only a short time, but the kingdom that God gives His children will last forever. I am so thoroughly convinced of this, that you are only losing your time in trying to draw me from the worship of the true God; for I can neither be tempted by your promises nor frightened by your threats." Diocletian was very angry to find that one of his own officers had the courage to contradict him, and be ordered St. George to be seized and carried off to prison. St. George was therefore led away to prison, where he was stretched on the floor, loaded with heavy chains, and a great stone was laid on his chest, so that he was pressed down to the ground, and could move neither hand nor foot.

The next day St. George was brought before the emperor, and as he continued true to his religion, he was placed upon a wheel covered with sharp points, contrived in such a way that, as it turned round, the sharp points pierced and tore his flesh. The pain was dreadful, for as the wheel went round and round, it cut new wounds, or pierced deeper into those which were already raw and bleeding; but the saint bore it all without a cry or a groan, or the least change of countenance. Then suddenly there was heard a voice from heaven, saying, "Fear not, George, for I am with thee," and a man clothed in white, and shining gloriously, was seen to stand beside him, and to give him his hand, and to embrace him, filling him with fresh courage and joy in the midst of his tortures, so that the greater were the tortures inflicted on him, the greater were his patience and fortitude. The Christians were filled with joy and thankfulness to see how bravely St. George stood up for their holy religion; while the pagans did not know what to make of his wonderful courage. Some of those who stood round, however, were converted, and among them Anatolius and Pretolius, two men of high rank, who were afterwards beheaded for the name of Jesus.

The emperor was very much surprised and disappointed to find, that in spite of all the tortures, St. George continued firm. He now thought he would try what could be done with him by fair words. He therefore went up to him, and speaking to him in a gentle and affectionate manner, he exhorted him to give up his folly, for that he would do great things for him, and would advance him to the highest honors, if he would obey him as his father. There was a pause of a few moments, and then St. George answered, "Let us go, O emperor to the temple and see the gods whom you worship." Diocletian was almost out of his wits with joy when he heard these words, for he thought that his old favorite, George, had come to his senses, and had changed his mind, and was about to forsake the Christian religion; so he invited the senate and the persons of his court, and all the people, to go up with them to the temple, to be witnesses of the sacrifice which George was going to offer. When they were all assembled, St. George went up to the statue of Apollo which was in the temple, and making the sign of the cross, he said to it, "Wilt thou have me offer sacrifice to thee?" The devil which was in the image could not resist the sign of the Holy Cross, and in spite of himself he was forced to answer the truth, saying, "I am no God, nor is there any other God except Him whom thou worshippest." Then St. George replied, "How darest thou, then, to stay here in the presence of such a one as me, who acknowledge and adore the true and living God?" As soon as St. George had spoken these words, there was heard a hideous noise like screeching and howling from the inside of the idols, and they all fell down on the ground and were broken to pieces. Many of the pagans who be held this miracle were converted, and cried out that Jesus Christ was the only true God. But the priests, who saw their idols broken to pieces, and who feared that their own credit with the people was gone, were very angry; and they stirred up the populace to seize St. George and bind him and beat him, and then to lead him before the emperor, calling out that this magician ought to be killed, for if he were not, the gods would punish them for standing by to see their images insulted and broken. The emperor was not less angry than the people at the destruction of the idols, and at the conversions which had taken place in con sequence of this miracle; and he was, therefore, very glad to have an excuse for putting the saint to death; therefore when the crowd shouted and cried out that George ought to be killed as a magician, he passed sentence on him, and condemned him to be immediately beheaded.

St. George was then led to the place where criminals were generally put to death, and when he arrived there he asked the executioners to give him a little time for prayer. This was granted him, when, lifting up his eyes to heaven, and sighing deeply from the bottom of his heart, he prayed aloud: "My Lord God, who art before all ages, and hast chosen me for Thy service from my childhood, and hast given me strength to suffer so many torments, and to confess Thy name, receive my soul and place it in those eternal mansions where Thy elect dwell with Thee. Pardon this blind people what they have done against me and Thy other servants, and give them light that they may come to know Thee. Stretch forth Thy hand to all that call on Thee, and fill them with such holy fear and burning charity that, loving Thee above all things, they may imitate Thy saints and follow in their footsteps, so that with them they may obtain of Thee pardon and glory, and everlasting happiness." As soon as St. George had finished this prayer, and while he was still on his knees, he stretched out his neck to the executioner, who with one blow cut off his head. So died St. George, the patron saint of England. His name is very famous, both in the East and the West, and among the Greeks he is generally called "The great martyr

St. George." His head is kept at Rome in a church dedicated to him.

In the foregoing history of St. George nothing has been said about his fight with the dragon, which one sees represented on the coin of England and in many pictures of him. The fact is, the story of St. George and the dragon is not supposed by anyone to be true. It may be looked on as an allegory, or sort of parable; for as the devil is called in the Bible the dragon, St. George may be said to have fought against the dragon when he underwent such severe tortures from the heathens, who were the servants of the devil; and when he triumphed over them in his glorious martyrdom, he indeed conquered the devil or dragon, and trod him under his feet. The legend of St. George and the dragon is, however, so interesting that we shall relate it. It is as follows.

Once upon a time it happened that as St. George was going to join the emperor's army he came to the city of Selene in Africa, or as some say, of Barytus or Bayrenth in Syria, the inhabitants of which were in great trouble. The cause of their distress was an enormous dragon, which, from time to time, came out of a neighboring marsh and devoured their flocks and herds. In order to keep this dragon in good humor, and to prevent him coming to the town and eating them all up, the inhabitants agreed to give him two sheep every day, and this they continued to do till all their sheep were eaten up. When the dragon found that no more sheep were sent to him he became very angry, and threatened to come and eat them all up, unless they would give him something to satisfy his hunger. The people were very much frightened, so they spoke very humbly to the dragon, and told him that they would do all they could to please him, and would willingly go on giving him sheep, but that they really had none remaining.

Thereupon the dragon answered, that he did not wish to be hard upon them, and that, since they had no more sheep to give him he would try to make the best of whatever they might have, and he thought he could put up with two fat children every day. The idea of giving the dragon their children to eat had never entered the heads of the poor people of the city, and at first they said it was impossible to let him have them; but at length, when they found that nothing else would satisfy him, they thought it was better to let him have two each day, as this was the only way of saving all the rest, and their own lives also. Accordingly every day two children, under fifteen years of age, were chosen by lot and sent to the dragon; and from this time nothing was now to be heard in the city but the lamentations of the parents who had lost their children, and the cries of the innocent victims on whom the lot had fallen.

At last the lot fell on Cleodolinda, the king's only daughter. The king was in despair at the idea of losing his only child, and he offered to give up all his treasures, and even half of his kingdom, to save her life. But the people answered:- " Is it just, O king! that you who have made us give up our children, should keep back your own?" And, when he still hesitated, they became very angry, and threatened to burn him in his palace if he would not give up the princess. So at last the king was obliged to give her up, and the only favor he asked was, that they would wait eight days before they took her away from him, which they agreed to do.

When the eight days were over, the princess came out of the palace, dressed in her royal robes, and looking very beautiful, and she knelt down at her father's feet and asked his blessing, saying that she was ready to die for her people. Then there was great lamentation and weeping, for everyone was sorry to lose such a beautiful and good young princess; but there was no help for them, and they led her forth out of the city, and shut the gates on her. Now at this moment St. George was passing by, and he wondered to see the ground all strewed over with the bones of the children whom the dragon had devoured. When he came up to the princess, who was walking slowly along and crying very bitterly, he was touched with pity, and he stopped and asked her why she was crying, and she told him the whole story. Then he answered, "Do not be afraid, for I will deliver you." But the princess replied, "Oh! do not stay here, brave knight, for you cannot help me, and you yourself will be eaten up. Fly! I beseech you, fly." St. George, however, had never, in his whole life, turned hist back on an enemy, and he would not now run away and leave this poor young girl to perish alone, so he said, "God forbid that I should fly! I will fight with this monster, and I will deliver you through the power of my Lord Jesus Christ." The princess was a heathen, and had never heard of the great name of Jesus, nor of the wonderful things that were done through His power; so when she saw the dragon coming towards them, half crawling, half flying, she began to tremble exceedingly, and she cried out again, "Fly! I beseech you, brave knight, and leave me here to die!" St. George did not say a word, but making the sign of the cross, and calling on the name of Jesus, he spurred his horse towards the dragon, and after a long and desperate battle, he pinned him to the ground with his lance. Then he called to the princess to give him her girdle, and he bound the dragon with it, and gave one end of it into her hand; and they walked back together to the city, the princess leading the dragon, who crawled after them like a dog. The people wondered to see St. George and the princess coming to the city, and when they perceived that the dragon was following them, they were dreadfully frightened; but St. George cried out, "Fear nothing, only believe in the God, through whose power I have conquered this monster, and be baptized, and I will destroy him before your eyes." Then St. George explained to them the Christian faith, and the king and all his people, to the number of 20,000, believed and were baptized, after which St. George killed the dragon and cut off his head. It is impossible to say how very grateful the king and all his subjects were to St. George, and the king wished to give him great treasures of gold and silver, but St. George would have none of them for himself, for he knew that it was not by his own courage or his own strength that he had conquered the dragon, and the only reward he desired was the love of Jesus and the treasures of faith laid up for him in the kingdom of heaven. So he thanked the king, and told him to give all the gold and silver to the poor, and then he bade him farewell, and continued his journey to the emperor's army.

The date of St. George's martyrdom, like all other details concerning him, is very uncertain; but some have supposed that it took place A.D. 303. The Church celebrates his feast on the 23rd April.

CHAPTER XXXIII
ST. JUSTUS AND ST. PASTOR

IT seems only natural that brave soldiers like St. George, St. Sebastian, and St. Maurice should not be afraid to die, and we are inclined to say that it is only what we should expect from them; but when we see that two little boys are just as brave, and act in the same heroic way, we must acknowledge that their supernatural courage was the fruit of God's grace in them, and we may well praise God in the words of the Psalm: "Out of the mouth of babes and sucklings Thou hast perfected praise."

These two little boys, Justus and Pastor, were Spaniards, and lived in a town called Complutum, now Alcala de Henares. Their parents, who were persons of rank, were Christians, and brought them up very carefully in the Christian faith. They were also taught all the things that children of their age generally learn, and for this purpose went every day to school.

The Roman governor of Spain at that time was called Dacian. He was a very cruel man, and hated the Christians; and when the emperor ordered them to be persecuted, he went about from town to town seeking them out, and torturing most cruelly everyone who would not sacrifice to the heathen gods. He came at length to Alcala de Henares, and immediately after his arrival he issued a proclamation commanding every one, under pain of death, to offer sacrifice to the gods who were the protectors of the Rome empire.

This proclamation caused a great stir in the town. The pagans, who had long been fretted to see the number of Christians constantly increasing, and their own temples deserted, were greatly rejoiced; while the Christians were terrified, and made preparations for leaving the town, or hiding themselves in some way or other. Justus was now seven, and Pastor was nine years of age. They were both at school, when a person came running in and told the news to the master. Most of the boys were so busy trying to finish their lessons quickly, in order to get out the sooner to play, that they took no notice of what the man said. But it was not so with Justus and Pastor. As soon as they heard about the governor's proclamation, a supernatural love and courage sprung up within them, and they were seized with such a wonderful desire to die for Jesus, that throwing down their books, they rushed out of school, and, running up to the tribunal of the wicked Dacian, they cried out that they were Christians, and that he must put them to death, because they would not sacrifice to the gods. At first Dacian would not listen to what they were saying. He thought they were foolish little children who were talking nonsense, and he ordered them to hold their tongues and not interrupt him, for he was very busy. But they would not be silent; they insisted on being heard; and they continued to speak so boldly that at last Dacian was obliged to attend to them. When he came to inquire who they were, and how they happened to have come to his tribunal, he was very much surprised. He could not understand how these two little boys, who had not been sought for, or brought up by any one, and had not been enticed by any promises or persuasion, could come freely of their own accord, and offer resolutely to die for Christ. If he had not himself seen it, he could not have believed it. He persuaded himself, however, that it was some childish fancy which had got into their heads; and he, therefore, ordered them to be privately whipped, being convinced that this would soon bring them to their senses.

So the two little brothers were led away, like innocent lambs, to be whipped. It was beautiful to see how, as they went along, they encouraged each other to bear every kind of torment for the love of Jesus. As Justus was the younger of the two, he thought that perhaps his brother would think that such a little fellow as he was could not have courage to bear the tortures, so he said to him:- "I hope, dear Pastor, you are not afraid of dying, or of the pain of being whipped, or of that sharp sword, with which they may perhaps cut off our heads. I am not the least afraid of them." "I am not afraid for myself," answered Pastor, "because I am getting on to be a big boy; but I am afraid for you, dear Justus. You know, brother, you are such a little fellow." "Don't trouble yourself about me, brother," replied Justus, "for though I am such a little boy, yet, by the grace of God, I shall be as strong as the biggest." "Are you quite sure, Justus?" rejoined Pastor. "Yes, quite sure," answered little Justus. "Though we are such little fellows, God, you see, has done us the honor to call us to die for Him, and do you think he will refuse to give us strength to bear our martyrdom?" "Dear Justus," cried Pastor, "I am so happy to hear you speak so bravely, for I think God must have given you His grace to do so. So now I am not at all afraid for you; and it will be quite easy for me to die with you, so that we may go together to live with our dearest Lord Jesus." "God will be sure to carry us through, even though we are such weak little things," replied Justus; "and He will take us quickly to that happy paradise which mamma and papa have so often told us about, where we shall be with His angels and saints, and shall see our kind, good Lord Jesus in glory." "Think, too, Justus," rejoined Pastor, "what a happiness it will be to shed our blood for that dear Jesus, who shed His precious Blood for us. Oh! how I hope we may deserve to see Him in heaven, and to be with Him for ever and ever."

In this way these dear children talked to each other, as they went along, showing clearly that it was the grace of God that spoke in them. The officers who heard what they said were amazed; and wondered how little children could be so ready to die; and they thought there must be something more than common about them. So they went to Dacian, and told him what they had seen and heard, and begged him to think once more what was to be done with these children. But though the cruel tyrant also was very much amazed at the courage of these two little children, he was too selfish and hard-hearted to be touched even by their angelic virtue. He thought only what a disgrace it would be to himself, a great and powerful man, if he were overcome by two little boys, and he was afraid that their heroic example might encourage other people to suffer martyrdom. So he ordered that they should be secretly beheaded in a place where none of the people should see them. The dear little boys were accordingly led out into a field, where they were beheaded upon a great stone; and, as if to show that even a hard stone was less hard than the heart of the cruel tyrant, there remains to the present day on this stone the mark of the knees of these innocent and holy little brothers. The Christians of Alcala de Henares took up their precious relics, and buried them, with great reverence on the spot which they had sanctified by their glorious death.

St. Justus and St. Pastor were martyred A.D. 304. There is a very beautiful and ancient hymn in the Breviary of Toledo, which was written in their honor, and which has preserved all the details of their martyrdom.

CHAPTER XXXIV

ST. AGNES

THERE lived in Rome, at this time, a young girl called Agnes. Her parents were rich and noble, and she was educated carefully in the way suited to her high birth. She was very beautiful, and so meek and lamb-like that everyone said she was rightly named Agnes. But, from the time she was quite a child, there was but one thing which she cared for, or thought of. Her heart was so filled with the love of Jesus, that it was her whole happiness to meditate on the mysteries of His life. Her only pleasure was to think about His sufferings, and the only thing she wished for was, to give her whole self entirely to Him. She loved Him so much, and thought so constantly about Him, that she seemed to be always living in His sacred wounds; and Jesus, in return, chose her for His spouse, and moved her, when she was still a child, to consecrate herself to love and serve Him as a virgin. In this way she passed a pure and innocent childhood, though few persons guessed what a bright and heavenly love burnt secretly in her breast.

 The devil hates everything that God loves; and so he hated this holy little girl, and resolved to do his best to rob her of the pure and holy thoughts which filled her heart. It happened one day that a young nobleman, son of Symphronius, governor of Rome, caught sight of Agnes; and, as she was remarkably beautiful, he fell desperately in love with her, and could think of nothing else day or night. He inquired who she was; and, finding that she was nobly born, and his equal in rank, he went to her parents, and asked them to let him marry her. Agnes was now only twelve years old, and her parents thought she was too young to marry; and so they did not encourage the young man's proposal. He was, however, so much in love that he would not easily give up the marriage; and he, therefore, determined to speak to Agnes herself, hoping that she would think better of his proposal than her parents had done. He constantly watched for her in the street, till at last one day he saw her pass; and then, going up to her, he told her how much he loved her, and he begged her to accept some beautiful jewels which he offered her. Long before this, Agnes had vowed herself to be the chaste spouse of Jesus Christ; and though she was so young and simple, yet when she heard a man speak to her of love, and ask her to marry him, she started back as if she had trod on a serpent, and she cried out, "Away from me! Leave me, and do not tempt me to be unfaithful to my dearest Spouse, whom I love so much that I live only in His love. Do not be so foolish as to think of being His rival, for He has six qualities of such perfection, that no one can be compared to him. He is noble, beautiful, wise, rich, good, and powerful. His birth is most noble, for His Father is God, and His mother is a pure virgin. He is so beautiful, that the sun and moon and stars look dark beside His brightness. He is so wise, and has made me love Him so much, that it is my greatest delight to speak of His excellence. He is so rich, that He has given me a treasure worth more than the whole Roman empire. But what shall I say to His goodness, which is so immense, that He has sealed it with His blood; while He is so powerful, that nothing in heaven or earth can withstand Him, for His touch heals the sick and raises the dead. He has chosen me for His spouse, He has given me rich clothes, and the most precious jewels, and He has pledged His word to me never to leave me. So I am His alone, and I love Him more than my own life and soul, and would be happy to die for His sake. Can you think, then, that anything could ever persuade me to marry you and be untrue to Him?"

The young man could not understand who it was that St. Agnes was speaking about in this rapturous way. He fancied it must be some man with whom she was in love, and he became so jealous, that he fell dangerously ill. When his father knew what was the cause of his illness, he sent for Agnes, and tried in every way to persuade her to marry his son; but she remained quite unmoved, and said she would rather die than be unfaithful to her first husband. Symphronius was then at some pains to find out who this husband could be; and at last someone told him that Agnes was a Christian, that she had been brought up from her cradle in sorcery, and that being a witch, she had espoused herself to Christ. Symphronius was very glad to hear this, for he knew that as she was nobly born, he could not accuse her of any other crime, and he hoped that by proceeding against her as a Christian, he should be able to force her to marry his son. He therefore had her seized and brought before his judgment-seat, when he did everything he could to bring about his wicked design; but her heart was so strengthened with the grace of God, that he had not the least success.

Among the idols which the Romans worshiped, there was one which they had called the goddess Vesta, and some of the Roman women used to make vows of perpetual virginity to her. When Symphronius saw that Agnes was determined not to marry, he thought to catch her in a very cunning trap which he laid for her, and he said to her: "Agnes, you must either marry, or if you wish to remain a virgin, you must offer up your virginity to the goddess Vesta, and serve her all your life as many Roman virgins do. If you do not do this, I will treat you as you deserve, and will send you to a house where there will be none but wicked men, who will insult you and ill-treat you just as they like."

But Agnes answered: "Do not be angry with me, my Lord, but the whole world shall not separate me from my Spouse. If for love of Him I refuse your son, who is a noble young man, how much more shall I despise the false gods who have neither life nor feeling. As to the insults you threaten me with, I am not afraid of them, for I have an angel always with me, and he guards and defends me; besides, my Lord Jesus himself, whom you have not the happiness to know, surrounds me on every side like a strong impenetrable wall."

The wicked judge was so enraged to hear Agnes defy him by these bold words, that he ordered her to be stripped naked, and to be led through all the public streets to the house which he had spoken of, while a crier went before her and proclaimed, with a loud voice:- "This is Agnes, a witch and enchantress, who is condemned by the governor for blaspheming the gods, and all men may insult her and ill-treat her in whatever way they like." This was a punishment very often inflicted on Christian women, and they feared it more than death itself, for they would rather be thrown among lions than among wicked men. But the Lord Jesus is so strong, that there is no hope for those who fight against Him. He came now to the assistance of Agnes, and made it appear plainly how much He prized her purity and chastity.

As they were stripping off her clothes, our Lord spread out her hair, and stretched it out in such a way, that it covered her completely, so that, while she passed through the streets, no part of her body could be seen to be naked.

And when she arrived at that dreadful house, which wicked people made their resort, she saw an angel standing ready to defend her, and there lay before her a beautiful robe whiter than snow, which she put on, while the room in which she was shone with a splendid heavenly light, such as no eye of man could bear to look at. Agnes was so transported with love and gratitude to her dearest Lord, who took such tender care of her, that she fell on her knees and thanked Him for His wonderful goodness to her. While she was praying, several wicked young men, one after another, came into the room where she was; but they were so struck with what they saw, that they did not dare to touch her. The heavenly light, the shining white robe, and the beauty of that spotless soul which they faintly portrayed, had a supernatural power which these sinners could not resist; and though they came in, stained and soiled with the most wicked thoughts, they went out chaste and sanctified.

At last came the governor's son, who had been the first cause of all this wickedness. He saw the other young men go in and come out quite changed, but he only laughed at them, for being such fools and cowards as to be afraid of a young girl. He went in with a bolder spirit of sin, and though he saw the same as the others had done, he hardened his heart and went up rudely and violently to Agnes. But just as he raised his hand to touch her, the angel who guarded her, struck him, and he fell dead at her feet. His companions who were waiting at the door, expecting him to come out as they had done, were surprised that he stayed so long; they waited on, but still he did not come; and at last, after waiting a very long time, they went into the room to see why he lingered. There they saw him dead on the floor, and Agnes on her knees looking pure and heavenly as an angel. They raised a great outcry, and it was quickly spread through the whole city, that Agnes, the Christian and the sorceress, had killed the governor's son by her enchantments. The dreadful news soon reached the ears of his unhappy father, who rushed like a madman to the place, and on seeing the dead body of his son, tore his hair, and made loud and pitiful lamentations. His grief was mixed with rage against Agnes, and turning in a fury to her, he cried out:- "Oh! thou witch, thou sorceress, thou infernal monster, born for my misery, why have you killed my son?" But Agnes answered: "It was not I who killed your son it was his own rashness and wickedness. Others came in here before him, and went out unharmed; for seeing this room full of brightness, they understand that the great King of Heaven guarded me, and defended my virginity, which I had consecrated to Him. But your son would not reverence my God who is here present, so the angel who is my guardian killed him miserably, as you see." These words calmed Symphronius a little, and he spoke more gently to her: "I entreat you, then, to restore my son to life again, so that all the world may know that you did not kill him by magic." And Agnes replied: "Your blindness and unbelief do not deserve that God should raise your son from the dead. But I will beg this favor of Him, in order that His glory may be made manifest, and that all the city of Rome may know, how happy are those who serve Him. Go then out of the room, and I will pray to God for your son." Everyone went out as she bade them, and when Agnes was alone, the threw herself on the ground, and with tears besought the Lord Jesus to restore the young man to life. Then an angel appeared to her, and comforted her, and told her that her prayer was granted. At the same moment the young man rose up, and going out among the people, cried out: "There is no God in heaven, or in the sea, or in the depths below, but only He who is almighty, whom the Christians adore. To him alone all honor is due. He only is to be adored. For the idols are devils who delude us in order to carry us with them into hell."

The news of the young man's being raised from the dead ran through the city even more quickly than that of his death had done. Everyone was talking of the miracle, and of what he said about the Christian religion being the only true one. This did not suit the purpose of the heathen priests, and of those who were zealous for the pagan idolatry; so they gathered together a mob of low and ignorant people, who made a disturbance, crying out:- "Death to the sorceress! Death to the sacrilegious and infamous witch who blinds the minds of men by her enchantments." The governor was very sorry to hear the clamors of this mob, for he was touched by the miracle which had been wrought on his son, and was inclined to repent of his former wickedness and to set Agnes free. He tried to calm the people, but all in vain; the more he spoke to them, the more violent they grew. He was very much troubled, and could not make up his mind what to do; for, on the one hand, he was afraid to disoblige the people, who would accuse him to the emperor of favoring the Christians, and on the other, he was afraid to offend the only true God, who loved and guarded Agnes. After hesitating a long time, he ended, as many other cowardly people have done, by doing wrong, but in such a way as he hoped would keep himself out of danger; for he determined to please the people by allowing Agnes to be put to death, and he fancied that he would keep clear of the anger of God by not doing this wickedness himself, but leaving it to be done by his lieutenant Aspasius. So he went away, and told Aspasius to do to Agnes whatever he thought best.

Aspasius commanded Agnes to be brought before him, and a great fire to be lighted in order to burn her alive. The fire was made, and it blazed so fiercely that it caught several of the pagans who stood near, and burnt them to ashes. But no sooner did Agnes enter it, than the flames divided on each side of her, and she remained in the middle of it without a hair of her head being singed, or any part of her body being scorched. The sight of this miracle only incensed the people the more against her, and they shouted out more wildly than before that she must be killed. But Agnes raised her voice in praise and thanksgiving to her Spouse, who had now saved her from this fire and these flames, in the same way as He had before saved her from the fire of impurity and the flames of hell; and she said to Him, "Lord, blessed be Thy holy name, since I now see what I desired, I enjoy what I hope for, and possess what I loved. Let my heart, my tongue, and my soul praise and magnify Thee. I desire fervently to come to Thee, true and eternal God, Who reignest with thy only Son, Jesus Christ, world without end." As she finished this prayer the fire, which a short time before had been burning so brightly, was quite extinguished, and the fuel suddenly became cold and black, as if it had never been lighted.

Still the people shouted furiously, and Aspasius became frightened at the uproar. He therefore ordered that Agnes should be thrust through the throat with a sword. The executioner, a hard man, accustomed to shed blood, coolly prepared to obey; but just when he was about to strike her, a sudden fear seized him, he turned pale and trembled, and durst not give the blow. But the holy virgin stood calm and undismayed, and thrilling only with impatient desire to behold the face of Him whom she loved and adored, reproved him for hesitating, saying, "What are you doing? Why do you wait? Who holds your hand? Make haste and kill this body, in order that my soul may live forever in the presence of God. O Lord who hast made choice of me for Thy Spouse, and whom alone I desire to please, vouchsafe to take me to Thine arms." While thus she prayed, the executioner recovered his courage and pierced her throat; and there flowed from the wound such a quantity of blood that it covered her whole body, and falling down she expired; while, at the same instant, her chaste and spotless soul was received into the loving arms of Jesus, and found its eternal home and rest in the secret and unfathomable depths of His sacred Heart.

The rage and hatred of the pagans were not appeased even by St. Agnes' death; for when the Christians went to pray at her grave, they attacked them, and wounded and killed several of them. Amongst those who were killed was St. Emerentiana, foster-sister of St. Agnes, who was still a catechumen, and had not yet been baptized. She reproved the crowd for their impiety, and they fell on her and stoned her to death; so that she was baptized, not in water, but in her own blood. Her body was laid close to that of St. Agnes, and the Church keeps her feast on the 23rd January, which was the day of her martyrdom, two days after that of St. Agnes, which took place and is celebrated on the 21st January.

The parents of St. Agnes clung so fondly to the memory of their pure and holy daughter that they remained night and day praying at her tomb. At length, on the eighth night after her martyrdom, they saw a great many virgins clothed in shining robes and crowned with garlands of pearls and precious stones, and in the midst of them stood St. Agnes, very bright and glorious, and by her side a Lamb more white than the driven snow. Then turning to her parents, she said: "Dear father and mother, mourn not for me as if I were dead. But rather rejoice with me that I have obtained in heaven the crown of glory with this holy company, and am happily come to Jesus, whom I loved on earth with all my heart and soul." Having said this, she disappeared with a choir of virgins who accompanied her. This vision soon became known all through Rome, and a particular feast in honor of it is celebrated by the Church on the 28th January.

St. Agnes is generally supposed to have been martyred A.D. 304 or 305.

CHAPTER XXXV

ST. DOROTHEA

ANOTHER virgin, who suffered martyrdom in the reign of Diocletian and Maximian, was St. Dorothea. She was born in Caesarea in Cappadocia, and was well known to everyone in the city on account of her great virtue; though it was known only to a few that she had consecrated herself, by a vow of virginity, to be the chaste spouse of Jesus, to whose service she devoted herself, passing her whole time in prayer and works of charity, and keeping herself ever in His presence by sweet and holy recollection.

There happened to come to Caesarea a governor, called Apricius, who was a great enemy of the Christians, and was very active in carrying into execution the laws which the emperor had made against them. He heard that Dorothea was a Christian, and though she was well-born, and had friends among the principal persons in the city, he had her seized and brought before him. After inquiring into her name and rank, he told her that he had sent for her to sacrifice to the gods, as the emperor had ordered everyone to do. St. Dorothea stood with her eyes cast down, as a timid young girl would naturally do, so Apricius thought she would not have the courage to disobey him; but her heart was raised up to God, and when she was called on, she was able to speak and act as bravely as the boldest man. When she heard what Apricius wanted her to do, she was not the least frightened, but looking up calmly, she said in a firm voice, "The true God and Emperor of Heaven has commanded me to serve Him alone, and to acknowledge Him for the only God. Whom then, Apricius, do you think that we ought to obey? The Emperor of Heaven or the emperor of the earth? God or man?" "Have done with such foolish talk," replied Apricius, "and get ready instantly to obey me and sacrifice to the gods, else it will cost you dear, for I shall make an example of you." "The example that I will give," rejoined Dorothea, "will be to teach every one not to fear man, but God. For all the torments you can inflict on me are temporal, and will soon be over, but those which God inflicts in hell are eternal, and without end." Dorothea's words provoked Apricius, and he ordered her to be placed on the rack, which was stretched out so that every sinew in her body was strained, and every limb put out of joint. But though the pain of this cruel torture was very great, yet Dorothea bore it with such fortitude that she seemed scarcely to feel it; and while she was hanging on this cruel machine, she said to Apricius in an undaunted tone: "Why do you give me such a slight torture? What are you waiting for? Dispatch quickly what you have to do, that I may the sooner see Him, for love of whom I even long for your torments. He is my Spouse, and He invites me to His paradise, which is a garden of pleasure, where the fruit is always delicious and beautiful, where lilies, roses, and all sorts of flowers are always in bloom, where the fountains of living water never dry up, and where the souls of the Saints rejoice in Jesus." "You had better give up all this nonsense," cried Apricius, "and sacrifice to the gods, and take a husband and live a quiet life like other people." Dorothea answered: "I will not sacrifice to devils, because I am a Christian and I will not take a husband, because I

St. Dorothea

am espoused to Jesus Christ."

Apricius saw that he gained nothing by torturing Dorothea, and he, therefore, determined to try what he could do by gentle means. So he sent for two sisters, Christina and Callista, who had formerly been Christians, but who had given up their religion; and he told them to take Dorothea home with them, and to talk to her, and persuade her to follow their example. They very willingly undertook the task, because they thought that their own sin in denying Jesus, would appear less if a holy virgin, like Dorothea, could be persuaded to do so too. They, therefore, took her to their house and treated her very kindly: they told her that they had once felt as she now did, and had resolved to suffer and die rather than deny their religion; but that they had afterwards thought better of it, and since they had given up the Christian religion, they had been very happy, and had often wondered they could ever have been so foolish as to think of dying for it. Then they pointed out to her how much they had gained by giving up their former stiff and queer notions, and they advised her to do the same: it might, to be sure, cost her a little at first, and perhaps for a short time after, her conscience would seem to tell her that she had done wrong; but they assured her she would soon get over that, and then she would be happy again, and would be very glad, as they now were, that she had not sacrificed her life for nothing at all. Dorothea listened patiently to all they said, and she answered them very gently but firmly, arguing with them, and telling them that they had really been very foolish in doing what they thought to be so wise, pointing out how much better it would have been for them to have died for Jesus, instead of living as they now were, servants of the devil, for whom the fires of hell were being prepared.

The end of all their conversations was, that the two

sisters, instead of persuading Dorothea to follow their example, were persuaded by her to repent of their sin in denying their religion, and to ask pardon for it with tears of true sorrow and contrition, so that now their only wish was to suffer the greatest torments for the love of Jesus, in hopes of making reparation to Him for the great sin they had formerly committed in denying Him.

After a few days Apricius sent for Dorothea and the two sisters, and taking the latter aside, asked them whether Dorothea had changed her mind. But they answered, "My Lord, she continues quite firm in her faith, and what is more, she has drawn us to her side, so that we have made up our minds to suffer all the torments you can inflict on us, hoping to wash away our former sin with our blood." Apricius was almost out of his senses with surprise and rage. In the first impulse of his fury he ordered the two sisters to be tied back to back, and thrown into the fire. While this was being done they cried aloud, "O Lord Jesus, Savior of the world! receive our penance and pardon us." While all this was going on, Dorothea stood by, filled with joy and thankfulness to think that though she was the cause of their bodies being burned, she had been the means of rescuing their souls from the fires of hell. And while the flames were rising on all sides around them, and their bodies were becoming blistered and black, she continued to encourage and comfort them, saying, "Go before me to heaven, my sisters. Be assured that God has pardoned you, and that by this martyrdom you have recovered what you have lost; for the Eternal Father will come to meet you and receive you into his bosom, and He will open to you the arms of His infinite mercy."

After Christina and Callista were burnt to death, Apricius turned his rage against Dorothea. He ordered her to be stripped and placed again upon the rack. But while

St. Dorothea 299

her limbs one after the other were being pulled out of joint, she was quite joyful and happy, as if she had got all that she wished for, so that Apricius wondered, and said to her: "What do you mean by this false show of joy? Why do you pretend to be so happy?" But Dorothea answered: "I never felt so happy in my whole life as I do now, both on account of those two souls which are restored to God, and of the hopes I myself have of enjoying Him in their company. So make haste, Apricius, and do not keep me long waiting." The cruel Apricius, on hearing her speak thus, bade the executioners put lighted torches to her naked sides, so that great holes were burned through her skin and flesh, even to her very inside. Then she was taken off the rack, and her beautiful face was buffeted by these ruffians, who could not bear her meek and gentle looks, which seemed to be a reproach to their own savage tempers. But the more they increased her pains, the more her joy increased, for the Spirit of God cheered her and dwelt more abundantly in her. At last, the executioners being tired out, Apricius condemned her to be beheaded, and on hearing this sentence she said: "I praise Thee, my Lord, chaste Lover of souls, because Thou hast called me to the marriage of the spotless Lamb and invited me to Thy heavenly banquet." While she was being led to execution, Theophilus, a lawyer, came up to her, and began to make sport of her; and having her say that in the paradise of Christ, her Spouse, there was delicious fruit in all seasons, and roses that never faded, he said to her in a joke: "Listen to me, you spouse of Christ. Pray do me one favor, and send me from your Spouse's garden some of the fine fruits und beautiful flowers which you have told us about." Dorothea answered gravely and confidently: "I will do so; I will not fail to do it." Then she knelt down to pray; and when she had finished her prayer, and was still on her knees waiting for the blow of the executioner's sword, there stood beside her an angel in the form of a little child, and he had in his hand a basket containing three fine apples and three most beautiful roses. And Dorothea said to him, "Go to Theophilus, and tell him that Dorothea has kept her promise, and has sent him these from the garden of her Spouse, Jesus Christ." Then she bowed her head, and receiving the blow of the sword, her soul was carried up by the angels to paradise, where she gazed and will forever gaze on the sweet and beautiful face of our Lord Jesus, to whose love she had devoted herself on earth.

Meanwhile Theophilus returned to his happy companions, and was telling them what he had said to the martyr, laughing and joking about the apples and roses she had promised him, for it was the 6th of February, and there was a severe frost, and neither roses nor lilies were in blow. But while he was still speaking, there came in a beautiful little child, who, going up to him, offered him the basket of apples and roses, and said to him: "Dorothea sends you these, according to her promise, from the garden of her Spouse, Jesus Christ." It was wonderful to behold the sudden change which came over Theophilus when he heard these words, and received the heavenly gift. He turned deadly pale, and for a moment he looked stupid and bewildered, as if he were going out of his mind; but the power of divine love, penetrating his soul, changed him into another man, and quickly recovering himself, he cried out, "Jesus Christ is the only true God." His companions thought he was mad, for he had always been an enemy to the Christians and had taken great pains to persecute them; and it was sometime before they could believe the sudden change had come over him. They talked to him, they questioned him, they argued with him, trying to prove either at he spoke in jest or was suddenly gone mad.

But they at last found that he was in his right mind, and spoke in sober seriousness, being resolute in confessing Christ to be God and in deriding the false gods of the pagans. When Apricius could no longer doubt of the wonderful change which had come over him, he ordered him to be placed on the rack and cruelly tortured; but the tortures only filled his heart with joy, and he cried out triumphantly, "Now I am a Christian, indeed, hanging as it were upon a cross." As the streams of blood poured down from his wounds Apricius said to him, "Unhappy man that you are, have you no pity on your body?" But Theophilus answered, "Unhappy you, take pity on your soul; for I will not spare my body now in hopes that God may pardon my soul eternally." Apricius bade them tear his sides with hooks of steel, and then burn them with lighted torches; but all the tortures they inflicted on him, did not in the least diminish his courage or his joy. At last Apricius ordered them to behead him, and on hearing the sentence the martyr answered, "I give Thee thanks, my Lord Jesus Christ, for this favor." So he finished his martyrdom, being baptized in his own blood. Thus did St. Dorothea, Theophilus, and the two sisters, Christina and Callista, all pass into the presence of God on the same day, which was the 6th of February, on which day the Church keeps the feast of St. Dorothea.

CHAPTER XXXVI

ST. BONIFACE

IT has been formerly said that the martyrs who suffered in this persecution were taken out of every rank and class of society. We have now heard of brave soldiers, little boys, and holy virgins, who died for the love of Jesus. The next story shall be about a great sinner, a man who spent many years of his life in sin, but who was afterwards converted, and was permitted to have the honor of being a martyr for Jesus' sake.

There lived at Rome at this time a noble lady called Agläe. She was very beautiful and very rich, and was connected with all the principal families in the city. But she made a bad return to God for all the gifts He had bestowed on her; for she fell into sin, and lived such a wicked life that she was quite a scandal to all who knew her. She had a servant, called Boniface, who acted as her steward and managed her estates; and as he was a very clever and sensible person she thought very highly of him, and at last became so fond of him that she lived with him, without being married to him. This conduct was the more wicked in Boniface and Agläe, because they were Christians, and knew what was right and wrong; and it was a great grief to all Agläe's relations that she should disgrace herself in such a way. Still, in the midst of their wickedness, they had one good quality, which was charity to the poor. They gave a great many alms, and did all they could to comfort and relieve people who were in distress; and these good works inclined our Lord to have mercy on them, and not to let them die in the miserable state of sin in which they were living.

It came to pass that after Boniface and Agläe had lived in sin for many years, our Lord touched their hearts and brought them to repentance. Then they wept for the wickedness of their past lives, and resolved to amend; but as they knew how grievously they had offended Almighty God, they wished to find some intercessors, through whose merits and prayers they might obtain mercy and pardon. So they determined to get the bodies of some holy martyrs, and to pay them great honor and reverence, hoping that in return these martyrs would pray for them in heaven, and obtain their pardon from our Savior Jesus Christ.

The Emperors Diocletian and Maximian had abdicated the empire a few years before, and had been succeeded by Galerius and Constantius Chlorus. Galerius was one of those who had persuaded Diocletian to persecute the Christians, and so, when he came to be emperor, the persecution raged as fiercely as ever in the East, which he governed. But Constantius Chlorus had married a Christian lady called St. Helena, and he was, therefore, very friendly to the Christians, who enjoyed peace and freedom from persecution in the West, which had fallen to his share. The consequence was, that as no Christians were now put to death in Italy, Boniface and Agläe could not get any relics of martyrs there. They therefore resolved to send to the East for them; and having heard that Simplician, the Governor of Cilicia, was a very cruel and covetous man, who put to death a great many Christians, and then sold their bodies for large sums of money, they agreed that it would be well for Boniface himself to go to Cilicia, where he was sure of getting what he wanted. Agläe made great preparations for his journey; she furnished him with horses and servants to accompany him; she gave him plenty of money to buy the bodies of martyrs; and she provided him with fine linen and spices, and perfumes of all kinds to embalm the precious relics which he should buy. When he was about to set out, he said to Agläe, as if in jest, "Madam, what will you say if, instead of my bringing you the bodies of other martyrs, my companions bring back mine to you? Will you look upon it as a relic?" "But Agläe reproved him, saying, "Boniface, this is not a time to jest; remember that we are not worthy to touch, or even to look upon the relics of holy martyrs. Take care, and behave yourself in such a way that you may deserve to obtain what I send you for."

Boniface set out from Rome with this pious purpose. As he journeyed along, the grace of God opened his eyes to see more and more the wickedness of his past life, and how unworthy he was even to touch the body of a martyr; and he gave himself to fasting and penance and alms deeds; praying our Lord to forgive his sins, and to do him the great favor of allowing him to die for His sake. At last they arrived at Tarsus, the capital of Cilicia, where Simplician was living. Boniface told his companions to look out for a lodging while he went to take a stroll through the town. His heart was burning with the love of martyrdom, and he turned his steps to the place where he was told that the Christians were put to the torture. Here he found twenty martyrs being tormented, some in one way and some in another, but all dreadfully torn and mangled. His heart was already with them, and he stood to gaze at them, wondering at their patience and fortitude. While he looked at them, a strange feeling came over him, and he became so inflamed with the love of God that he could not contain himself, so that running up to them he threw himself at their feet and began to kiss their wounds, and to bathe them with his tears, and to anoint his eyes with their blood. He also cried out with a loud voice, "Oh, blessed martyrs! oh, friends of God! stand firm and endure these torments courageously, for they cannot last long, and our Lord will reward you for them by giving you everlasting joy and consolation."

Boniface's strange behavior attracted the attention of Simplician, who ordered him to be seized, and began to question him as to who he was. He soon found out that he was a Christian, and he therefore condemned him to be tortured. They tore his body with iron hooks till his bones were laid bare, and they thrust sharp reeds into his hands and feet under his nails; and seeing that he made light of these sufferings and never ceased to thank God for them, they poured boiling lead into his mouth. Boniface prayed to our Lord to give him strength to bear whatever was done to him, and he begged the other twenty martyrs to pray for him, that by their intercession he might obtain what he himself was unworthy to ask, because he was so great a sinner. They joined their prayers with his, and our Lord gave him grace to bear all the tortures with such a serene and angelic countenance, that even the pagans who were present, cried out, "Shame!" on the tyrants. Many of them were so moved by the sight of his constancy, that they exclaimed, "Great is the God of the Christians; we all believe in Thee, oh, Lord Jesus Christ." And they threw down a small altar which had been erected for the Christians to offer sacrifice at, and they flung stones at Simplician, so that he had to fly in order to save his life.

All this, however, was no help to Boniface, for he was put into prison, and the next day Simplician had him thrown head foremost into a cauldron of boiling pitch. But our Lord delivered him as He had formerly done the blessed apostle St. John; for He sent an angel who preserved him from the boiling pitch, while the flames around the cauldron burnt several pagans who were lookers on. At last he was sentenced to be beheaded. Then he begged they would allow him a little time to pray. This favor being granted him, he knelt down and prayed, saying: "Lord Jesus look not on my former sins, but on the desire with which Thou hast inspired me to die for Thy dear name's sake. Be graciously pleased to reckon me among Thy happy and blessed martyrs, and vouchsafe to enlighten all the pagans here present and to deliver them from their blindness."

When he had finished this prayer his head was cut off, and his blessed soul rose up to heaven. His prayer for the pagans found such favor with God, that five hundred and fifty of them who were present at his martyrdom, were converted.

Meanwhile St. Boniface's companions began to wonder what had become of him. At first they had thought little of his absence, for, knowing what a wicked life he had formerly led, they fancied he had fallen into bad company and was amusing himself. But when the night passed on and he did not return, and morning came, and no Boniface appeared, they went out to look for him. After searching and enquiring in the neighborhood and hearing nothing of him, they happened to meet an officer of justice, whom they asked if he had seen a Roman stranger who had come to town the day before. "This very day," answered the officer, "the governor has put to death a Christian who seemed to be a stranger. Perhaps he is the person you are looking for." "No, no," replied they, "he whom we are looking for, is not one of that sort. We are more likely to find him in bad company than dying for Christ." But the officer went on to describe the stranger who had been martyred that day, and his description answered so exactly to Boniface's appearance, that they were tempted to go to the place of execution and see if indeed it could be he. There they saw the body of the martyr with his head cut off, and lo! it was none other than Boniface himself. At this unexpected sight they burst into tears, partly for grief at losing him, but still more for sorrow and shame that they should have had such evil thoughts of one, who was now a glorious martyr. And while they wept and asked his pardon, the saint, opening his eyes, looked sweetly and lovingly on them, as if to say that he forgave them. Their next thought was to do the business for which their mistress had sent them so far; and feeling sure that no other martyr's relics would be so precious to Agläe as those of Boniface, they bought his body for five hundred pieces of gold, and after embalming it they returned with it to Rome.

Agläe already knew by revelation all that had passed; for an angel had appeared to her and had told her to receive Boniface, not as her servant, but as her lord, for that he was now a martyr of Jesus Christ, who for his sake and by his intercession would do her many favors. When she was aware that his body was near Rome, she assembled many of the clergy and went out with great solemnity to meet it; and she built a church in his honor over the spot in which he was buried. After this she lived thirteen years, giving herself up entirely to prayer and fasting and penance; and after attaining to great perfection in holiness, she at last died in peace, and was buried near St. Boniface.

The martyrdom of St. Boniface is supposed to have taken place on the 14th May, A.D. 306, on which day the Church keeps his feast.

CHAPTER XXXVII

DEATH OF GALERIUS; CONVERSION OF CONSTANTINE

EIGHT long years had now passed away since Diocletian published the laws which were intended to root out the Christian religion, and it was more than twenty years since Maximian had begun to persecute the Christians. The persecution had been so severe, such numbers had been thrown into prison or put to death, and so many more had either renounced their faith, or had hid themselves in desert places, that very few Christians were to be seen in public. Then the pagan emperors flattered themselves that they had conquered the God of the Christians; and, in the pride of their hearts, they erected pillars with inscriptions on them, in honor of the great victory they had gained in overthrowing and rooting out the Christian religion, some of which pillars are still to be seen in Spain.[20]

But just when the triumph of the pagans seemed to be the greatest, God stretched out His almighty hand and made His power known. The Emperor Galerius, who, as has been before said, was the chief persecutor, was attacked[21] with a very horrible disease. The upper part of

---

[20] Baronius *in ann.* 304, 9.

[21] Lactantius, *De. Mort. Persec.* 33. Euseb. 1. 8, c. 16.

his body was so thin that it was only skin and bone, and looked like a skeleton, while the lower part was swollen and covered with ulcers, from which quantities of worms crept out, while the smell was so horrible that it was scarcely possible for anyone to come near him.

The best doctors were sent for from all parts of the empire, but they could do nothing for the wretched emperor. Great offerings were made to the heathen gods, but whatever their priests recommended only increased his sufferings. This continued for a whole year, and Galerius, who was almost mad with pain, caused several of the doctors to be put to death because they could not cure him. At last one of them, seeing that in any case he was likely to be killed, had the boldness to speak the truth to the emperor. He said to him: "My Lord, you deceive yourself if you think that men can remove what God sends you; this disease is not a natural one, and our medicines cannot touch it. Remember what you have done against the servants of God and against His holy religion, and you will at once see to whom you should apply for relief. You may kill me, as you have killed the other physicians; but mark my words, no human power will cure you." These bold words opened the eyes of the dying emperor. His conscience told him that the doctor was speaking the truth, and that his illness was a punishment from God for his persecution of the Christians: so, being struck with remorse, he cried out that he would rebuild the churches which he had destroyed, and would make reparation for the great sin which he had committed. He lost no time in acting up to his word, and he issued an edict (A.D. 311), in which he gave the Christians leave to profess their religion publicly, and to assemble for divine worship, asking them in return to pray for his restoration to health. Very soon after this he died.

This edict restored peace to the Church in all parts of the empire. It was so unexpected that it seemed like bright light shining after a long dark night, or like the resurrection of the dead. The Christian religion had seemed to be dead, but all of a sudden it started again into life; for though men may persecute and afflict the Church, they cannot kill it, because God dwells in it and gives it a supernatural life. The Christians who had been shut up in prisons or forced to work in mines, were now set free, and returned to their homes; so that the roads were covered with troops of these holy confessors, who sang psalms of joy and thankfulness as they walked along; while the bodies of most of them showed what they had undergone for the faith; some having lost one eye, some a leg or an arm, some being crippled, and others being scarred all over. The Christians who had fled and hid themselves during the persecution, now appeared again in public; those who had denied their faith, ran eagerly to confess their sins and ask for penance and absolution. The churches were reopened, and divine worship was celebrated just as if it had never been interrupted. This sudden revival of the Christian religion was, in fact, so wonderful, that even the pagans could not help being struck with it, and many of them exclaimed aloud, "The God of the Christians is the only great and true God."

The death-bed repentance of the Emperor Galerius was a great triumph to the Christians. But God was preparing for them a still greater and more lasting triumph; for the time was now close at hand when that great city of Rome, which had long been the chief seat of the devil's power, was to confess the faith of Christ, and to be acknowledged by all the world as the capital of Christ's kingdom. This great change was brought about by the conversion of the Emperor Constantine, which took place in the following manner, the year after the death of Galerius.

After the death of Diocletian, the empire continued to be governed by several emperors: at one time there were no less than six, and after Galerius' death there were still four: namely, Maxentius and Constantine in the West, and Licinius and Maximin Daïa in the East. Maxentius was the son of the cruel Emperor Maximian, and was quite as cruel, and even more wicked than his father. He reigned over Italy, and spent his time chiefly in Rome, the inhabitants of which hated him for his crimes, and were prevented only by his large army from rebelling against him, and putting him to death. Constantine was the son of Constantius Chlorus, who has been already mentioned as being very friendly to the Christians; and his mother was the great St. Helena, who several years after this time had the honor of finding the true Cross, and of discovering the holy sepulcher. Constantine was educated as a pagan, but as his mother was a Christian, and he was accustomed from his youth to associate with Christians, he was very friendly to their religion. He reigned over France and Spain, and was much respected as a wise and good prince.

It happened[22] about a year after Galerius' death that Maxentius quarreled with Constantine and made war against him. Constantine did everything he could to avoid going to war, because he knew that Maxentius' army was much larger than his own; but at last finding that it was impossible to keep peace any longer, he thought his wisest plan would be to march and attack Maxentius in Italy, instead of waiting to be himself attacked by him in France. He accordingly crossed the Alps, and marched into Italy with the best army he could muster; but though he

---

[22] Gibbon, c. 14.

collected all the troops he could, he had only 40,000 soldiers while Maxentius had 188,000.

Constantine felt very anxious about the issue of the war because he knew that Maxentius was a very cruel enemy, and if he should happen to be defeated, he would probably lose both his empire and his life. When people feel their own weakness, they are inclined to think a great deal about the justice of their cause, and to place their trust in God; and Constantine seems to have done so on this occasion; though when he came to hope that God would help him, he was puzzled to know what God to trust in, whether in Jupiter, the god of his pagan father, or in Jesus, the God of his Christian mother.

But Constantine was not the only one who was anxious, for Maxentius shared his anxiety. A strange feeling seemed to have taken possession of people's minds, that this was not a common war between two emperors, but that there was something supernatural about it, and that the powers of heaven and hell were interested in it. In Rome nothing was talked of but prophecies and superstition, signs and omens, which foretold some great misfortune to Maxentius, so that the tyrant trembled in spite of his fine army, for he thought that God was against him, and his conscience told him that he did not deserve God's favor. In Constantine's army,[23] too, there was a great talk about signs from heaven; for it was said that armed hosts had been seen in France, as if fighting in the sky; and wonderful tales were told of their gigantic limbs, the awful flashing of their arms, and the bright light which shone around them; and while men were gazing in fear at these heavenly combatants, they were heard to say: "We seek

---

[23] Gibbon, c. 20.

Conversion of Constantine

Constantine; we go to help Constantine."

The accounts of this vision which reached Constantine, cheered him a little, but still he continued to be very anxious. He was now at Saxa Rubra, within nine miles of Rome, and the next day a great battle which would decide his fate, was to be fought.[24] It was mid-day; the sun shone bright; his army was drawn out and passing in review before him, and he and his generals were looking carefully to see that the soldiers were well prepared for the next day's battle, when lo! a wonderful sight appeared in the sky; a shining cross of bright light was seen, and under it were written the words, "By this conquer." It was seen by Constantine, his officers, and the whole army, and so great was its splendor that the noon-day sun looked dark beside it. Most of those who saw it were struck with terror, for they were pagans, and what had they to hope from the cross, or what victory could they gain through it. Constantine also was troubled, and though he had long thought a great deal about the Christian religion, he could not make up his mind how to interpret this vision. That night he lay on his bed awake, for he was too anxious to sleep, and he could not get the vision of the cross out of his head; and while he was thinking and musing, our Lord Jesus came to him, and stood by him, and showing him a cross like that which had appeared in the sky, with the same words written under it, desired him to use it as his standard. Constantine did not now hesitate any longer, but, with the morning's dawn, he gave orders that the commands of our Lord should be obeyed. For above a thousand years the standard of Rome had been an eagle, and the Roman soldiers had always been in the habit of

---

[24] Euseb. *Vit. Constantin.* 1. 1.

worshiping it as their favorite god, and they had believed that it had led them to the conquest of the world. But now this proud pagan eagle was torn down and trampled underfoot, and in its place was raised the despised Cross of Christ, with the motto, "By this conquer."

The next day's battle proved the truth of the heavenly vision. Maxentius' army was entirely defeated; he himself was drowned in crossing the river Tiber; and Constantine entered Rome in triumph. In honor of his victory he erected a statue of himself with a cross in his hand. and an inscription declaring that he owed his victory to that saving sign; and his triumphal arch, which may still be seen at Rome, has an inscription to the same effect.

Constantine's victory over Maxentius had made him master of the western half of the Roman Empire, which included Italy, France, Spain, Portugal, Britain, a part of Germany, and the north of Africa. He now professed the Christian religion, which was gradually established in all these countries, so that from this time they may be said to have ceased to form a part of the kingdom of the devil, and to have become a part of that of Christ.

CHAPTER XXXVIII

MAXIMIN DAIA; ST. CATHERINE

BUT though Italy and France and Britain, and all the countries of the west had been conquered by the Church, the eastern division of the empire still continued under the dominion of Satan; for it was governed by Licinius and Maximin Daia, and they were pagans.

Licinius was at this time very well disposed to the Christians, and for many years he behaved kindly to them. But was not so with Maximin. When Galerius, on his death bed, had published the edict forbidding everyone to persecute the Christians, Maximin did not dare to go against his orders. But he obeyed him very reluctantly, because he hated the Christians, and had already persecuted them very cruelly; and in a very few months after, when Galerius was dead, he recommenced the persecution.

On this occasion Maximin[25] did what none of the former persecutors of the Church had ever dared to do. For he caused some writings to be forged which contained the most horrible blasphemies against our Lord, but which he pretended were the true account of our Lord's trial and condemnation by Pontius Pilate; and he sent those

---

[25] Euseb. 9. 5

blasphemous writings into all parts of his dominions, where he had them stuck up in the most public places, so that everyone must see them; and he ordered that they should be used as lesson-books in all the schools, and that the children should be obliged to learn them by heart. He did this because he hoped that in a few years, when people had been in the habit of hearing these blasphemies constantly repeated, they would begin to think that what everyone said must be true; and also, that when the children in the schools grew up to be men, they would believe what they had learned from their very childhood; just in the same way as Protestants now-a-days believe a great many false and foolish stories about Catholics, merely because everyone says so, or because they have been told so ever since they were children.

Maximin also gave orders that the Christians should be very cruelly treated. In some places he put great numbers of them to death; but in others, instead of having them killed, he had the eyes of some put out, and the hands, and feet, and noses, and ears of others cut off; and when he had crippled them in this way, he sent them to live in unhealthy mines underground, or he drove them out into desert places, where they led a miserable life, and were in constant danger of perishing from cold and hunger.

The most celebrated of the martyrs who suffered under Maximin, though at an earlier period of his reign, was St. Catherine. She was born in Alexandria, and her parents belonged to the imperial family. She was very beautiful, and so good and amiable, that everyone who knew her loved and admired her. She was also very clever, and though it was not the custom at that time for women to be highly educated, yet her parents had her taught much more than other women generally learned; and as she was very fond of study, and very eager to be always learning

St. Catherine

something new, she lost no opportunity of improving herself; and so, in course of time, she became so learned that very few men were more clever than she, or knew more than she did. Among other things, she learned all about the Christian religion; for, as it has been already said, since Christianity had spread so widely, it had become a sort of fashion for pagans to know something about it, and many people who did not care to become Christians, liked to talk about Christian doctrines; and as there was a famous Christian school at Alexandria, Catherine frequently fell in with good and learned Christians, and so, in the natural course of things, she came to know all about our Lord Jesus and the principal doctrines of the Church. But though she believed the Christian religion to be the only true one, and she even wished to love and serve our Lord, she was not baptized.

Though Catherine was too good and amiable to be conceited because she was more clever than other people, or to despise those who did not know so much as herself, yet there was another kind of pride into which she seemed to have fallen. The gift of reason is one of the noblest natural gifts which God has bestowed on man, and clever people who enjoy the largest share of this gift, find such pleasure in exercising it that they are apt to make too much of it, and to put it into the place which belongs to God alone. This was the case with Catherine. As she found that whenever she tried to learn anything she succeeded, and that whenever she did not understand any subject she had only to apply her mind to it in order to understand it more clearly, she naturally, and almost unconsciously, came to feel that there was nothing which it was beyond her power to understand if she only chose to study it, and so she got into the habit of refusing to believe anything until she could understand it, and of never consenting to do what appeared to her contrary to her reason. Though this habit was of great use to her in worldly matters, since it made her think before she acted, and thus prevented her doing many silly and foolish things, yet it was a terrible hindrance to her in the things of God, which are so high and incomprehensible that human reason cannot reach up to them. Our Lord, too, has said, that they are hid from the wise and prudent, and are revealed to little ones; which means that if a person thinks that he can learn them and understand them by dint of his own reason and cleverness, he will be sure to fail, whereas if he humbles himself like a little child, and receives in simple faith what God has revealed to the Catholic Church, and through the Church to us, God will bestow on him more and more of this heavenly wisdom. Now this was where Catherine went astray. We have said that though she believed all the Christian doctrines, and wished to love our Lord, yet she was not baptized. She knew that the Church ordered all believers to be baptized, and that she could not receive Holy Communion till she was baptized; but she would not obey the Church, because she could not understand how it was that the sacraments could confer grace, since they seemed to her to be no more than mere empty ceremonies, very good for ignorant people, but of no use to those who were better informed, and could worship God in the depth of their own hearts. And so instead of obeying our Lord, and doing as He had ordered His apostles to do, and as the Church has done ever since, she thought she would be a Christian in a more rational and simple way than by being baptized into the Catholic Church, and that she would go direct to our Lord and receive grace from Him, through her own prayers alone, instead of through the sacraments which He Himself has ordained to be the food and support of all His children. It was very wrong of Catherine thus to neglect the sacraments, but she was only a pagan, and perhaps nothing better could have been expected of her. However, as she was sincere in her belief, and really loved God, He had compassion on her, and taught her what was right in a wonderful and supernatural way.

One night when Catherine was in bed and asleep, she dreamt that our Blessed Lady appeared to her, holding in her arms the Infant Jesus, who looked more beautiful than words can tell, and was caressing His mother with such fond and winning tenderness, that Catherine was transported with love and admiration, and her whole soul seemed riveted on this heavenly sight. And as she gazed, our Lady came up to her, and took her very graciously by the hand, and offered her to her Divine Son; but the Holy Child gave her only one hurried glance, for as soon as His eyes rested on her, an expression of pain and disgust came over His sacred face, and turning quickly away from her and pushing her from Him, He cried out that He could not bear to look at her, because she was so ugly, since she had never been baptized. Catherine had been almost in an ecstasy of joy when our Lady took her hand and offered her to the Infant Jesus; and now when He pushed her away, and would have nothing to do with her, her heart seemed about to break with grief, and she burst into such a violent flood of tears that she awoke.

But though Catherine awoke she could not get the dream out of her head; and when she came to think quietly over it, she had no doubt that it was more than a common dream, and that our Lord had sent it to her to teach her, that notwithstanding all her natural goodness and amiability, and her belief in Jesus, and even her wish to love Him, she was not fit to see His face so long as she was not adorned with the supernatural gifts, which He bestows on His children in baptism. As soon as Catherine saw her fault she was very sorry for it, and lost no time in repairing it; but going immediately to a priest she had herself baptized, and before long our Lord showed her how pleased He was with her ready obedience.

A few nights after her baptism, when Catherine was asleep, our Lady again appeared to her, carrying in her arms the Infant Jesus. Catherine remembered her former disappointment, and feared to meet with another dreadful repulse. But still the Infant looked so beautiful and winning, and such sweet feelings of love and confidence gushed through her soul, that, in spite of her fears, she could not help running up to our Lady, and throwing herself at her feet, trembling with hope and joy. This time it needed only one word from our Lady to make the Divine Infant turn His eyes on Catherine; and as soon as He looked on her, He smiled most sweetly on her, and calling to the angels who stood around, He bade them look at this creature of His who was very beautiful in His eyes, and whom He loved very much, because she had done all she could to please Him. Then raising her up, He threw His arms lovingly round her, and pressed her to His sacred heart, and putting a ring on her finger, He said that He took her to be His spouse, and would love her to all eternity. Then Catherine fell into a heavenly ecstasy, and remained for some time in a state of rapture which no human tongue can describe. After this she awoke, and to her inexpressible joy she found, that though she had been asleep, all this was not a mere dream, but had really taken place, for lo on her finger was the ring with which our Lord had made her His spouse.

From this time Catherine lived as became the spouse of Christ. Placing herself under the patronage of our Blessed Lady, who had presented her to the Infant Jesus, she took a vow by which she bound herself never to marry any

St. Catherine

human being, but to devote herself, body and soul, in all her thoughts, words, and actions, to love and serve our Lord Jesus, and Him alone. She had never been fond of dress or care-free society, or of being praised and admired, nor was there any man whom she wished to marry, and so it was not by giving up these things that she could show her love to her heavenly Spouse. But there was one thing on earth to which she was very much attached, and which she had once preferred to Jesus, and this was the very thing she now resolved to give up out of love for Him. Her greatest enjoyment had been the exercise of her intellectual powers; she had loved to read and study, and to be ever learning more and more, and she had known no greater pleasure than that of talking with the philosophers of Alexandria, picking up fresh knowledge from them, or hearing them discuss deep questions of philosophy, or getting them to explain to her the reasons of things which she did not understand clearly. It was this love of philosophy which had led her to make an idol of her own reason, and to follow its dictates instead of obeying our Lord in His Church. It was, then, by giving up her love of argument and her philosophical studies that she could best please our Lord; and though it was hard to give up that in which there seemed to be nothing sinful, and which was a part of her very self, she joyfully resigned it all for love of Him. She avoided the society which she had formerly enjoyed; she gave away the books which had been such a source of pleasure to her; and she shut herself up in her own house, never going out except to church or on some work of charity. There, hidden from men and alone with God, she led a sweet and holy life, thinking of nothing but doing His will, and wishing for nothing except to love Him more and more.

The only book which she now cared to read was the

Sacred Heart of her beloved Spouse; and so she spent her whole time in meditation on the mysteries of His life, kneeling with our Lady and St. Joseph by His lowly crib in Bethlehem, or watching Him at His humble work in the little house of Nazareth, or joining the crowds who followed Him in His weary journeyings through the cities of Judea, or weeping with Him in the garden, or collecting His precious Blood at the foot of the cross, or kneeling with Magdalen at His feet on the resurrection morn, or prostrating herself with the seraphim before the throne of His glory. Thus she made for herself a home in the Sacred Heart of Jesus, and there she dwelt like the dove in a cleft of the rock, languishing with love of her Beloved, and refreshed and supported only by the living water which flowed from His wounded Side.

It was some time after Catherine had begun to lead this solitary life that the Emperor Maximin happened to come to Alexandria. As he found that there were a great many Christians in the city, he at once began a violent persecution by issuing an edict ordering everyone to sacrifice to the heathen gods, and threatening with death all who refused to do so. As soon as this edict was published, Alexandria was filled with people who flocked from the neighboring country to offer sacrifice; and though the greater part of them were pagans, yet there were found among them some Christians, who loved their lives more than they loved God, and who were, therefore, ready to do anything to please the emperor. The temples were crowded with worshiper; the blood of the victims flowed in streams from the altars; and Maximin and the heathen priests were overjoyed when they saw that, in spite of the great noise which had been made about the Christian religion, their master, the devil, had still so many faithful servants remaining.

But though the devil seemed to triumph, yet at the very moment when his servants were most proud and joyful, our Lord raised up a weak woman to confound him and them. When Catherine heard the shouts of the crowd who were singing and dancing before the heathen altars, and was told the cause of the uproar, her heart was pierced with sorrow at the thought of the insults which were offered to her dearest Lord, and with pity for the poor souls of the idolaters. She redoubled her devotions, and knelt night and day before her crucifix, offering her own heart to our Lord in reparation for the outrages done Him by the idolaters, and beseeching Him to have mercy on them, and to pardon them, as He had prayed to His Father to pardon those who crucified Him on Calvary. And one day as she knelt and prayed, our Lord told her that He accepted the offering of herself which she had made Him, and He bade her, in token of her love for Him, to go to the emperor and reprove him publicly for his wickedness. It was an unseemly thing for a young girl to go and reprove the emperor, and still more for the modest spouse of Christ to appear in the midst of a tumultuous crowd; but our Lord had bade Catherine go, and so she did not stop to consult her own judgment, but calling her attendants, she set out immediately for the temple where Maximin was presiding at the sacrifices.

As Catherine had of late been seldom abroad, her appearance in the crowd made a great sensation. Those who did not know her stared, with curiosity, and asked who was this beautiful and noble lady, who looked more like an angel than a woman; while those who did know her were even more surprised, since they thought she was come to sacrifices to the heathen gods, and they could scarcely believe it possible that one, whose love for Christ was the talk of the whole town, could be coming so quickly and so willingly to deny His Holy name. But Catherine was unconscious of the stir that she had created, for she could think of nothing but the work which the Holy Spirit had inspired her to undertake. She did not look to the right or to the left; she did not notice the loud whispers of the crowd which opened to let her pass; but she walked straight forward, with her eyes bent on the ground, and a look of holy recollection, till she reached the place where the emperor stood. When she came up to him she saluted him very respectfully, and then addressing him in a firm but modest tone, she said: "Maximin, God has sent me to reprove you for your great wickedness in worshiping dumb idols, and leading astray the people whom He has appointed you to govern. I exhort you, therefore, in His Holy name, to repent of your sin, and to humble yourself before this One only true God, who created you, to whom alone you owe your empire, and who, though he was God, made Himself man for the love of us, and died upon a cross to deliver us from the death which we had deserved by our sins."

Maximin was troubled by Catherine's words, for his conscience told him that she was speaking the truth, and for a few minutes he was confused, not knowing what to do or say. But at last there came into his head the proud thought that he was a Roman Emperor, and that it was beneath his dignity to care for the words of a weak, young girl; and so, plucking up his courage, he turned to her with as careless an air as he could assume, and bade her wait till he had finished his sacrifice, for he would not be disturbed and could not listen to her just now. Catherine, accordingly, went to the palace, and waited there till the emperor should return home.

When Maximin returned to the palace he sent for Catherine; and, when she came into his presence, he said to her: "Tell us now who you are, and what it was you were talking about this morning?" Catherine answered: "My family is well known in this city; my name is Catherine; and I have spent my time chiefly in studying philosophy. But the only thing I think worth knowing, is the knowledge of the One, true God; and the only thing I glory in, is that I am a Christian, and that I have the Lord Jesus Christ, true God and true Man, for my Spouse." Then she went on to give an account of her faith, and of her reasons for believing the Christian religion to be the only true one; and she spoke with such power and. eloquence, and, at the same time, in such a modest, gentle manner, that Maximin was quite astonished at her wisdom, and charmed with her grace and beauty. He did not know what to say in answer to her arguments; but, instead of looking on this as a proof that what she said was true, he hardened his heart, and persuaded himself that the reason he could not answer her, was because he was not so learned as she was, and had not studied philosophy as she had. So he said that he would send to all parts of the empire for the most learned men that could be found. Meanwhile, thinking that Catherine: would be afraid to meet them and argue with them, and might run away before they could all be collected, he gave orders to have her shut up and kept a close prisoner in his palace.

In due time there came to Alexandria fifty of the most learned and eloquent men in the empire; and a day was appointed for them all to assemble in a public place, where they were to meet Catherine and argue with her in the presence of the emperor and all the people of the city. When the philosophers found out that they had been brought so far only to argue with a young girl of eighteen years of age, they were very much offended; and they represented to the emperor, as strongly as they dared, that it was beneath the dignity of learned men like them to dispute with a woman, however learned she might pretend to be. The emperor, however, would not listen to them, but insisted that they should argue with Catherine in public.

On the day appointed for the disputation he went in great state to preside on the occasion, and the whole city flocked to hear what the philosophers would say to confound this foolish, conceited girl, as they thought her, who had set herself up to put all the world right, but who, of course, would not be able to resist for one moment the arguments of these learned men. It was enough to frighten any woman, much more a modest, retiring girl like Catherine, to be led out before such crowds, and to be obliged to stand up alone and argue with so many men. But our Lord had ordered her to serve Him in this way; and though her heart beat quick and her limbs trembled under her, the thought of His love supported her, and she went forth unhesitatingly and joyfully. And as she was going along to the place where the disputation was to take place, and was praying very earnestly to our Lord to be with her and to tell her what to say, an angel suddenly stood before her, and bade her not to fear, for that God would give her a divine knowledge which would be far better than all earthly wisdom and eloquence, and that by its means she should get the victory over the fifty philosophers, and should convert them and many others to the Christian religion, and that both they and she should be crowned with martyrdom. Catherine was greatly comforted by the angel's visit, and by the promises which he made her. She entered the place of assembly with a light and firm step; and though she looked down modestly, because she was not accustomed to appear before so many people, yet it was easy to see that, so far from being frightened, she was quite calm and joyful, like one who felt

St. Catherine

confident of gaining a great victory.

When the emperor had taken his seat, and had given the signal for the disputation to begin, the philosopher who was considered to be the most clever of them all, stood up, and turning to Catherine with a scornful air, said: "Art thou she who hath been reviling our gods with foolish and insolent words?" "I am she," answered Catherine, "but my words were neither foolish nor insolent; for, on the contrary, all that I said was most reasonable and true." Then the philosopher began to set forth his arguments in favor of his own gods, calling them by many high-sounding names, and insisting that Jesus Christ could not be God, because He had been crucified, and because none of the poets and philosophers had ever mentioned Him in their writings. When he had finished his speech, Catherine got up to answer him. She first proved by many clever arguments, as well as by common sense, that there could not possibly be more than one God, who must be the creator of all things. Then she went on to show that all the high-sounding names which the philosopher had given to his gods were only empty words, without any truth or real meaning, since many of these very gods had been no more than wicked men, whom the heathens themselves believed to have been guilty of all sorts of horrible crimes. And lastly, she reminded him, that though the poets and philosophers had not written about Jesus Christ, yet that a long time ago there had been certain women, called Sybils, whom every one believed to have been inspired by God, and that they had prophesied about our Lord, and had predicted that He would be put to death by His own people, and would rise from the dead, and would ascend up to heaven, whence he would come again to judge the living and the dead. While Catherine was saying all this, she did not tremble, or hurry, or become confused; but she spoke slowly and calmly, quoting the different writings of the Sybils, and going through her arguments with such clearness and distinctness, that the philosopher, who just before had been too proud even to look at her, was astonished, and began to listen to her with great attention, for he thought he had never before heard any one speak so well. As she went on he became more and more impressed, and listened more and more attentively, till at last, being quite overcome by the supernatural wisdom and fervor with which she spoke, he came boldly forward and exclaimed, that Catherine was not speaking the words of human learning, but that she was inspired by God, and therefore it was impossible for anyone to resist her arguments.

Maximin was not a little surprised and vexed that Catherine should have defeated this learned man; but still he was only one out of the fifty philosophers; and not doubting that the other forty-nine would have better success, he turned to them and ordered one of them to come to the assistance of their companion, and help him to convince this obstinate girl of her folly. But all of them rising, as with one accord, cried out together, that their companion was the most clever and learned of them all, and that so far from being able to help him to conquer this young girl, they, as well as he, were conquered by her; so that they were all ready to confess that, up to this time, they had been blind and ignorant in adoring as gods those who were no gods, but that now they knew there was only one God, Jesus Christ, and would never henceforth worship any other.

It is impossible to describe the fury into which Maximin flew when he heard what these learned men said, and saw indeed that they had been conquered by the divine wisdom which issued from the lips of Catherine. He stormed and raged with passion, and when he could not give further utterance to his violence, he commanded that a great fire should be made ready, and that all of them should be thrown alive into it and burnt to death. The emperor's servants instantly set about obeying his orders; and while they were preparing and lighting the fire, the philosophers threw themselves at Catherine's feet, and most earnestly besought her to pray to God to pardon their sins, since, through His mercy in opening their eyes, they were now ready to receive baptism and to die for Him. Catherine was overjoyed when she saw that these men, who had just before been so proud of their worldly learning, had now humbled themselves before the power of the Holy Spirit, and were ready to give up all, even to their very lives, for love of the true God. She therefore spoke to them most lovingly, comforting and encouraging them by the assurance that God would not fail to pardon their sins, since they had preferred His love and favor to those of an earthly monarch, and bidding them not to be afraid because they could not be baptized, for that the fire would serve them for baptism, and would completely cleanse and purify their souls. These promises cheered them, and as soon as the fire was ready they were thrown into it, calling on the name of Jesus, and signing themselves with the sign of the cross. The flames rose quickly round them, and in a short time they were burnt to death; but in the course of the following night some Christians having gone to collect their relics, they found to their great surprise, that their bodies had been miraculously preserved, so that there was no appearance of their having been burnt, nor was a single hair of their heads singed. The wonderful conversion of these philosophers and the miraculous preservation of their bodies, had such an effect on the pagans of Alexandria, that many of them were converted and baptized.

Maximin was very much mortified and enraged at the turn which this affair had taken. There was nothing he would not have given to bend Catherine to his will, and he was resolved to do so either by fair means or foul.

He first tried gentleness and kindness, speaking to her with the affection of a father, and making her great promises, if she would submit to him and worship his gods. But Catherine's heart was so filled with the love of Jesus Christ, that she cared neither for the love nor the promises of the emperor. He next threatened to put her to the most cruel tortures. But she answered, calmly, "Do what you will, you will not be able to make me worship your gods. For your torments, however cruel they may be, will have an end, but the reward that I shall receive for them, will last forever. Besides, I hope in God that many of your own family and household will be saved through my means." Then the emperor commanded that her clothes should be taken off, and that she should be scourged with whips made of the sinews of animals. This was done, and for two long hours the executioners took it in turns to scourge her, till her whole body was so torn and streaming with blood, that those who stood by could not help shedding tears. But Catherine was quite unmoved, and all the time she was being scourged, she gave no more sign of feeling than if she had been a stone statue instead of a living being. After the expiration of two hours, when the executioners were quite tired out, she was thrown into a dark prison, and the emperor commanded that she should have nothing to eat, hoping that she would either be starved to death, or that the pangs of hunger would conquer her resolution, and force her to worship his gods.

The whole town was now talking about Catherine. Some praised her beauty, and others her gentleness and modesty; some were astonished at her learning, and others admired her courage in reproving the emperor; while all united in wondering at the fortitude and constancy with which she had borne the scourging. The common talk of the town spread even to the palace, and reached the ears of the empress, who longed to see this young girl, in whom there seemed to be something supernatural. She was afraid to send for her, or to go and visit her by day, lest the emperor should hear of it and be angry; so she went to the prison by night attended by Porphyry, a captain of the imperial guard, and several soldiers, and she remained there a long time talking to Catherine, and expressing her wonder that she should have been able to argue so cleverly with the philosophers, and to bear the scourging with such fortitude. Catherine answered her with great humility, saying: "It may seem wonderful to you that a young girl like myself could confound so many wise men; but I assure you that it is nothing more than any Christian, however ignorant, could do, if God so willed it. I did not speak of myself, but the Spirit of my Heavenly Father spoke in me, according to the promise which the Lord Jesus has made to us, that when we are taken before kings and governors for His sake, it will be given us in that hour what to speak. And as for the scourging, though it tore my flesh, yet it made me so happy that I scarcely felt the pain; for you must know, that He whose spouse I am, and whom I love more than my own soul, was once scourged much more severely on account of my sins, and the thought of suffering some little thing for Him, who has suffered so much for me, was so sweet to me, that I seemed to be in Paradise all the time that they were scourging me." Then Catherine went on to tell the empress all about the boundless love and wonderful sufferings of her dearest Lord Jesus, and about the Christian faith, speaking as the

Holy Spirit inspired her; and her words had such a Divine power, that the empress and Porphyry, and two hundred of the soldiers, were converted and baptized, offering themselves at the same time to our Lord to die for Him whenever He would give them an opportunity of doing so.

Catherine remained in prison day after day, and the jailers strictly obeyed the emperor's orders and gave her nothing to eat. Our Lord, however, did not forget her or allow her to want; for He sent His holy angels to visit her, and comfort her, and cure all her wounds; and every day a little dove came flying into the prison and brought her food enough to support her. Jesus Himself, too, appeared to her, and calling her His dear spouse, bade her not fear, because He was always with her, and would take care of her amid all the tortures which His enemies would inflict on her; and He promised her that before very long He would take her to Himself to live with Him in glory forever.

As day after day passed away, Maximin expected to hear either that Catherine was willing to sacrifice to the gods, or that she was dead; but no such news came to him. After waiting twelve days, he became so impatient that he could wait no longer, and he ordered that she should be brought before him; when to his unspeakable surprise, he found her neither thin nor half starved, nor scarred with the wounds of the scourging, but quite cured, and looking as well and as beautiful as before she was thrown into prison. He was so struck with her grace and beauty, that he began to speak kindly and flatteringly to her; but Catherine was not the least moved by his praise, and only answered coolly: "My Lord, it is not worth our while to think much about the beauty of the body, since, like a flower, it withers and dies away; but we ought to think a great deal about that of the soul, which will last forever,

St. Catherine

and which we shall possess even in heaven." Then Maximin, finding that his flattery made no impression on her, became very angry, and ordered her to be tortured on a very horrible machine. This machine was made of four wheels covered with sharp pointed nails, and contrived in such a way, that if a person was tied to one of the wheels and the wheel was turned round, his body would be torn to pieces by the nails on the other wheels. The executioners tied Catherine to the wheel and began to turn it round; but no sooner did they move it, than an angel of the Lord came to her rescue, and breaking the cords with which she was bound, set her at liberty; while, at the same time, he tore the wheels of the machine asunder with such violence, that they flew away from each other, and dashing against the pagans who stood by, killed several of them. As for the rest of the spectators who escaped unhurt, they were so wonderstruck at the sight of this miracle that they cried out, with one accord, "Great is the God of the Christians."

Maximin, however, remained unmoved, for as he had quite given himself up to serve the devil, and had shut his heart against Divine grace, all the wonders which God worked, only served to harden him more and more, and to make him more and more fierce. So far, then, from being touched by what was enough to convert the other bystanders, he only thought of inventing some new and more terrible tortures to inflict on Catherine.

When the empress heard all that had happened, and how the emperor was bent on having Catherine put again to the torture, she could no longer conceal that she herself was a Christian; and so, going to the emperor, she reproved him for his horrible wickedness and hardness of heart, and she confessed that she herself had been baptized, and that her heart was so filled with the love of

Christ, that she was ready to die for Him. Maximin was almost mad with rage when he heard that his own wife had turned against him, and become a Christian. He commanded her to be instantly taken out of his presence and beheaded; and as Porphyry and the two hundred soldiers of the guard also confessed that they were Christians, he ordered that they should all be beheaded together with her. The empress was rejoiced to receive the sentence of death, and she besought Catherine to pray for her that she should have grace to die a good death. And Catherine answered, "Do not fear, God is with you, and you shall reign with Him forever." Then the empress took leave of her joyfully, and, immediately after she, and Porphyry, and the two hundred soldiers were beheaded. Thus did God fulfil the prophecy of Catherine, that some of the emperor's own family and household would be converted by her means.

Maximin was very much frightened to find that Catherine had been able to convert so many persons out of his own palace; and being afraid lest she should turn all the people the city against him, he determined to get rid of her as quickly as possible, and he accordingly ordered her to be beheaded.

As soon as this cruel sentence became known in the city, every one, young and old, rich and poor, flocked to witness the execution of the saint. As she went along, she looked so young and so beautiful, and her face glowed with such seraphic joy and fervor, that many of the crowd wept for grief and pity. But she herself was in a rapture of delight at the sure and certain hope of being in a few minutes with her beloved Spouse; and, raising up her hands to God, she thanked Him for all His mercies, and most of all for having given her this opportunity of offering herself to Him, and shedding her blood in token of her true love for Him; and she besought Him to receive her spirit and not to leave her body in the hands of these unbelievers. As soon as she had finished her prayer she bent her head to receive the executioner's blow; and one of the soldiers cut it off with a single stroke of his sword. Our Lord did not forget the last earthly wish of His virgin spouse, for He gave her body into the charge of His holy Angels, and they carried It miraculously to Mount Sinai and buried it there; and after many years the Emperor Justin built a beautiful church and a monastery over the spot where she lay.

The Church celebrates the memory of St. Catherine on the 25th November. She is generally painted with a wheel beside her, a sword in her hand, and an emperor's head at her feet. The sword and the head mean that she obtained the crown of martyrdom by the sword, and that she thus triumphed over the wicked emperor who had her beheaded.

CHAPTER XXXIX

MISFORTUNES AND DEATH OF MAXIMIN DAIA

WHEN Maximin recommenced the persecution of the Christians, he boasted[26] that the empire was very prosperous, and that there were no wars or famines or pestilences, and he ascribed these blessings to his false gods, Jupiter and Mars. But the only true God, the God of the Christians, whom he was persecuting, and against whose love and mercy he had hardened his heart, punished him for his ingratitude and wicked blasphemies, and brought him at last to such a miserable end, that he became a terrible example of God's justice and vengeance.

Armenia, the inhabitants together with their king, Tiridates, had become Christians. As the Armenians were not a powerful nation, they were dependent on the Romans, and therefore Maximin, when he began to persecute the Christians, ordered the Armenians to give up their religion and to worship his gods. But the Armenians refused to obey him, and rather than do so, they went to war with the Romans, who were much stronger than they, and had often overrun and conquered their country. Maximin assembled a very large army and marched into

---

[26] Euseb. *Hist. Eccles.* 1. 9, c. 8.

Armenia, expecting to carry all before him. But the Armenians fought very bravely, and God was with them; and so it came to pass, that instead of Maximin having the best of it as he expect ed, he was shamefully beaten, and great part of his army perished, and he himself underwent a great many hardships and dangers before he could get safely back into his own country.

But this unfortunate war did not bring near so much misery on the empire as the famine and the pestilence which followed it. There was first a great drought, the consequence of which was such a terrible famine, that in some parts of the country almost everyone died. In the towns, provisions rose to such a price that the poor could not buy them at all, and were forced to live on grass and herbs, and all sorts of scraps and rubbish which they picked up in the streets. Even those who were rich, had soon parted with all they possessed, and then ladies of rank were to be seen going about asking alms; and people who looked like skeletons, walked tottering through the streets, begging for a morsel of bread, till they fell down exhausted and died; dead bodies lay unburied in all the streets and squares, and no one would take the trouble of burying them, and at last the dogs came and tore them to pieces.

The famine was followed by a pestilence which fell on rich and poor alike. A great many magistrates, governors of provinces, and persons of high rank, who had been rich enough to escape the sufferings of the famine, were the first to be carried off by the pestilence. Two or three bodies were often borne together to the grave; in many cases whole families were swept off; and nothing but cries and groans, sighing and sobbing, were to be heard in the streets. The distress was so great and so general, that people's hearts became hardened; no one troubled himself about his neighbor, but each thought only of how to take care of himself, and how to escape the infection. This was a fine opportunity for the Christians to revenge themselves on the pagans for all the ill treatment they had met with, and they did not fail to do so in the true Christian way, by returning good for all the evil that had been done them. They gave up themselves and all that they possessed to help their poor pagan brethren, for whom, no less than for themselves, their Lord Jesus had died; they went about the streets looking out for persons who were dying of hunger, and seeking out the sick, and collecting the dead bodies which there was no one to bury, supplying the wants of all to the best of their power, and working so hard at this labor of love, that even the pagans were forced to praise the God of the Christians, and to confess that no one except the Christians, knew what true charity was.

But this was not all that befell Maximin as a punishment for his blasphemies and his other great sins. He made war on Licinius, who, as has been said, was his partner in the Empire of the East, and governed one half of it. After making several long marches, the two armies came in sight of each other near the town of Adrianople, and a battle was expected to take place the next day. The night which preceded the battle was a night of great anxiety to both Maximin and Licinius, because they knew that whichever was conquered, would lose his crown, and most probably his life; and so both of them did everything they could to make sure of the victory. Maximin[27] made a vow to his god Jupiter, promising to kill all the Christians, and root their religion out of his empire. As for Licinius, he had of late been very kind to the Christians, and this night

---

[27] Lactant. *De Mort. Persecut.* 46. 47.

God rewarded him; for while he was asleep an angel appeared to him, and promised him the victory, on condition that he and all his army would pray to the One true God in the words of a prayer which he repeated to him.

As soon as the angel was gone, Licinius awoke, and calling for his secretary, made him write down the words of the angel's prayer; and he had a great many copies of it made and distributed among the officers, who taught it to their soldiers.

Early the next morning news was brought to Licinius that Maximin was coming to attack him; whereupon he drew out his men in battle array and advanced to meet him. In a short time the two armies came in sight of each other, and as there was only a barren and open plain between them, they could see each other quite distinctly. At this moment, just when the battle was going to begin, Licinius gave a signal, and in a moment all his soldiers took off their helmets, and laying down their bucklers, raised up their hands to heaven, and solemnly repeated after the emperor, the prayer which the angel had desired them to use. They repeated the prayer three times, and then putting on their helmets and taking up their bucklers, they felt their courage rise at the thought of the victory which had been promised them, and they longed to rush on their enemies.

Meanwhile, Maximin's army had no supernatural hope to support them. They had seen Licinius' soldiers laying down their arms and raising their hands to heaven; they had heard the words of the prayer which they used; and though they had themselves talked very loudly the night before about the victory, which their god Jupiter would be sure to give them in return for the vow which their Emperor had made to kill all the Christians, yet now their hearts sank within them, for they knew that Licinius' army had prayed to the God of the Christians, and they trembled to think that this Great and Almighty God was fighting against them.

When the battle began, Licinius' soldiers rushed boldly and confidently to the attack, while those of Maximin disheartened and downcast, scarcely dared to draw their swords or to throw their javelins. Maximin rode from rank to rank, trying both by threats and promises to rouse them, but all in vain. Some stood still to be quietly cut down by Licinius' soldiers, while others, seized with a strange and sudden panic, took to their heels and ran away as hard as they could go. It was plain that God was with Licinius and that the day was his; and after a time, Maximin seeing there was no hope of victory for him, disguised himself as a slave and fled.

Maximin fled across the straits which separate Europe from Asia, and Licinius followed him, hoping soon to come up with him. But Maximin was in such a fright that terror seemed to give him wings, and he fled so quickly that Licinius was always disappointed. But still Licinius followed, and still Maximin fled further and further. Then Maximin felt that he had been fighting against God, and being in a great fright he issued an edict,[28] giving the Christians leave to build their churches, and ordering their lands and their goods, which had been seized, to be restored to them. But Maximin could not atone for his former wickedness by being kind to the Christians merely because he was in danger, and without repenting of his sins. The hand of God was on him, and Licinius still pursued him, and still kept coming closer and closer. Then

---

[28] Euseb. Hist. Eccles. 1. 9, c. 10

Maximin,[29] in despair, took poison; but the poison was not strong enough to kill him at once, and for four days he lingered on in horrible agonies, rolling on the ground like a madman, dashing his head against the wall, and forcing handfuls of earth into his mouth, as if to allay the fire which was burning within him. At last he seemed to see God seated in judgment, and surrounded by numbers of spirits clothed in white robes, whom he knew to be the souls of the martyrs whom he himself had put to death; and being seized with horror at the sentence which our Lord seemed to be on the point of pronouncing against him, he would at one moment cry out, "It was not I who did it; it was the priests who deceived me and at the next, he would confess that he himself was guilty, and he would pray our Lord Jesus to have mercy on him. Then he would utter the most horrible cries, as if he were already in the fires of hell; till at last worn out by the interior tortures which he was suffering, he expired in agony. Thus (A. D. 313) died Maximin Daia, the most cruel of all the persecutors of the Christians.

---

[29] Lactant, *De Mort. Persecut.* 49.

CHAPTER XL

Tenth Persecution

LICINIUS: FORTY MARTYRS OF SEBASTE

LICINIUS owed his victory to the favor which God showed him; but though he knew and felt this he did not become[30] a Christian, and he did not care for our Lord Jesus except in so far as it was to his worldly interest to get His assistance. For some years he was very kind to the Christians, because he wished to be on good terms with Constantine, who was the Emperor of the West. But after some time there sprang up quarrels between him and Constantine, and then he began to be suspicious of the Christians who, he thought, must be fonder of Constantine than of him; and this wicked jealousy took such hold of him that at last (A. D. 320) it led him to begin another persecution.

This persecution lasted but a short time, and it fell only on that part of the empire which Licinius governed. He began by suddenly turning all the Christians out of his palace; he seized their goods; he sold some of them as slaves he sent others into banishment in distant countries, and he threatened others with death. He next ordered all who held any place under government to sacrifice to his

---

[30] Tillemont, t. 5, p. 503.

Forty Martyrs of Sebaste

gods, and he deprived of their offices a great number who refused to do so. The bishops, as usual, suffered severely, for as Constantine was accustomed to treat them with great reverence, Licinius looked upon them as his greatest enemies. St. Blaise, Bishop of Sebaste, in Armenia, and St. Basil, one of the bishops of Pontus, and several other bishops, were cruelly tortured and put to death. Not only men, but women and even little children were martyred; and all the Christians were in such danger, that they fled from the towns and hid themselves in mountains, and caverns, and desert places.

In the town of Sebaste the persecution raged very fiercely. Among the martyrs were two little children, who were beheaded at the same time as St. Blaise; and just after them seven women, who were put to death because they had been observed to be collecting the drops of St. Blaise's blood, for it was the custom of the Christians to collect the blood of the martyrs, and to keep it as a very precious relic. There is also a very interesting history told of forty soldiers, who were all martyred together, and who are generally known as the forty martyrs of Sebaste.

Among the Roman soldiers who were quartered in Sebaste, there happened to be forty men who were all natives of the same province, and who were famous for their courage and their great love to each other. As they were fellow-countrymen, it did not seem strange that they should be great friends; but they had a better reason than that for being friends; for they were Christians, and the love of Jesus in their hearts was a stronger bond of union than any tie of blood and kindred. They were always together, meeting for prayer, helping each other in their daily duties during the time of peace, and encouraging each other to fight bravely in time of war. They were so kind to their comrades, and did their duty so perfectly, that everyone spoke well of them.

Now it happened that the governor of Sebaste, whose name was Agricola, was a great enemy of the Christians, and he could not therefore bear to hear these Christian soldiers so well spoken of by everyone. Accordingly, when the emperor, published the edict requiring all those who were in his service to sacrifice to the gods, Agricola was very glad to have it in his power either to force these soldiers to sacrifice, or to punish them if they refused to do so. So he sent for them, and pretending to be their friend, he spoke hypocritically to them, telling them that he had heard a great deal about their brave deeds, for which he knew that the emperor intended to reward them, and so he advised them to lose no time in obeying him and sacrificing to the gods, lest if they delayed, it might interfere with their promotion. But the soldiers answered with one voice, "If, as you say, we have fought so bravely for the Emperor of the earth, what do you think we shall do now, that we are called on to fight for the Emperor of Heaven? You may be sure that we shall fight even more bravely than we are in the habit of doing; and we will not lay down our arms as long as there is any breath in our bodies." This was just what Agricola wished they would say; so he indulged his spite against them by abusing them violently, and threatening to degrade them from their rank, after which he sent them to prison, saying he would give them time to think better of the matter and to change their minds before it was too late.

But these brave soldiers of our Lord had no thought of changing their minds. As soon as they got into the prison they fell on their knees, and besought our Lord that as He had so often helped them, and given them the victory when they were fighting for earthly things only, so He would not forsake them in this battle which they were about to fight for His glory, but would strengthen them with His grace, and at last crown them with victory. After this they sang the 90th Psalm, which begins with the words, "He that dwelleth in the aid of the most High, shall abide under the protection of the God of Jacob;" and so they passed the whole night in praying to God and singing psalms. And in the middle of the night, while they were singing and praying, our Lord Jesus stood in the midst of them, and said to them: You have begun very well. Take care now that you go on well and persevere to the end; for the crown of victory is given only to those who fight well to the very last."

The next day the governor sent for them out of prison, and when they came before him he spoke to them in the same way as he had done the day before, praising them very highly for being such brave men, and recommending them to sacrifice at once, because he wished to promote them to high honor. But he had no better success than he had had the day before, for they would not even listen to his fine promises, and they did not care a straw for his threats; so that at last, when he found that his words made no impression on them, he sent them back to the prison, to be kept there till their captain, who happened to be absent, should return and decide what was to be done with them.

When the soldiers found themselves again in their prison they did as they had done before, and spent their whole time in praying to our Lord Jesus to help them, and in singing psalms and hymns which would cheer them, and make them more confident in Him. And one of them, who was called Quirion, encouraged his companions by reminding them, how often in their former battles, they had prayed to our Lord, and He had always heard them, and therefore they might be sure that He would not fail to help them now.

After seven days had elapsed their captain returned home, and then they were taken out of prison again, and were led before him and the governor, in order that they might have a last chance of saving their lives. As they went along Quirion said to his companions, "We have now three enemies to fight with, namely, the devil, the governor, and our captain; or, rather, we have only one enemy, the devil, who, being himself invisible, makes use of the other two as his servants and soldiers, to do his bidding and fight against us. Surely, then, one single enemy cannot overcome forty brave soldiers of the Lord Jesus Christ? No, no, it is quite impossible." When they came into the presence of their captain, he did everything he could to persuade them to sacrifice; now making them great promises, and then again threatening to punish them very cruelly. But all in vain, for nothing made the least impression on them. Then the governor and the captain became very angry, and ordered that their jaws and teeth should be struck with stones, so as to break them all to pieces; but our Lord took care of them, and ordered it so that, though the executioners struck them till they themselves were tired out, and their own hands were all cut and bleeding, those brave soldiers remained quite uninjured. The captain, seeing this, flew into a rage, and taking up a stone tried to throw it at one of the martyrs; but our Lord guided the stone, and, instead of hitting the soldier, it struck the governor on the mouth and hurt him terribly. After this the forty martyrs were led back into prison, to remain there till the governor and captain should resolve what more to do with them.

As soon as the brave martyrs returned to prison they resumed their old occupation of singing and praying; and now they did so even more earnestly than before, because the fight was begun, and they knew that they would soon have to go through many sufferings and strong temptations, and that unless their Lord was with them, they should never have strength and fortitude to gain the victory over the devil and his servants. They, therefore, sang the 122nd Psalm, which begins with the words, "To Thee have I lifted up my eyes, who dwellest in heaven;" and when they had come to the end of it, our Lord Jesus stood before them, and He said to them in a voice of tender love, and yet of great majesty and authority: "He that believeth in Me, although he be dead, shall live. Have great confidence in Me, and fear not the torments which last only for a short time. Fight bravely to the end, in order to gain the crown of victory." This vision was a great joy to them; it made their hearts burn with love for their dearest Lord, and it inspired them with such courage and fortitude, that they spent the rest of the night in singing songs of thanksgiving and triumph.

When it was morning they hoped to be taken out of prison and put to death, but no one came near them. Hour after hour passed on, and still all was quiet in the prison, and they longed so much to suffer and to die for Jesus that every hour they had to wait, seemed to them an age. At length, towards evening, they heard footsteps approaching their prison. Then there was the rattling of keys in the door, and their hearts leaped for joy, when the jailers came in and told them that they were to go with them to the governor to receive their sentence of death. The kind of death to which this wicked governor sentenced these brave soldiers, was a very cruel and trying one.

Close to the town of Sebaste there was a lake, or large pool of water, which was deep enough to cover a man up to his neck, though it was not deep enough to drown him. It was now the midst of winter, and as the weather was very cold it seemed probable that this lake would be frozen hard during the night; and so this wicked judge thought that the most severe suffering he could inflict on the martyrs, was to have them stripped naked, and put into the lake to remain there all night. At the same time, by way of tempting them to give up their religion, he had a large fire lighted, and a warm bath prepared within sight of the freezing lake, and they were told that any one of them who would consent to sacrifice to the gods, would be instantly taken out of the icy water, and led to the blazing fire and the warm bath.

When the forty martyrs heard their sentence they were overjoyed, and there was no need of executioners to pull off their clothes, for they undressed themselves with great joy and haste, and encouraged each other to make light of their tortures, saying: "The soldiers stripped our Savior of His garments, and He endured it willingly for our sins. Let us, then, strip off our clothes for love of Him, and to make satisfaction for our sins. The cold will be hard to bear, but it will take us to heaven. The frost will nip our flesh, but our souls will rejoice in the hope of the reward that awaits us. Our torments will soon end, but the glory of the Lord will be everlasting, and one night of suffering will win for us a day that will never end. If our feet are frozen, they will be the more fit to stand with the angels round the throne of God. If our hands drop off with cold, they will one day embrace the Lord, who gave them to us. How many of our comrades have died in the wars for an earthly prince, and how many criminals have suffered worse torments than these in punishment for their crimes! Let us, then, thank God that we are about to die, not for an earthly prince, nor for our crimes, but for justice, for virtue, and for the faith of the Lord Jesus Christ." Then turning to the Lord they offered themselves to Him as a sacrifice, to be consumed in the water by the fire of His love, and, being filled with the spirit of God, they leaped joyfully into the freezing lake, praying to God that as forty of them were entering the fight, so forty also might come out conquerors, and not one of their number be wanting.

The sun had set before the forty martyrs were brought out of prison, and very soon after they had jumped into the lake, night closed in. It was a night of more than usual severity. The air was clear, the stars twinkled brightly, a cold cutting wind sprang up, and ice was forming quickly over the surface of the lake. Guards were set to watch that none of the martyrs escaped from the lake, and to keep ready the blazing fire and the warm bath, which were to be the reward of him who would deny Christ; and though these guards were wrapped up in cloaks and blankets, and sat by the blazing fire, it was as much as they could do to keep themselves warm. They laughed and joked at the misery of the poor wretches who were in the freezing lake, and they foretold that, before very long, their boasted courage would be at an end, and they would all come flocking to the fire and the bath, and give up their former folly in thinking so much about the name of Jesus. But hour after hour passed on, and not one of the martyrs shrank from his icy bed; and as the wondering guards went out in turn to look at them, they saw that each stood in the spot in which he had first placed himself, and round which the ice was fast closing, while as the wind whistled over the lake, it brought with it no sound of sighs or groans, but only the voice of prayer and of thanksgiving. At length most of the guards settled themselves down to sleep, and one only remained awake to keep watch over the martyrs.

Then it came to pass that as the man on guard cast his eyes on the lake, he saw a bright light shining in the heavens; and as he looked, he perceived a host of angels descending, bearing in their hands bright crowns, which they were about to place on the heads of the martyrs. But when he counted the crowns he discovered that there were only thirty-nine, at which he was filled with surprise, since there had been forty soldiers who had so joyfully offered themselves to die for Jesus. But as he was wondering why there were only thirty-nine crowns, the mystery was explained; for at the same moment one of the martyrs, shrinking like a coward from the fight, called to him to help him out of the lake and put him into the bath, since he could bear the cold no longer, and must go near the fire, let it cost him what it might. The guard hurried to the lake, and helped the frozen man out of the ice, and brought him to a small altar which stood by, where he sacrificed to the gods and abjured the holy Name of Jesus. After this he was allowed to go near the fire, where he rubbed his numbed hands, and stretched his stiffened limbs, and basked in the genial blaze; then he stepped into the bath, and chuckling with joy, as he felt the delicious warmth steal over his frozen body, he seemed for a moment to forget all his late sufferings in the enjoyment of his present luxury. But it was only for a minute-for scarcely had he laid himself down in the water than a sudden pain shot through his frame, his limbs were convulsed, and with a piercing shriek and a look of horror, as if he saw before him the flames of hell into which he was falling, he expired.

The guard now understood why the angels had brought only thirty-nine crowns from heaven, and moved by the grace of God, he felt within him a sudden desire to win the fortieth crown, which had been destined for the wretched apostate, but which he had lost so miserably in exchange for one moment's pleasure. So he awakened his comrades in haste, and stripping off his clothes he jumped into the lake, crying out that he was a Christian. As for the other thirty-nine martyrs, they had been terribly grieved and downcast when they first saw their unhappy comrade desert them; but afterwards, when they beheld his awful fate, their courage rose, and they were more firmly resolved than ever never to give up the fight, but to die a thousand deaths, if necessary, for Jesus sake. And now, when the guard jumped into the lake, and took the place of the unfortunate apostate, they raised their voices in praise, and triumph, and thanksgiving to God, whose ways are unsearchable, and who had chosen a heathen to win the crown which the Christian had lost.

In the morning the executioners returned to the lake, and found the forty martyrs nearly frozen to death. They were not a little surprised to see that one among them was the soldier who had been on guard the night before, and who had been converted, by seeing the heavenly light and the vision of the thirty-nine crowns, which the angels were bringing from heaven for the martyrs. They went to Agricola, and told him, with awe and wonder, all that had occurred; how one of the martyrs had fallen away, and how the pagan guard had taken his place and won his crown: but Agricola cared not for the tale, and only flew into a rage, and ordered that all the martyrs should be taken out of the water, and that their legs should be broken and they should be beaten with clubs till they died. This was accordingly done, and while they were being beaten to death, they kept constantly repeating the words of the Psalm "Our soul hath been delivered as a sparrow out of the snare of the fowlers. The snare is broken, and we are delivered. Our help is in the name of the Lord, who made heaven and earth;" till at last they expired, committing the souls to Him who had created them, and had redeemed them with His blood, and would now crown them gloriously in heaven.

When they all seemed to be dead the executioners

began to take up their bodies, and to lay them on a cart to carry them to be buried. But as they were doing so, they saw that one of them, whose name was Meliton, who had been younger and stronger than the others, was not quite dead; and so they did not put him on the cart, but left him on the ground, hoping that he might yet change his mind and forsake Christ. But Meliton's mother was standing by, and when she saw the cart going away without her son, and understood why they had left him, she was terribly grieved; and though she was only a weak old woman, she went up to her son, and taking him in her arms, ran with him after the cart on which were the bodies of the other martyrs, crying out as she went along, "My dearest child, how happy shall I be if I see thee die for Jesus' sake! Pluck up thy courage, and stand firm to the end, for the angel who brought thy crown from heaven, is waiting to give it thee at the gates of Paradise. Suffer then the little which still remains to make thee a martyr, and me a happy mother. Other mothers weep for their children when they die, but I can only rejoice with thee, because I know that eternal glory is awaiting thee. I can only pray thee to expect me in heaven, and to make intercession to God for me, who once brought thee forth into this transitory life, and who now desires to bring thee forth a second time by martyrdom into eternal life!" As she spoke these words, her brave son, smiling on her brightly, as if to thank her for her love and care of him, expired in her arms; and she seeing that he was now in safety, threw his body into the cart with those of the other martyrs and following the cart, would not leave it till she had seen all the bodies burnt to ashes.

These brave soldiers were martyred on the ninth of March, on which day their feast used to be celebrated; but it is now transferred by the Western Church to the tenth, in order to leave the ninth for the feast of St. Frances of Rome, which also falls on that day.

CHAPTER XLI

DEATH OF LICINIUS; TRIUMPH OF THE CHURCH

VERY soon after the forty soldiers were martyred, war broke out between Licinius and Constantine. The two emperors made great preparations for this war, which would decide which of them was to be master of the world; and when each had assembled as large an army as he could, they marched to give each other battle. Constantine had not so many soldiers as Licinius, but he remembered that God had once given him a great victory; so trusting in Him alone, he took with him several Christian bishops, whom he engaged to pray for him, and at the head of his army he caused to be carried the famous standard, called the Labarum, which he had had made in imitation of the bright shining Cross, which he had seen in the sky the day before he fought the battle with Maxentius. Ever since that time Constantine had used this standard. It was always placed in a tent at some distance from the camp, and the day before a battle was to be fought, it was Constantine's custom to keep a strict fast, and to spend some time in prayer before it.

Licinius as well as Constantine, had formerly gained a great victory in consequence of obeying God, and making his army use the prayer which a heavenly vision had taught him. But since that time he had forgotten how much he owed to our Lord, and had persecuted His people;

and so our Lord had forsaken him, and had allowed Satan to blind him and to harden his heart. Licinius, therefore, instead of taking Christian bishops with him, called round him a host of magicians, sorcerers, and heathen priests, who promised him a certain victory. He assembled all these servants of the devil in a wood which they considered sacred, and after they had gone through a number of horrible and idolatrous ceremonies, he said to them: "My friends, these are the gods of our fathers, whom we honor as they taught us to do; but Constantine has forsaken them and taken up with some strange God, whose standard he carries before his army. We shall now see which of us is in the right. If Constantine's God gives him the victory, we must acknowledge Him to be the true God; but if, as I do not doubt, our gods give us the victory, we shall make war on these sacrilegious Christians, and root them out of the face of the earth."

The words which Licinius thus spoke in impious pride and confidence, soon became true. The two armies met on the plains of Adrianople, and Licinius was defeated. A short time after, a second battle was fought at sea near Byzantium, and Licinius was again defeated and forced to fly. Constantine pursued him. A third battle was fought near Chalcedon, and Licinius was defeated for the third time. Licinius fled again, and shut himself up in Nicomedia, where Constantine besieged him. At last, when all hope was lost, Licinius went out to Constantine's camp, and throwing himself at his feet, resigned his crown, and begged only to have his life spared. Constantine sent him as a prisoner to Thessalonica, and after some time had him put to death. Thus was it proved which was the true and living God.

The defeat of Licinius, A.D. 323, made Constantine sole emperor, and thus the Eastern Empire as well as the

Western, was brought under the dominion of the Church.

Though there were still a great many pagans remaining in the empire, yet the Church had now got the upper hand, and she had therefore more power to preach the Gospel, and to lead people to live holy lives.

Before this time, when the emperor was a pagan, his ministers were pagans, and the governors of provinces, and all who were in authority were pagans, he showed greater favor to pagans than to Christians, so that it was more for a man's worldly interest to be a pagan than a Christian; and therefore all people who cared little about religion, or who wished to be respectable in the eyes of their neighbors, called themselves pagans. Pagan temples, too, were built in every place; pagan priests were paid by the State, and pagan worship and pagan schools were kept up at the public expense; while the Christians had to build churches for themselves, and to pay their own clergy, and to keep up schools as they best could. All the laws, too, were made according to pagan notions of right and wrong, and not according to the law of God; and so it came to pass that a great many wicked things were done with the permission of the laws, and many horrible crimes were committed without anyone thinking that such things were wrong.

But when the emperor became a Christian all this was changed. Though he did not persecute the pagans, or turn them out of their employments under government; yet, he naturally had more confidence in Christians, and he therefore gave them all the offices of greatest trust, and showed them greater favor than the pagans. Now it was more creditable to be a Christian than a pagan; and many worldly and careless people began to turn their thoughts towards learning something about the Christian religion and many who would otherwise have lived and died in sin and idolatry, were brought into a state of grace, and not a few of them were really converted, and gave up the world, and led holy lives. Now, too, Churches were built and endowed, and schools were kept up by the State, and so of course, much more was now done to teach the people the faith of Christ, than could have been done when these works were carried on only by means of the offerings, which Christians were able to make out of their private fortunes. The laws, too, were reformed so as to agree with the law of God, and people began to know what was really right or wrong; and they learned that many things which they had formerly done in ignorance, were very sinful and displeasing to God. Instead of thinking only about the pleasures of this world, they now began to consider what was their duty to God and to their neighbor, and how they were to avoid the fires of hell and to gain the glories of heaven; and in this way, as year by year passed on, the devil's power over their hearts became less and less, and more and more souls were converted to the knowledge and love of the Lord Jesus Christ. And so, though there were still a great many pagans remaining in the empire, even after Constantine's conversion, yet, every year, they became fewer and fewer, and it was very plain that the Church of God, after fighting for nearly three hundred years, had at last overcome the great pagan idolatry, which had held possession of the world for so many centuries.

CHAPTER XLII

JULIAN THE APOSTATE

THOUGH the Church was now established throughout the Roman empire, we must not suppose that the devil was conquered, or that the war which he was waging against our Lord Jesus Christ had come to an end. No, this war still went on, and it will go on till the end of the world. But from this time, the devil carried on the war in a different way from what he had done before. He is always fighting against our Lord in people's hearts; sometimes by making them pagans; at other times by making them Muslims; sometimes by leading Christians into heresy and schism; and at others again, by tempting those who hold the true Catholic faith to commit mortal sins. His only object is to make them his servants and to take them with him to hell; and so long as he can manage to bring that about, he cares not whether they are pagans, or Muslims, or heretics, or bad Catholics, since he can get hold of them under one name as well as under another.

After Constantine's conversion, the devil saw that he must change his way of fighting against the Church; and so, instead of stirring up the pagans as formerly to persecute the Christians, he called in the aid of a set of heretics, called Arians, and by their means brought great troubles on the Catholics. These quarrels between Christians created great scandal, for the pagans began to

Julian the Apostate

think the Christian religion could not be true, since the Christians could not agree among themselves as to what a man ought to believe; and the consequence was that many, who might otherwise have been converted, turned away in disgust from thinking on the subject, while others thought that things went on much better in "the good old times," when the pagan temples were open, and all sorts of feasting and merriment were kept up in honor of the heathen gods, and no one cared what his neighbor believed, or troubled himself about deep questions of theology which people could not understand.

This was just the state of things which the devil had been wishing to bring about, and he took advantage of it to make one desperate effort to revive the pagan idolatry. The time which he chose for making this last attempt, was about forty years after the death of Licinius, when the Catholics had been so dreadfully persecuted by the Arians that the true faith seemed to be on the point of being lost and the person whom he selected for his instrument was a nephew of Constantine's, who is always known by the terrible name of Julian THE APOSTATE.

When Constantine died he left three sons, Constantine, Constans, and Constantius, who succeeded him, and divided the empire between them. He also left two brothers, and several nephews. Constantius, one of the young emperors, was of a very cruel and suspicious temper, and being afraid that these brothers and nephews of his father might try to usurp the throne, he encouraged his soldiers to murder them all, except two young children, who owed their lives to a bishop, called Mark of Arethusa, who took pity on them, and hid them till the massacre was over. These young princes were called Gallus and Julian.[31] Several years after, when Gallus was grown to be a man, Constantius quarreled with him, and had him also put to death; so that Julian was the only one of the imperial family who survived.

But though Julian's life was spared he met with very unkind treatment from his cousin Constantius. He was not allowed to live as was suited to a prince of the imperial family, but was kept shut up in a fortress, surrounded by guards and spies, who watched his movements, and repeated all his words and actions to the jealous and suspicious Constantius. All this must have been very irksome to a high spirited young prince like Julian; added to which, it must often have made him very sad to think that all his family had been murdered, and that he had no other relative than his wicked cousin. Still, in spite of all this, Julian might yet have been happy; for he had been baptized, and he was educated as a Christian; and therefore, if he had taken his trials in the same spirit as the martyrs did theirs, he might have been happy in this world in the enjoyment of the peace and love of God, and might have merited eternal glory in the next.

But while Julian was educated as a Christian he nourished in his heart a bitter hatred, which was quite opposed to the spirit of Christ. Our Lord has said that no one who loveth not his brother, can love God; and so it was with Julian. He began by hating his cousin Constantius, and he ended by hating our Lord Jesus. He hated Constantius as the murderer of his family, and this hatred gradually increased, and took such possession of his mind, that it made him hate everything connected with

---

[31] The History of Julian is taken from Gibbon, c. 23, 24.

Constantius. He knew that Constantius was a Christian, and, consequently, the enemy of the pagan gods. But he hated Constantius so much that he could not bear to be of the same religion as he was, and therefore, though he had been baptized, and had received in baptism the supernatural gift of faith, he longed to be able to think that the Christian religion was false, and the pagan idolatry was true. So he was always finding fault with Christian practices, and caviling at Christian doctrines, while at the same time he sought the acquaintance of pagans, and listened eagerly to whatever they had to say in defense of their own religion and against that of Christ. In this way he laid himself open to be deceived; and it is not therefore surprising that he was deceived, or that he soon came to hate our Lord Jesus, and to love the heathen gods.

When Julian was twenty years of age he made up his mind to become a pagan, and, in order to do so more perfectly, he determined to go through certain magic ceremonies, which were supposed to do away with his Christian baptism. He was accordingly taken down into a subterranean cave, and the magicians, into whose hands he had put himself, went through the incantations which they were in the habit of using when they wanted the devils to appear before them. When these were finished there was a most frightful noise, as if the whole place was coming down about their ears, and after this the cave was filled with devils, who appeared to them under the form of fiery spirits. Julian was so frightened when he saw these devils, that, without thinking of what he was doing, he made the sign of the cross, which he had been accustomed to make from his earliest childhood, and instantly all the devils vanished. The magician was very angry with him for having made this holy sign, and told him he must not do so again, because the devils did not like it. Julian promised to obey him, and then the magician repeated the same incantations and, in course of time, the same horrible noise was heard and the cave was again filled with fiery devils. At the sight of these wicked spirits Julian was again so frightened that he forgot what the magician had told him, and he made the sign of the cross involuntarily, whereupon the devils instantly fled. Julian was very much startled when he saw what wonderful power there was in this holy sign, and for a moment he hesitated whether he would give it up. The magician saw his hesitation, and was afraid that he might yet repent; so, by way of strengthening him in his former wicked resolution, he told him that the devils, or the gods, as he called them, had not fled because they had been frightened by the sign of the cross, but because they were offended with him for making it, and would have nothing to do with him so long as he used the sign of their great enemy. Julian was very glad to believe this lie, for his heart was bent on becoming a pagan, and so he willingly received what the magician told him, and from this time forth he never again made the holy sign of the cross.

For above ten years Julian did not dare to acknowledge that he was a pagan, because, if he had, Constantius would have put him to death. He continued to attend the Christian churches; he received the tonsure; he was sometimes employed to read the Scriptures aloud in church; and he even talked of becoming a monk. But all this was only hypocrisy, for even while the name of Jesus was on his lips, his heart was filled with blasphemous thoughts: and at night, after every one was gone to bed, and when there was no danger of his being seen, he would spend whole hours in praying to the heathen gods, and offering sacrifices to them, and going through magic ceremonies which he thought would please them. He offered himself to be their devoted servant; he believed that they had chosen him to be the restorer of their worship; and he longed to be emperor only in order that he might re-open their temples, and celebrate their festivals, and put down the hated religion of Christ.

At length, Constantius died, and Julian succeeded him. Julian's first act was to place himself publicly under the care of the "Immortal Gods," as the pagans called the devils whom they were in the habit of worshiping; and after doing this, he lost no time in restoring their worship. All the heathen temples were re-opened, and many of them which had been given to the Christians, and consecrated for Christian churches, were now taken from them, and given back to the pagans.

Whenever Julian arrived in a city, his first business was to inquire about the temples and altars which he knew had formerly been there; and if he found that they were thrown down or neglected, he gave immediate orders to have them built up; and he made rich presents to them, by way of encouraging others to do the same. He took away from the Christian clergy the revenues which Christian emperors had bestowed on them, and gave them to the pagan priests. He turned all the Christian courtiers and servants out of his palace, and supplied their places by heathen priests, philosophers, soothsayers, magicians, and a host of worthless people; many of whom had formerly pretended to be Christians, but who now courted Julian's favor by talking loudly about the "Immortal Gods," and blaspheming our Lord Jesus.

But Julian was not satisfied with merely restoring the pagan worship; for he felt that only half his work was done so long as any of his subjects adored the God, whose enemy he had openly declared himself. The Church had had many persecutors, but Julian surpassed them all;

because, while they were actuated merely by enmity against a new religion, be was urged on by a bitter personal hatred of the Savior whose love he had spurned, and whose Blood he had trampled underfoot. He would have wished, like a Roman emperor of old, that all his Christian subjects had had but one neck, that he might have got rid of them all with one blow. He had, however, too much good sense to fancy that he could put down Christianity by open persecution; besides, he was on the eve of a war with the Persians, and it would not have been politic to have begun a persecution just then. He hoped, therefore, to effect his purpose better by petty, wearing tyranny, and by doing all he could to bring the religion gradually into discredit. He always spoke contemptuously of our Lord Jesus; and instead of giving Him His own name, he called Him "the Galilean;" and, in like manner, he never called those who believed in Him Christians, but only Galileans, as if in contempt and ridicule. He also pretended that he was very anxious that all his subjects should live together in peace, and should not persecute each other for matters of religion; and on this pretense he recalled from banishment all those wicked and dangerous persons, who had been banished for spreading heresy in the Church, while, at the same time, he would not allow the chief Catholic bishops to remain in their sees. He also allowed the populace to maltreat the Christians; and on some occasions his own temper got the better of his wiser judgment; for when he saw persons paying open honor to our Lord, he would be so irritated that he would fly into a rage and ordered them to be cruelly punished.

It has been mentioned, that, in heathen times, it was the custom on certain occasions for the emperor to make a present to his soldiers, each of whom, on receiving the gift, used to throw a little incense on the altar, by way of making an offering to the heathen gods for the emperor's prosperity. This custom had been long given up, and was almost forgotten; but Julian revived it. He assembled all his soldiers, and gave each a piece of money, requiring each at the same time to throw a grain of incense into the fire on the altar. Most of the men thought more about the money than about their religion, and made no difficulty about throwing the incense into the fire; some, having heard what they would be required to do, pretended to be ill, and stayed away; others, again, openly refused to receive the money on such terms; while several, who were very ignorant, were deceived and made to believe that the whole ceremony was only a form, and had nothing to do with religion, and so they innocently offered the incense and received the money, without intending to deny our Lord, or to worship the heathen gods.

It happened that several of these last, who had been deceived by their pagan comrades, sat down together to the feast which followed the distribution of the money. Before they began to drink, they made the sign of the cross as usual, and one of their pagan comrades, seeing them do this, cried out, "What are you doing? What do you mean by calling on Jesus Christ just after you have denied Him?" "How? What do you say? When did we ever deny our Lord?" exclaimed the Christians, terrified and astonished. "You did so," replied the pagan, "when you threw the incense into the fire." When the poor simple men heard these terrible words, they tore their hair, and uttering the wildest cries of grief and horror, they rushed into the public square, exclaiming, "We are Christians in our hearts. We wish everyone to know it, and we declare it before God, to whom alone we wish to live, and for whom we are ready to die. Dearest Lord and Savior, we have never denied Thee! Dearest Jesus! we have never refused to confess Thy name! We have sinned with our hands, but not with our hearts. The emperor has deceived us; we renounce our impious deed, and we wish to atone for it with our blood." Then, running to the palace and throwing the gold at the emperor's feet, they cried out, "We will not have your gift; for it is a sentence of death to us. We ask only one favor, which is, that you will sacrifice us to the Lord Jesus Christ. Throw us into the fire; cut off our hands, which have been guilty of this sin; but give your gold to those who will take it without remorse." Julian was so provoked at the boldness with which these simple fellows confessed their love and devotion to the Lord and Savior whom he himself hated, that, in the first impulse of passion, he ordered them all to be beheaded. They were accordingly led out of the town to be executed, and a crowd of people followed them, admiring their courage. When they reached the place of execution, the oldest of them begged the executioner to begin with the youngest, who he feared might not be so courageous as the others, and might get frightened if he were to see all his comrades executed before him. Accordingly, the youngest, whose name was Romanus, knelt down, and stretching out his neck, was just going to receive the blow of the executioner's sword, when a messenger ran in haste, and stopped the execution. The emperor had thought again of the matter, and seeing how much glory the Church would receive by their deaths, he would not allow them to have the honor of martyrdom. "Alas!" said Romanus, as he rose from his knees, "my Lord has not thought me worthy to be a martyr." Julian did not, however, pardon them, but banished them to the most distant parts of the empire, where he condemned them to live in wild and desert places, and forbade their entering any town or village.

Another person who was very cruelly treated in this

reign was Mark of Arethusa, the bishop who had saved Julian's life when he was a child.

In the reign of Constantius, Mark had been very zealous in making converts from paganism, and he had taken a principal part in the destruction of a very famous temple. As soon as Julian ascended the throne, Mark was ordered to pay a large sum towards the rebuilding of this temple; and, as he was firmly resolved not to do so, he at first fled; but some of his flock having been taken up in his stead, he came back and gave himself up to the persecutors. The pagans were rejoiced to get hold of one who had been the great enemy of their gods. A mob assembled round him, seized him, and pelted him with stones and mud; they dragged him through the streets by the hair of his head, and at last threw him into the public sewer. After a time they pulled him out of the sewer; they collected round him a crowd of children, who pierced him with sharp-pointed writing instruments, called *styles*; they cut off his ears with strong fine wire; they tied cords round his legs so tightly as to cut them to the very bone; and, finally, they stripped him naked, rubbed his body over with honey, and hung him up in a basket, in the mid-day sun, where he was scorched by its burning rays, and tormented and stung by the flies, and bees, and other insects, which the honey attracted to settle on him. While they were tormenting him they gave him to understand, that if he would pay the money for rebuilding the temple, they would set him free; but he obstinately refused to do so. While he was hanging exposed in the basket, they thought that perhaps he was not rich enough to pay so large a sum, and so they said they would be satisfied if he would pay half of it; but so far from consenting, he only laughed at them, telling them that he was much better off than they were, since he was raised up to heaven, while they were groveling on the earth. Still they could not believe that he was inflexible in his resolution, and they constantly went on reducing their demands, and asking him less and less; but he was still immoveable, assuring them that it would be as wicked to give a single farthing as to give the whole sum, and therefore he would rather die than give even this one farthing. At length, finding that nothing could conquer him, they let him go. Julian owed his life to Mark, and yet when he heard how the pagans of Arethusa had treated him, he did not give orders to punish them, nor even utter one word blaming their conduct.

The populace in many places were encouraged to attack and ill-treat the Christians, because they knew that the emperor would be pleased, and no one else would dare to punish them for breaking the laws which protected the Christians. In Ascalon, they seized a great number of priests and virgins, dedicated to the service of the Church, and after tearing them to pieces, set a herd of swine to devour them. In Gaza, they dragged three brothers out of their houses, scourged them severely, and threw them into prison. After some hours, they rushed from the theater, in which they were assembled, took the brothers out of the prison, and dragged them through the streets, sometimes on their faces, sometimes on their backs, dashing them against the pavement, cutting them against the stones, and breaking their bones with cudgels, or whatever else came to hand. Even the women left their spinning and pierced them with their spindles; while the cooks from the public eating-houses ran their spits into them, or poured boiling water over their bodies. At last, when their skulls were fractured, and their brains were scattered on the pavement and their whole frame was torn and smashed, they dragged them into the place outside of the city, where the carcasses of dead animals were thrown, and there they buried them.

The governor of the province was a pagan; but he was so shocked at the violence which had been committed, that he thought it his duty to put the ring-leaders into prison; and the people, when they returned to their senses, trembled to think what punishment would be inflicted on them by the emperor, who was known to be generally very strict in having the laws observed. But they were all quite mistaken; for when Julian heard of what had happened, he was so far from punishing the rioters, that he banished the governor for having put the ringleaders into prison, at the same time saying, with a laugh, "What great harm was there done if a troop of pagans did murder half a dozen Galileans?"

But there was one way especially in which Julian thought more certainly than in any other to bring dishonor on our Lord Jesus. This was, by proving that His words had been false. Our Lord had prophesied that the temple at Jerusalem should be destroyed, and that it should never be rebuilt; and so Julian determined to rebuild the temple, and thus to prove that our Lord had been a false prophet. He accordingly gave the Jews leave to return to Jerusalem, and to rebuild their temple; and, by way of encouraging them to do so, he gave them large sums to buy the necessary materials, and sent for workmen from all parts of the empire to help them; and desired the governor of the province to assist them in every way he could.

The Jews, who had now been wanderers on the earth for nearly three hundred years, were overjoyed at this sudden and unexpected piece of good fortune. They hastened from all parts to help on the glorious work. Those who were young and active worked day and night; those who were rich gave enormous sums to buy materials; some sent shovels and hods of silver to be employed in the holy work; the women offered their jewels and most precious ornaments; and many of them even worked with their own hands, collecting the rubbish, and carrying it away in gowns of the richest silk. The work went on briskly and prosperously. The Jews and Pagans were in the highest spirits, and loudly boasted of their triumph over the Christians.

At length the ground was cleared; the day was fixed for laying the foundations of the new temple; and an immense concourse of Jews were assembled to witness the happy event. But the night before, an earthquake took place; and not only removed to a great distance the stones which were to have formed the foundations, but threw down the surrounding buildings, under the ruins of which a great many Jews were buried. There was also a whirlwind, which scattered the lime and sand, and other materials which had been collected. A supernatural fire, too, burst out of the ground, and burnt up the workmen's tools. The next day, the Jews who had witnessed the disasters of the preceding night, returned to their work, and tried to repair the damage which had been done. But it was impossible; for as soon as they began to work, the fire burst out afresh from the spot on which they intended to build the temple, and ran about hither and thither, burning all those whom it met. The same thing happened several times, so that they were at last obliged to give up the work, and to return in grief and disappointment to their own houses. Thus, what Julian had intended to bring dishonor on our Lord became the means of proving His Divine Mission.

CHAPTER XLIII

JULIAN THE APOSTATE—CONCLUSION

JULIAN spent the second winter of his reign in Antioch, where St. Peter had first set up his bishopric; and as the people were almost all Christians, and very full of zeal, he and they were constantly getting into some dispute on matters connected with religion. There was a deaconess, called Publia, who was at the head of a religious community; and when Julian was passing, she and her nuns would sing, in the words of the Psalm, "The idols of the Gentiles are silver and gold, the works of the hands of men. Let them that make them become like unto them, and all such as trust in them." Julian was very angry when he heard them sing these words; and he commanded them to be silent when he was passing. But they took no heed of his orders; and the next time he passed they sang: "Let God arise and let His enemies be scattered." Julian now flew into a rage, and sent for Publia; and though she was an old woman, and greatly respected, he made his guards strike her violently on the face. But she looked upon her bruises as marks of honor, and going home in triumph, she and her nuns went on singing just as they done before.

Another cause of quarrel between him and the citizens of Antioch was, the removal of the relics of St Babylas, About five miles from Antioch there was formerly a beautiful temple, called the temple of Daphne, which had been very famous in pagan times for its oracle of the heathen god, Apollo. This temple had been much neglected since the people of Antioch had become Christians; and for several years the oracle had refused to answer the questions which were asked it. The heathen priests said that Apollo would not speak, because the martyr, St. Babylas, was buried in the cemetery which surrounded the temple; whereupon Julian ordered the Christians instantly to remove the body of St. Babylas. The Christians made no difficulty about obeying the emperor's orders; but instead of doing so quietly or secretly, as they would have done if they had been afraid or downcast, they made it the occasion of a sort of triumph.

The relics of the saint were placed on a very high car; all the clergy and almost the whole population of Antioch walked in procession after it, and the whole way, as they went along, they sang hymns and psalms, while, at every pause, the crowd joined in with the chorus, "Let them be all confounded that adore graven things, and that glory in their idols." Julian was greatly enraged and ordered the principal Christians to be punished. Several persons were taken up and put to the torture. Among them was a young man called Theodore, who was tortured from morning till night; but all the time he was being tormented he continued to sing, with a calm and smiling countenance, the some words which the crowd had sung the day before. After he was sent back to prison he was asked if he had not felt dreadful pain; to which he answered, that at first he had felt a little pain, but that afterwards there stood beside him a young man, clothed in snow-white linen, who wiped his face, and gave him some cool, sparkling water to drink, and this water filled him with such joy and consolation that he was quite sorry when the tortures ceased and the young man left him. A few nights after, the temple of Daphne caught fire without any one being able to say how; the image of Apollo and all the ornaments of the temple, were burnt to ashes; the roof fell in, and the bare walls and columns alone were left standing.

At length the spring came round, and all the preparations for the Persian war were completed. Julian was very anxious to begin and finish this war, because he could not set in good earnest to persecute the Christians till it was off his hands. However much he had already ill-treated them, it was nothing to what he wished to do; and he made a vow, that as soon as he returned victorious he would exterminate the Christians. He never for a moment doubted that he would be victorious, because he had consulted the most celebrated pagan oracles, and they had all promised him success. Besides, he was confident that the gods would give him the victory, in return for the vow which he had made to exterminate the Christians.

He marched out of Antioch with great pomp, surrounded by a host of pagan priests and philosophers. All the pagans were in high spirits, and insulted the Christians in every conceivable way. As for the Christians, they watched the preparations for the war with even more interest than the pagans did, for their lives and their whole fate hung on its issue. The common people were terribly cast down, for the insolence and the threats of the pagans depressed them, and they thought a persecution close at hand: but the more devout Christians felt confident that God would come to their rescue, and bring some terrible judgment on the apostate, whose impiety and blasphemy had risen to such an awful height. One of Julian's friends happening to meet a Christian, said to him, in an insolent and mocking tone: "Well, what is the carpenter's son doing now?" Whereupon the Christian answered solemnly: "Making a coffin for your Master." The pagan laughed in scorn; but some few months after people remembered the Christian's words, and saw that they had been prophetic.

Julian marched through the countries which lay between Antioch and Persia; and wherever he went the blood of sacrifices streamed from the pagan altars, and the fragrance of incense perfumed the air. He arrived at the River Chaboras, which was the boundary of Persia, and crossing it he continued his march through the Persian territory, burning down the villages, and laying waste the whole country through which he passed. He came to two or three very strong fortresses which were considered impregnable, but he took them and leveled them with the ground. His pride and insolence increased with his good fortune. The omens in the sacrifices began to be unfavorable, but he did not care for them; for he now defied the heathen gods, as he had already done the Christian God, and, puffed up with pride, he trusted only to his own strength and valor. The Persians always retired before him; and being persuaded that the King of Persia was afraid of him, he formed the bold design of pursuing him into the heart of his dominions. The King of Persia, however, was retreating only with a view of drawing him into a position, where he could surround him and more surely effect his ruin. But Julian did not suspect this and marched boldly on into Persia.

The march of Julian's army lay through a rich and fertile country, and Julian, therefore, took few provisions with him, trusting to find plenty as he went along. But though the country was very rich and fertile, the inhabitants had turned it into a desert, for they had set fire to the corn fields, and had driven away their cattle, and had fled from the villages; and thus, as the Romans advanced, they found nothing but black and smoking ruins. In a few days they began to suffer from famine, but

Julian still made them go on, assuring them that they would soon come up with the Persian king. But still the Persian king retreated before them, and the further they advanced, the less hope there seemed to be of finding him. At last Julian was obliged to make up his mind to retrace his steps, and turn homewards.

Up to this time the Romans had never seen any enemy, except a few horsemen who seemed to watch them, and run away when they were attacked. But scarcely had they turned than a cloud of dust was seen in the distance. They thought that it might be a herd of wild asses, or some of their own troops whom they were expecting to join them; and with this hope they pitched their camp, and the night closed in. But as soon as the morning dawned they discovered their mistake, and found that they were surrounded by the whole Persian army. Julian's courage, however, did not forsake him. He determined to continue his march, and he himself led the way. His soldiers were sinking with hunger and fatigue; they marched through a country which had been laid waste, and where no food was to be had: their little stock of provisions was daily becoming smaller and smaller; but still they marched steadily on, fighting every step of their way, constantly defeating their enemies, but gaining nothing from their victories, since fresh bands of Persians were constantly coming up to renew the fight. In this way they marched on for ten days.

For some time, past bad omens had been noticed in the sacrifices, and Julian was now terrified and distressed. But still, he could not stop. His only hope lay in continuing his march. At length, on the tenth morning, the omens were worse than usual, and the soothsayers told him he must not fight that day, because some misfortune was hanging over him. But at the same moment the trumpet sounded to arms, and he heard that the Persians were attacking his rear guard. He happened to have laid aside his cuirass, because being the month of June, the weather was very hot; but as soon as he heard the trumpet call to arms, he rushed out to the rear guard and drove back the enemy. The next moment the trumpet sounded in front, and he galloped forward; and after a desperate fight obliged the Persian cavalry and elephants to fly. Julian was foremost in pursuing them, and by his voice and gestures, animated his soldiers to follow him. His guards called after him reminding him that he was without armor, and beseeching him to return: but their advice came too late. At the same moment a javelin struck him and pierced his side. He tried to draw it out, but the steel cut his fingers and he could not stir it. Then catching the blood in his hand, and throwing it into the air, he exclaimed: "Galilean, thou hast conquered," and sunk senseless from his horse. His guards hurried round him and carried him to his tent. In the first impulse of disappointment, he had confessed that he was conquered by no earthly arm, but this awful thought could not bring him to repentance. He lived only a few hours, and expired with words of blasphemy on his lips, A.D. 363.

A dark cloud had been lowering over the Church, and seemed to be on the point of bursting on it; but the love of God, like a bright sun-beam, broke through it, and the wild storm of persecution was suddenly turned into gentle showers of grace. The death of Julian broke in a moment the power of Satan and of hell. Men awoke as from frightful dream, and looking around for the cause of their terror, perceived that it was only a phantom of the night, which had faded away before the light of day. Julian's efforts to give a new life to paganism had only served to show how vain, and hollow, and lifeless was that system of idolatry, which had once held the greatest intellects of earth in its thrall; and when his support was withdrawn from it, it was cast away by common consent, and may be said to have been buried in his grave. A succession of Christian emperors now filled the imperial throne of Rome, and under them paganism lost ground so rapidly, that in the course of sixty years it was a matter of doubt whether any pagans were still to be found within the empire;[32] and yet, this great change, like all other operations of God's grace, was brought about in such a gentle and scarcely perceptible way, that men could not say how or when it took place, and were forced to ascribe the glory of the world's conversion to the sovereign power and love of God.

It has been formerly said that our Lord chose for His Church, the same mode of conquest through suffering, which He had chosen for Himself. In like manner, He was pleased to make her His associate in the circumstances of His victory over death and hell. The hour of that victory was the darkest hour in the world's history. He came unto His own, and His own received Him not; Jews and Gentiles alike scorned and rejected Him; the powers of the world, agreeing in nothing else, united to condemn Him and nail Him to His cross; His very friends betrayed Him, denied Him, fled from Him; even His Heavenly Father seemed to have forsaken Him; and though a few loving souls followed Him, only one heart, that of His immaculate Mother, clung closely and firmly to Him, and shared His

---

[32] Gibbon, c. 28.

dying agony. Well might the sun hide its face for grief, for the Hope of the world was expiring, and the powers of hell seemed to have conquered the Son of God. But when all around was darkest and most hopeless, there arose a loud and thrilling cry; there were heard the joyful words, "It is consummated," and bowing His head, Jesus gave up the ghost. This cry, and these words, rang through the highest courts of heaven, and pierced down to the lowest depths of hell; and they proclaimed to the whole universe that the God of love had triumphed over the powers of hell, and that man was freed from the bondage of Satan.

And so it ever has been, and ever will be, with the Church. Clouds will lower over her, persecutions will come upon her, trials will afflict her, and sorrow and suffering will pierce her through and through. But the darker is the hour, the nearer will be her light; for in the darkest gloom, our loving Lord will be closest to her, and He will whisper to her, "O poor little ones, tossed with tempest, without all comfort, behold I will lay thy stones in order;" and when the storm is about to crush her, He will come to her rescue, and give her peace.

The infallible word of prophecy bids us to look for a time of sorrow and of trial such as has never been since the world began. At that time the sun shall be darkened, and the moon shall not give her light, and the stars shall be falling; and there shall be, not only wars and pestilences and famines, and earthquakes, but there shall be scandals, and hatred, and false prophets, and lying wonders, so that iniquity shall abound, and charity shall wax cold, and many shall fall away from the faith. But while the world will be shaken, and men's hearts will be withering away for fear and expectation of what shall be coming upon them, the Church will look up and lift up her head, because her redemption is at hand. Let us then never forget what we are to look for and to hope for as Catholics. We must look for sorrow and trials, since without suffering we cannot be one with Jesus; but when this sorrow and these trials press heaviest on us, and our hearts are ready to faint, we must lift up her heads and look up, and if we listen with patient and loving hope, we shall not fail to hear the sweet words, "Surely, I come quickly;" and our hearts will answer joyfully, "Amen. Come, Lord Jesus."

FINIS

www.ingramcontent.com/pod-product-compliance
Lightning Source LLC
Chambersburg PA
CBHW030245010526
44107CB00031B/1332/J